MODERNIZING URBAN LAND POLICY

Papers by

RICHARD F. BABCOCK
DAVID L. CALLIES
MARION CLAWSON
DANIEL WM. FESSLER
MASON GAFFNEY
IRA MICHAEL HEYMAN
HARVEY S. PERLOFF
JOHN W. REPS
WILBUR A. STEGER
ROBERT C. WEAVER

MODERNIZING URBAN LAND POLICY

Papers presented at an RFF Forum held
in Washington, D.C., 13–14 April 1972

EDITED BY MARION CLAWSON

Published for Resources for the Future, Inc.
By The Johns Hopkins University Press, Baltimore and London

Resources for the Future is a nonprofit corporation for research and education in the development, conservation, and use of natural resources and the improvement of the quality of the environment. It was established in 1952 with the cooperation of the Ford Foundation. Part of the work of Resources for the Future is carried out by its resident staff; part is supported by grants to universities and other nonprofit organizations. Unless otherwise stated, interpretations and conclusions in RFF publications are those of the authors; the organization takes responsibility for the selection of significant subjects for study, the competence of the researchers, and their freedom of inquiry.

RFF editors: Mark Reinsberg, Vera W. Dodds, Nora E. Roots.

ACKNOWLEDGMENTS

The assistance of several people in the production of this book is gratefully acknowledged. First of all, there are the authors of the various papers, who gave generously of their time, thought, and experience. Erwin D. Canham, editor-in-chief of the *Christian Science Monitor* and chairman of the board of Resources for the Future, was the skillful moderator for the first day of the Forum, and Charles M. Haar, professor of law at Harvard Law School, played a similar role for the second day. Some of my colleagues at Resources for the Future, notably Joseph L. Fisher and Lowdon Wingo, helped to formulate the plan of the Forum at which these papers were first given, and to recruit those who participated. The papers were edited by Nora E. Roots, and we are all indebted to her for better readability, more clarity, and fewer errors. Arrangements for the Forum, communications with the participants, and typing of the papers have all been aided by the diligent efforts of my secretary, Diantha Stevenson.

Marion Clawson

CONTENTS

MODERNIZING URBAN LAND POLICY

EDITOR'S INTRODUCTION

MARION CLAWSON

The city, as a form of human settlement, is changing. And as it changes, urban land policy must also change. But to what end, and how? Who will direct the new urban land policy?

Barring some wholly new development not now foreseen, or perhaps foreseeable, the population of the United States will continue to concentrate in metropolitan areas. The nonmetropolitan areas, which contain no city as large as 50,000 but many small cities and most of the nation's open country, are essentially stagnant. Even the building of new towns on a large scale (a development that seems unlikely) would probably not change this situation. There is ample room for many new towns within present metropolitan areas, and these areas might well be the most economic location for them.

On the metropolitan scale, the population movement is outward from city center to suburb, and has been for much longer than is often realized. Census data on city populations conceal the fact that since 1880 at least, and probably earlier, city boundaries have pushed outward almost as fast as population has increased.[1] The decentralization is far more than merely numbers of people, and far more than simple residences for them. Taxable wealth and investable capital have also moved outward; so have jobs, and retail trade; and, perhaps most serious of all, so have social and political leadership. Moreover, the outward trend holds for blacks as well as for whites. A preoccupation with overall statistics on racial change in the older urban cores has obscured the significant migration of middle- and upper-income blacks to the suburbs — a movement that is likely to continue and to accelerate.

All this raises significant questions as to the future form of the American metropolis. One picture has been a black core surrounded by a white ring.

[1] Marion Clawson, *Suburban Land Conversion in the United States: An Economic and Governmental Process* (Johns Hopkins University Press for Resources for the Future, 1971), pp. 33–37.

3

Another has been a doughnut — a decayed and largely abandoned core surrounded by growing suburbs. Melvin Webber advanced the intriguing idea of
community without propinquity, suggesting that technological advances in
communication would make actual physical proximity unnecessary and that
groupings of people into cities would therefore have little purpose.[2] The
trend, however, has been in the opposite direction; as metropolises have
grown, business (which is basically human contact) has grown to replace, and
more, the losses of industry from the central city. Face-to-face contact
acquires increasing values as metropolitan size and impersonality increase. In
my opinion, metropolitan cores have such strengths and values that they
should be revitalized and reconstituted at some time in the future. But, for
the present and for the next decade or two at least, land use policy might be
most effective in the suburbs where the largest changes are now taking place.
If action is taken soon, it may be possible to direct these changes to social
ends.[3]

One point that is sometimes overlooked is that change occurs gradually in
city and suburb alike. Buildings typically last 50 to 100 years, and annual
residential construction is rarely as much as 3 percent of standing stock. Even
more permanent and pervasive than the buildings are the streets and other
major features of the city, including the vast underground network of sewers,
water pipes, telephone lines, electric power lines, and the rest. New construction typically takes place incrementally. When a building is under construction, all the surrounding buildings and streets are part of its environment; but, once built, it becomes part of the environment for newer
structures. A city cannot change immediately and drastically — a fact that
one may regard as an asset or as a liability. Nevertheless, within a few
decades, or even a few years, substantial changes can take place, and choice is
possible.

The expansion of the city into the suburbs and the rebuilding of the older
city center will be characterized by a mixture of private and public efforts. It
is a complex process, with many actors. City building and rebuilding to
accommodate new residents and to provide better housing for present residents will be largely an activity of private business; public housing has been,
and is likely to continue to be, relatively unimportant as a source of shelter.
But the private activity will take place within a framework of laws and
institutions established or imposed by the public, operating through government at various levels.

[2]Melvin M. Webber, "Order in Diversity: Community without Propinquity," in
Lowdon Wingo (ed.), *Cities and Space: The Future Use of Urban Land* (Johns Hopkins
University Press for Resources for the Future, 1963).
[3]Clawson, *Suburban Land Conversion*, see pp. 243 ff.

LAND USE CONTROLS

Urban and suburban growth and development are, or can be, controlled in a variety of ways: by the location and timing of public improvements, by lending policies and restrictions of private lending agencies and of the government agencies that supervise them, by governmental subsidies and other programs, as well as by public land use controls. The most important land use control — and the one emphasized here — is zoning, but subdivision regulations, building codes, and health requirements can also be influential in guiding land use.[4]

The various groups involved in urban land use zoning and other controls are each seeking their own ends, using all the economic, political, and legal powers they possess. If the results are disadvantageous to other groups, this is not by evil intent; it is an unavoidable outcome of each group seeking its own ends. Zoning may properly seek to preserve the quality and the value of an established area, but this objective rather easily slides over into a purely exclusionary one. Zoning, to be effective, must restrain some person or group from doing what he otherwise would have chosen to do; otherwise, it is worthless. But are its restrictionary outcomes in a general social interest, or not?

On the affirmative side, zoning and other land use controls have provided a significant degree of stability in land use in established residential and other areas. They have operated to keep the intrusion of discordant land uses to a practical minimum; service stations, funeral parlors, grocery stores, and scores of other uses do not readily invade an established residential area, for instance. By keeping out what are generally considered discordant land uses, zoning has helped to maintain land values in each zone. And by assuring some permanence of land use within an area, zoning may have encouraged private investment, thus adding to the attractiveness and stability of the protected area. Zoning has reduced the ease of land use change within established areas; whether one regards this as an advantage or a disadvantage, that seems to have been its effect.

On the negative side, zoning and other land use controls have operated to exclude some groups from settling in the growing suburbs. The effects have often been indirect; that is, a zoning ordinance would rarely if ever specify that a poor person or a minority group member be excluded from a particular area, but it might establish conditions that would virtually guarantee this outcome. Large lot-size requirements, building codes that seem defensible but

[4]F. Stuart Chapin, Jr., "Taking Stock of Techniques for Shaping Urban Growth," *Journal of American Institute of Planners*, May 1963.

ensure expensive houses, and lending policies that make it difficult if not impossible for a member of a racial minority to get a loan have operated to exclude the blacks and the poor almost as surely as an outright prohibition would have done. Seymour Toll has described how this aspect of zoning was embedded within land use zoning from the beginning.[5]

These same controls have been of limited value, however, in guiding new suburban land development. While the whole community might unite to help exclude the unwanted poor, the typical developing suburb has been unable or unwilling to enact zoning and other controls that were strong enough to effectuate a general plan for the area. The difficulty has been primarily political, not legal; dominant elements in the developing area have successfully resisted any major limitations on their operations.

In the past, land use zoning has been used by units of local government (counties and cities) for local ends. Within such local areas, it has been dominantly the concern and the creature of certain special interest groups — the real estate developers and the zoning lawyers primarily, with limited participation by the electorate at large. Each local zoning area has sought its own objectives; one area may want to attract industry to secure its tax contribution, another may want to exclude industry to preserve a style of suburban life desired by its upper-class residents.[6] Both figuratively and literally, local communities have dumped their sewage upon their neighbors. There has been no regional or metropolitan or overall concern except for special functions such as fire fighting, police control, parks, and highways. The absurdity of fire-fighting companies refusing to help fight fires in neighboring jurisdictions, or of police not cooperating to help capture criminals fleeing from one jurisdiction to another, overcame even the localism of local government. But, when it comes to overall economic and social development and implementing a metropolitan strategy, local land use zoning and controls have been notably deficient. The result has been Spread City — an amorphous spreading texture lacking strong nodal points and real metropolitan form — combined with the exclusion of the poor and the blacks and the degradation of the environment. De facto, we have allowed a major part of national land policy to be formed by the sum of many disparate local actions.

ORIGINS OF THIS BOOK

Considerations such as the foregoing led some of us at Resources for the Future to consider a more comprehensive and formal review of the problems

[5] Seymour Toll, *Zoned American* (Grossman Publishers, 1969).
[6] Robert C. Wood with Vladimir V. Almendinger, *1400 Governments: The Political Economy of the New York Metropolitan Region* (Harvard University Press, 1961).

of urban land policy, particularly the exclusionary aspects of land zoning and associated local land controls. In March 1971, we drew together a small group of planners, economists, and lawyers with particular interest and competence in the subject for a one-day informal discussion. As a result of the interest displayed at that meeting, we decided to hold a Forum. Those who were invited to give papers met for a day in November 1971 to outline what they expected to include in their papers, so that a degree of coordination could be achieved.

At the Forum itself, which consisted of four half-day sessions on April 13 and 14, 1972, each speaker summarized his paper. This was followed by a panel discussion by all the Forum speakers, and then audience participation was sought. There was a lively discussion about each pair of papers. After the Forum, those who had prepared papers revised them in light of the reactions of their colleagues and the audience; and it is the revised papers that are presented in this book.

A virtue of this type of seminar or forum is that a group of able professional workers can contribute knowledge and experience that no one author could hope to marshall in a single book. A weakness is that the various papers are not always closely related to each other or are not addressed to the same audience. Reviewers of books reporting such seminars or forums nearly always refer to the papers as "uneven." In this particular case, I think there is rather more compatibility and comprehensiveness than is typical for such volumes partly because the authors had an opportunity to coordinate their presentations. Each of the papers stands alone, in the sense that it can be read separately from the others. Together, they provide a more complete picture of our urban land policy — how it developed, what it has and has not achieved, and how it might be modernized to serve current and future needs.

A SUMMARY OF THE FORUM PAPERS

In the opening paper, John W. Reps discusses the historical aspects of urban land use planning and, more particularly, the history of public land-ownership in city development. He reviews some of the ways in which modern city and suburban development is less than fully satisfactory, and how a number of recent commissions and individual authors have indicated the desirability, if not the necessity, for large-scale public acquisition of land for later development by private individuals or firms. Reps notes that the nation's hesitancy to undertake such a program may reflect the notion that public land acquisition is somehow un-American — a notion that is not borne out by a study of the country's history. Public landownership was the basis upon which many American cities were developed: Washington, D.C., under the driving force of George Washington and Thomas Jefferson; many colonial tidewater towns and cities, including Baltimore, Annapolis, and Williamsburg; a number of cities in the South and Midwest; and cities of Spanish origin, including Los Angeles in the West. Much of Manhattan was once publicly owned. For many years the city raised revenue for its public services by selling off land, only to have to buy some of it back at a greatly increased price when Central Park was established. Had New York City retained the land it once owned and leased rather than sold it, the city today would be rich with low taxes. Its use of land to raise revenue for current operating costs must rank as one of the most short-sighted and expensive municipal financing systems in history.

Reps traces at some length the planning and development of Savannah, where planning and public landownership played major roles. The merit of the city's original plan is attested by the fact that most of the original squares have survived. As long as the supply of public land lasted – until about the middle of the nineteenth century – Savannah's development was orderly and the result attractive and efficient; after the public land was used up, development proceeded on private land, largely unplanned and uncoordinated, with predictably bad results.

Reps concludes by pointing out that historical precedent is no substitute for careful and rational analysis of problems and of alternatives for the future. But he does substantiate his thesis that public landownership in growing cities is an old American institution, which might well be revived for future urban development.

In the next paper, Robert C. Weaver draws on his extensive research and administrative experience for a discussion of the effects of land use zoning and other local land use controls on minority groups. He starts with a carefully documented description of the many ways in which minorities are discriminated against, and the role that zoning and other land use controls play in that process. He feels that two important new elements entered the scene in 1968: the Housing Act, with its new programs for moderate-income housing and the Civil Rights Act, which made it more difficult to practice discrimination in housing. The subsidies for low- and moderate-income people in the 1968 Housing Act were highly important, yet in many respects the federal programs could be, and have been, thwarted by local governments.

Weaver points out the need to improve housing for the poor and the minorities, in *both* the suburbs and central cities – not just in one or the other. He further points out that removing zoning restrictions alone is not enough: it does not solve the equally serious problem of an inadequate supply of suitable housing at costs the lower-income people can afford. He feels that aid to renters – rent supplements, paid to them as individuals – is helpful, but that subsidies for the production of more housing for low-income people are also necessary. He explores the possibilities of denying grants of all kinds to units of local government that do not make a significant effort to provide housing for low-income people within their boundaries.

Weaver concludes with a brief analysis of some of the complex problems that face the poor, of whatever racial or ethnic group they may be. He concludes, as have others, that their problems are not confined to housing alone. But better housing will help them to deal better with other problems; and liberalized zoning regulations facilitate housing construction for lower-income people.

The next two papers were presented at a session given over to the economists. Wilbur A. Steger considers the economic effects of racial discrimination, and Mason Gaffney explores the effect of local governmental action, particularly real estate taxes, on discrimination in housing and in land use.

Steger starts by a careful review of the economic literature about the costs of racial discrimination, in terms of low incomes, increased cost of housing, low labor force participation, unemployment and underemployment, and the like. He recognizes that many of the problems of the poor are interrelated, but he seeks to measure the net effect of discrimination as such. For example, a poorly educated worker is more likely to be unemployed or to receive a lower wage than a well-educated one; but how much less does a poorly educated black receive, because he is black, than he would receive if he were white? He concludes that part, but by no means all, of the difference in earnings between whites and blacks is explainable in terms of differences in age, education, health, labor force participation, and similar observable factors, but some is due to discrimination, as such.

Perhaps the outstanding contribution of Steger's paper is that, proceeding as best he can on the basis of admittedly inadequate data, he makes an estimate of the national cost of discrimination. "Together, the poverty and nonpoverty aspects of black income opportunity deprivation due to residential segregation are estimated to exceed $10 billion annually." Steger concludes with some policy suggestions and an outline of the fields where additional research is most seriously needed. Most informed observers of the modern urban scene would agree that discrimination against minorities is serious and undesirable; Steger has given us an estimate of its monetary significance, to reinforce and to quantify our general impressions.

Gaffney notes that local governments "have objectives and operate under constraints and incentives just like persons and firms." Some of these incentives give rise to the local exclusivism that conflicts with national goals. To avoid diluting their tax base, for example, local governments may put obstacles in the way of those who will demand more in services than they contribute in taxes.

In pursuit of their own self-interest or municipal "mercantilism" local governments practice such policies as: balkanization, or subdivision into small local enclaves; administrative modifications of the property tax; forcing property consumption by direct controls over land use; by regressive regulatory bias; allocation of municipal funds; and other ways. Of all the tools used by municipal governments to affect land use, Gaffney feels that the property tax is by far the most important. In particular, the real estate tax falls too heavily on buildings, not heavily enough on land. As a result, land tends to be used less intensively than would be desirable; sites tend to be cleared and rebuilt more slowly than would be best; taxes halt many building and rebuilding projects by making them submarginal or marginal ventures and lead to the use of larger parcels of land than would be the case if land taxes were higher. "The combined effect is to reduce the service from any given amount of land and diffuse demand over a wider area than necessary, economical, or socially desirable."

In his closing section Gaffney suggests that remedial policy should be radical enough to change local incentives and nudge local decision in the humanist direction. At the same time he suggests that it be conservative in retaining local control over local matters and in recognizing that small changes can tip the scales.

The third half-day of the Forum was given over to the lawyers, who considered some of the legal problems in discriminatory land use zoning and related controls. Ira Michael Heyman considered the legal assaults made in recent years on land use regulation, while Daniel Wm. Fessler explored some of the ways in which discriminatory controls might be attacked in the courts. Each paper was assigned, and was designed to fit into the overall plan of the Forum.

Heyman starts by making clear his assumption that land use controls are here to stay, but not as a municipal monopoly. He notes that zoning and subdivision regulation by local governments have failed to meet many of the original objectives and have buttressed exclusionary tendencies.

Heyman then reviews the recent assaults on municipal land use regulation, and finds that there have been six major sources. The environmentalists who have opposed land use controls because they have been "inadequate to treat rationally of ecological systems that transcend local boundaries"; the lawyers or, more particularly, the American Law Institute, which has been drafting model statutes for land use regulation; the participants in the land development market or the very large builders who have both the legal talent and the economic power to fight restrictive local land use controls; the proponents of open housing who have sought to overthrow local land use regulations that have had the effect of excluding racial or other minorities; state governments, which have created various instruments with power to override local land use controls under some conditions; and federal stimulants, which are a powerful force against restrictive municipal land use regulations, and may become still more powerful.

Heyman concludes: "We are witnessing a substantial transfer of land use control from the local to regional and state levels." He judges that this transfer of power will continue under the influence of the several sources of change described above; in particular, he feels that environmental considerations will be particularly important in leading to metropolitan or state powers to override local zoning actions. The process is primarily a political rather than a legal one, and new political alliances and power-groupings may be in the making.

Fessler's task was to examine the bases upon which discriminatory land use controls might be challenged over the next several years. He starts by describing the rapid development in recent years of a system of legal services for the poor, who were previously effectively excluded from recourse to the courts, because they lacked funds to employ legal talent. "A dramatic shift in the heretofore sporadic government involvement was achieved with the advent of the Office of Economic Opportunity." The legal services thus made available have scored a number of notable gains for low-income people, although few would contend that the balance has yet been fully redressed. Fessler traces some of the difficulties the blacks and the poor face, when they seek to leave the undesirable city centers for a better life in the suburbs, as upper-class whites have so long done; and he feels that such disadvantaged groups, joined by those seeking a profit from building houses for low- and moderate-income people, will seek to overthrow the exclusionary land use measures.

If an attempt is made to have courts overturn local discriminatory land use controls, Fessler thinks the courts, especially the Supreme Court, will be wary of substantive Due Process or of substituting its judgment and standards for those of the legislative and executive branches of government. In particular, in the past it has been nearly impossible for those excluded from a local area to bring suit, for they neither lived nor owned property in the area concerned. Although the courts in recent years have greatly relaxed the "standing" requirements, the "noninterventionist standard of review adopted by the courts" remains a major obstacle.

A more promising avenue seems to lie in the Equal Protection Clause of the Constitution. It might be well be claimed that decent housing is a "fundamental right" to which all citizens are entitled. "If the disparity in land use opportunities dictated de facto or de jure by the mandate of zoning ordinances happens to coincide with the racial composition of the favored and disfavored neighborhoods, a garden variety strict review equal protection suit is theoretically before the court." While racial exclusion might be the basis for a successful court suit, discrimination along economic lines is much less likely to be stricken down by the courts. He notes that "in no case has the Court ever found in the fact of economic discrimination, standing alone, an invidious classification."

Fessler feels that the most promising ground upon which to attack discriminatory land use controls is the doctrine of federal supremacy. This doctrine has been the basis for legislation and court actions on many racial discriminatory matters, including some land use zoning cases. If a clearly articulated federal policy sought to outlaw discriminatory local land use zoning, it is highly probable that the courts would uphold such legislation.

Fessler concludes by pointing out that state courts are, in many important respects, freer to deal with discriminatory land use cases than are federal courts — where the judges hesitate to interfere with the rights of a lower unit of government, for instance. Although most civil rights attorneys have sought to sue in federal courts, Fessler argues that "serious consideration should be given to seeking relief in a state court where the quest is a direct appeal to the state courts to order their own house, and a national housing law is not at stake." And he concludes that there is reason for "cautious optimism that the habitually disadvantaged, now for the first time possessed of a litigating capacity, may extricate themselves from the discriminatory impact of snob zoning schemes."

On the final half-day program, Richard F. Babcock and David L. Callies discussed the conflicts that sometimes emerge between ecological or environmental concerns and the provision of housing and jobs, especially for the lower-income segments of the urban population. In their view, "any beneficent public policy, if prosecuted vigorously, is bound to conflict with an equally beneficent public policy." They cite a number of instances in which ecological or environmental protection efforts have imposed hardships on groups that are less able to enjoy the preserved environment than the advocates of the preservation programs are. Concluding that compromise is a moral as well as a practical goal, they make a number of specific suggestions for reconciling the environmental-housing conflicts. One of their suggestions is that consideration be given to housing impact statements as well as environmental impact statements. Another is that the state take back some of the police power that is the legal basis for municipal zoning.

In the final paper, Marion Clawson and Harvey S. Perloff consider policy alternatives for the future. They divide their suggestions into two broad categories: procedural reforms and substantive reforms. Land use planning and zoning are often administered in a sloppy fashion, and reform of procedures has much to commend it. The states might establish and enforce criteria for local land use planning and zoning; in general, conformity to recognized principles of good government practice would bring the level of practice up to that of some of the best units of local government today. The standing of citizen groups to sue might well be broadened, to remove undesirable local inadequacies of governmental process. Provision might be made for appeal of zoning cases to some unit of government with broader jurisdiction; this would leave responsibility for initial and for local action with the local body, while at the same time providing a degree of metropolitan, regional, or state control over the process.

One of the substantive reforms would be to require every land use plan or zoning ordinance to make specific provision for lower-income people — provision proportionate to the need; this might be done at subdivision, suburban community, or metropolitan levels. The potentialities of public land purchase, with later sale or long-term lease to private developers, is explored at some length; "one is forced to conclude that nothing less than major public involvement in the suburban land market will make any real difference in the kinds of urban growth that will take place." Ways in which private speculation in land could be reduced and "de-profitized" are also considered. The present suburban land market has been strongly influenced, if not determined, by various laws and regulations. Other suggestions for future urban land policy are briefly mentioned.

Among the many points made by the several authors in this book, two general conclusions seem to stand out.

Urban land use policy is now under such scrutiny and attack that substantial changes seem highly probable, but the degree and precise direction of change is still uncertain.

Policies with respect to control over urban and suburban land use are important but only part of the whole picture; public works and services, housing programs, and other governmental measures greatly affect the public welfare and have a special bearing on the opportunities of the poor and the disadvantaged.

PUBLIC LAND,
URBAN DEVELOPMENT POLICY, AND
THE AMERICAN PLANNING TRADITION

JOHN W. REPS

The defects in the present system by which we attempt to control urban development should now be apparent to all. As James Rouse put it in testimony before the House Committee on Banking and Currency in 1966, "The most advanced planning and zoning concepts in America today are inadequate to preserve our forests and stream valleys and maintain open spaces. They cannot produce well-formed communities with a rich variety of institutions and activities and a wide range of choice in housing density, type, price and rent. As a matter of fact, zoning has become almost a guarantee of sprawl rather than protection against it."[1]

The exclusionary aspects of much current suburban zoning have now been highlighted in a series of state court decisions.[2] And Seymour Toll has recently documented the suspicion that back of the fine rhetoric supporting the

---

J O H N W. R E P S is professor of city planning at Cornell University. He has written and lectured extensively on urban land policy and land use controls, and is the author of four books on the history of American city planning – *The Making of Urban America*, *Monumental Washington*, *Town Planning in Frontier America*, and *Tidewater Towns*. Mr. Reps was born in 1921 and has an A.B. from Dartmouth College and a Master of Regional Planning Degree from Cornell University. He has also studied at Liverpool University and the London School of Economics.

[1]*Demonstration Cities, Housing, and Urban Development, and Urban Mass Transit*, Hearings before the Committee on Banking and Currency, 89 Cong. 2 sess. (1966), pt. 2, p. 1048.

[2]These cases have become the subjects of many law review articles; see, for example, Robert Silkey and Lawrence Dickie, "A Survey of the Judicial Responses to Exclusionary Zoning," *Syracuse Law Review*, vol. 22 (1971), p. 537, and Lawrence Sager, "Tight Little Islands: Exclusionary Zoning, Equal Protection and the Indigent," *Stanford Law Review*, vol. 21 (1969), p. 767. See also Richard Babcock, "The Courts Enter the Land Development Marketplace," *City*, vol. 5 (January–February 1971), pp. 58–64.

earliest comprehensive zoning ordinances were motives of almost unblemished selfishness and discriminatory intent.[3]

Our present planning and zoning system thus does not work well for rich or poor, for black or white, for central city or suburb. Blight, noise, and congestion characterize some areas, while sprawl, inconvenience, and visual monotony are the rule in others. Residents of low-income racial ghettos and those from affluent exurban preserves are both deprived of a satisfactory urban environment. Separate but equal exclusion from opportunities to enjoy the full richness and wonderful diversity that the city could provide seems to be the rule that shaped our urban guidance system.

Our total failure to control development at the metropolitan scale should be regarded as a national disgrace. We have nothing equivalent to such achievements in planned metropolitan growth as Rotterdam, Amsterdam, or Stockholm — three cities among many whose development during much of this century closely followed patterns of expansion determined by public authorities. The present preoccupation of many American metropolitan planning agencies with alternative configuration models has no current relevance whatsoever, because the power is lacking to carry out even the least drastic proposed departure from a straight-line projection of past trends.

We lack not technical skill but political will. The state of the art of environmental planning in America at least equals that in the many European cities whose quality of design stands as proof that the modern metropolis can be shaped to meet man's needs. Nor is it lack of financial ability; the Netherlands in 1902 and Sweden in 1904 were surely less affluent than we are today even with all of our pressing obligations. Yet it was then that cities in those countries were authorized to acquire by purchase or condemnation all land that would be needed for urban purposes well in the future, to hold it until required for expansion, and then release it to the market by sale or lease under covenant or leasehold restrictions guaranteeing its use for the purposes designated in the long-range development plan.

This is the key to successful implementation of environmental plans. As its director of planning and building control stated in 1965, "Stockholm's ability to plan its physical, economic, and social development must be attributed mainly to one all-important factor: public ownership of the land."[4] Recent studies by American and Swedish authorities have documented fully the truth of this assertion.[5]

[3] Seymour Toll, *Zoned American* (Grossman Publishers, 1969).

[4] Goran Sidenbladh, "Stockholm: A Planned City," *Scientific American*, vol. 213 (September 1965), p. 107.

[5] Ann Louise Strong, *Planned Urban Environments* (Johns Hopkins University Press, 1971), pp. 1–64; National Housing Board, National Swedish Institute for Building Re-

The difference between there and here is not in planning ability but in the location of decision-making power over the place, tempo, sequence, and pattern of urban development. There, the power resides in public bodies charged with promoting the general welfare and under conditions that make private economic goals secondary to social benefit. Here, the power rests primarily in private hands; it is motivated mainly by profit and personal gain, and it is modified only slightly by public controls.

By ignoring a recommendation on this point that was made by the National Resources Committee in 1937, we lost the opportunity to initiate a system of urban guidance that could have been fully and successfully operating in 1972. Thirty-five years ago that agency, an advisory planning body to the president, issued a masterly statement on the nation's urban problems. That report, *Our Cities – Their Role in the National Economy*, traced the development of America from a rural to an urban nation, analyzed existing issues, and recommended a series of remedial measures. Even then it was evident that there were deficiencies in zoning, subdivision regulation, and other police power measures and in community plans that were essentially advisory or inspirational in nature. The Committee felt there were benefits to be gained from municipal land acquisition and management, and its recommendation on this matter reads as follows:

> Better to control urban development, to combat land speculation and to have land available for low-rent housing, recreational, educational and other public facilities likely to be increasingly required in the future, the Committee advocates a more liberal policy of land acquisition by municipalities and accordingly recommends the liberalizing of the fundamental laws of the States in order to permit urban authorities to acquire, hold, and dispose of land . . . .
>
> Since opportunities for land acquisition often are best when the urban community is least able financially to make such outlays, the Committee recommends that the . . . [federal government] . . . should be authorized to make loans to urban communities for the acquisition of both improved and unimproved real estate for the purposes mentioned above.[6]

The Committee based that recommendation on an intensive investigation of urban land policy carried out by the staff of its subcommittee on urbanism. Their extended monograph included a long section written by Harold S.

search, *Municipal Land Policy in Sweden*, Document D5:1970, Stockholm, 1970; Shirley S. Passow, "Land Reserves and Teamwork in Planning Stockholm," *Journal of the American Institute of Planners*, vol. 36 (May 1970), pp. 179–88; John E. Cribett, "Some Reflections on the Law of Land – A View from Scandinavia," *Northwestern University Law Review*, vol. 62 (1967), p. 277.

[6] U.S. National Resources Committee, *Our Cities* (1937), pp. 76–77.

Buttenheim on the experience of European cities with this means of development control and a searching analysis of the arguments for and against its
possible application in the United States.[7] Despite the thoroughness of the
Committee's research and the force of its arguments advocating the adoption
of this policy, no executive or congressional support for such a program ever
materialized.

We now have before us not a proposal from a single agency but a near-
consensus by those who have examined the issue of how additions to the
urban fabric should be provided. A growing number of individuals during the
past few years have examined and recommended vastly increased land acquisition by public bodies for development control and related purposes, the most
recent being Marion Clawson in *Suburban Land Conversion in the United
States.*[8]

Several broadly based ad hoc committees, professional societies, and
national organizations have also supported this position either for guiding
expansion at the urban fringe or for creating more remotely located entirely
new communities. They include the American Institute of Planners, the
National Committee on Urban Growth Policy, the National Urban Coalition,
and the American Institute of Architects.[9] The draft of a model planning and

---

[7] U.S. National Resources Committee, "Supplementary Report of the Urbanism Committee," vol. 2, *Urban Planning and Land Policies* (1939), pt. 3, sec. 6, pp. 312–28.

[8] Johns Hopkins University Press for Resources for the Future, 1971. See also the
following: Donald G. Hagman, "Public Acquisition and Disposal of Lands," in Virginia
Curtis, ed., *Land-Use Policies*, papers presented at the land-use short course held at the
1970 ASPO National Planning Conference, Chicago (1970), pp. 5–17; John W. Reps,
"The Future of American Planning – Requiem or Renascence," in American Society of
Planning Officials, *Planning 1967*, pp. 47–65, and *Land-Use Controls*, vol. 1 (1967),
pp. 1–16; Grace Milgram, *The City Expands* (Institute for Environmental Studies, University of Pennsylvania, 1967), pp. 131–38; Edward Higbee, *The Squeeze: Cities Without Space* (Morrow, 1960), pp. 327–38, and *A Question of Priorities* (Morrow, 1970).
pp. 160–65; Dennis O'Harrow, "Proposals for New Techniques for Shaping Urban
Expansion," in U.S. Housing and Home Finance Agency, *Urban Expansion – Problems
and Needs*, papers presented at Administrator's Spring Conference, April 1963 (1963),
pp. 137–59; Shirley Siegel, *The Law of Open Space* (New York Regional Plan Association, 1960), p. 58; James W. Rouse, *Demonstration Cities . . . ,* Hearings, pp. 1047–52;
Henry Bain, *The Development District*, prepared by the Washington Center for Metropolitan Studies for the Maryland–National Capital Park and Planning Commission (1968);
Marion Clawson, "Suburban Development Districts," *Journal of The American Institute
of Planners*, vol. 26 (May 1960), pp. 69–83; and Fred P. Bosselman, *Alternatives to
Urban Sprawl*, Research Report No. 15 prepared for the National Commission on Urban
Problems (1968), pp. 2–3, 41–68. For the arguments against adopting a policy of this
kind see Sylvan Kamm, *Land Banking: Public Policy Alternatives*, Urban Institute Paper
112–28 (Washington, 1970).

[9] American Institute of Planners, *Policy Statement on New Communities* (Washington, 1968); National Committee on Urban Growth Policy, *The New City* (New York,
1969), pp. 169–74; National Urban Coalition, *Counterbudget: A Blueprint for Changing*

development control act, now in its final stages of revision by the American Law Institute, would authorize substantially increased powers of land acquisition for such purposes.[10]

Large-scale public land acquisition was examined and endorsed by the many urban policy task forces reporting in recent years. The 1968 proposal by the National Commission on Urban Problems (the Douglas Commission) may be cited as a typical example:

> The Commission recommends that state governments enact legislation enabling state and/or local development authorities or agencies of general purpose governments to acquire land in advance of development for the following purposes: (a) assuring the continuing availability of sites needed for development; (b) controlling the timing, location, type, and scale of development; (c) preventing urban sprawl; and (d) reserving to the public gains in land values resulting from the action of government in promoting and servicing development.[11]

Similar proposals can be found in the reports of a number of policy task forces and study groups.[12] The unanimity of support for what might have been regarded a few years ago as a wildly radical solution suggests that at long last this is an idea whose time has come, especially as the membership of most of these groups included more than token members of political and economic conservatives.[13]

National Priorities, 1971-1976 (1971), pp. 132–46; American Institute of Architects, "The First Report of the National Policy Task Force," *Memo* (January 1972 special issue), p. 4.

[10] The American Law Institute, *A Model Land Development Code*, Preliminary Draft No. 13 (Philadelphia, 1971).

[11] National Commission on Urban Problems, *Building the American City* (1968), p. 251.

[12] President's Committee on Urban Housing, *A Decent Home* (1969), pp. 144–46; President's Council on Recreation and Natural Beauty, *From Sea to Shining Sea* (1968), pp. 115–16; President's Task Force on Suburban Problems, *Final Report* (1968), pp. 76–81; Advisory Commission on Intergovernmental Relations, *Urban and Rural America* (1968), pp. 152–61; Canadian Federal Task Force on Housing and Urban Development, *Report* (1969), p. 43; California Governor's Advisory Commission on Housing Problems, *Report* (1963), pp. 60–62; Puerto Rico Planning Board, *Urban Land Policy for the Commonwealth of Puerto Rico* (1968), pp. 95–106; New York State Office of Planning Coordination, *New Communities for New York* (1970), pp. 64–66.

[13] There were no stated reservations by any of the 26 members of the Advisory Commission on Intergovernmental Relations, whose recommendations are perhaps the most detailed and specific on the subject of land acquisition. It is clear that the commission believed that effective guidance of urban development could be achieved only through massive public intervention in the urban land market by large-scale purchase or condemnation. Membership consisted of the following: Farris Bryant (*chairman*), a former governor of Florida; Price Daniel (*vice chairman*), director, U.S. Office of Emergency Planning; Ben Barnes, speaker, Texas House of Representatives; Neal S. Blaisdell,

The advantages of a public land acquisition system are both numerous and compelling. It would enable the community at large to determine the character of its expanding man-made environmental framework and to create convenient, safe, and attractive neighborhoods. Used to prevent sprawl, it would reduce public capital costs and annual operating expenses. It would aid the private building industry by assuring a constant flow of improved and conveniently located sites for construction — preplanned, approved for immediate use, and with no uncertainties as to cost. It could dampen pressures by private interests to subvert and destroy public plans for wise land use by eliminating the speculative profits so often gained through successful attacks on zoning. It might help to curb spiraling prices of land, which have become a major factor in raising the cost of housing.[14] It may be the only method that can assure a more balanced social and racial mix in new urban neighborhoods. It can and should be employed to facilitate central city renewal by providing relocation sites for persons and businesses displaced through slum clearance and redevelopment.

Those who doubt the validity of these propositions should examine the achievements of the many cities in northern Europe that have had long experience with such programs. They might also look at the experience of Puerto Rico where the Puerto Rico Land Administration has in a few years acquired substantial holdings of land for eventual planned development in eleven urban areas of that small island.[15] Even more persuasive are the accomplishments in

---

mayor of Honolulu; Ramsey Clark, U.S. attorney general; Dorothy I. Cline, professor of government, University of New Mexico; John Dempsey, governor of Connecticut; C. George De Stefano, member, Rhode Island State Senate; John F. Dever, commissioner, Middlesex County, Mass.; Florence P.Dwyer, representative from New Jersey; Buford Ellington, governor of Tennessee; Sam J. Ervin, Jr., senator from North Carolina; L. H. Fountain, representative from North Carolina; Henry Fowler, secretary of the treasury; Alexander Heard, chancellor, Vanderbilt University; Jack Maltester, mayor of San Leandro, California; Angus McDonald, commissioner, Yakima County, Washington; Karl E. Mundt, senator from South Dakota; Edmund S. Muskie, senator from Maine; Arthur Naftalin, mayor of Minneapolis; James A. Rhodes, governor of Ohio; Nelson Rockefeller, governor of New York; Gladys N. Spellman, commissioner, Prince George's County, Maryland; Al Ullman, representative from Oregon; Jesse M. Unruh, speaker, California Assembly; William F. Walsh, mayor of Syracuse.

[14] Professor Grace Milgram's study of land development in a major sector of the Philadelphia area between 1945 and 1962 indicates that land typically sold for $1,350 an acre in 1945 and for $10,250 in 1962. She estimated that, with a program of advance purchase by some public body, the 1962 selling price would have been only $3,250. Note her conclusion: "The difference between these prices is the economic cost which can be attributed to maintenance of a private market in vacant land." Milgram, *The City Expands*, p. 128.

[15] The Puerto Rico program was first suggested in the report to the Puerto Rico Planning Board, prepared in 1961 by Mohinder S. Bhatia and Alvin Mayne, but not published by the Board until November 1968 as *Urban Land Policy for the Common-*

guiding urban development through advance and massive public land acquisition by several cities in western Canada, including Red Deer, Saskatoon, and Calgary.[16] There, under social, political, economic, and legal conditions closely resembling those in the United States, public officials, private builders, and consumers alike report fully satisfactory results. It was after an examination of this experience and an exhaustive study of the flaws of police power regulations that the Canadian Task Force on Housing and Urban Development — the equivalent of our Douglas Commission — issued the following unequivocal recommendation: "Municipalities or regional governments, as a matter of continuing policy, should acquire, service and sell all or a substantial portion of the land required for urban growth within their boundaries."[17]

Yet we hesitate. The present administration has called for a national urban growth policy, but has submitted no proposals for federal legislation of the type I have been discussing. Title VII of the Housing and Urban Development Act of 1970, enacted under Democratic congressional leadership, addresses itself only to new communities, and even for projects such as these it contains no provisions for advance land acquisition and extensive holding periods. The open space acquisition program in the same act permits advance acquisition, but not for land that would eventually be developed; in fact, the Conference Committee went out of its way to note that the measure was not intended to permit what they referred to as "land banking."[18]

---

wealth of Puerto Rico. The basic legislation was passed in 1962 as Act No. 13, Puerto Rico Land Administration. Its provisions were upheld by the Puerto Rico Supreme Court in 1967 (Opinion No. 67–172, December 7, 1967), and an appeal to the U.S. Supreme Court was denied in the following year. For a discussion of the Puerto Rico program and an examination of the decision in *Commonwealth of Puerto Rico* v. *Jorge I. Rosso*, see David L. Callies, "*Commonwealth of Puerto Rico* v. *Rosso*: Land Banking and an Expanded Concept of Public Use," *Land-Use Controls*, vol. 2 (1968), pp. 17–31. The case (and its implications) is also examined in Ernest Roberts, "The Demise of Property Law," *Cornell Law Review*, vol. 57 (1971), p. 1.

[16]Denis Cole, "The City of Red Deer," *Habitat*, vol. 6 (1963), pp. 28–33; S. Buckwold, "Land Policy in Saskatoon," *Habitat*, vol. 5 (1962), pp. 2–5; and N. S. Trouth and A. L. Martin, "Land Development in Calgary," *Habitat*, vol. 5 (1962), pp. 14–23.

[17]Canadian Federal Task Force on Housing and Urban Development, *Report*, p. 43. Their earlier condemnation of reliance on zoning and subdivision regulations to assure planned development should be noted (p. 42): "Where is the 'grand design' in zoning by-laws, sub-division requirements and the like? . . . Instead of positive planning of transportation corridors, public and open spaces, and other broad elements of urbanization, there exists a flood of negative minutia dictating minimum lot sizes, setbacks and other requirements virtually inconsequential from a planning viewpoint. At best present municipal development by-laws can be said to prevent the worst. In point of fact, as often as not they merely inhibit the best."

[18]Report of Senate and House Conference Committee on HR 19436, *Congressional Record*, Dec. 17, 1970, p. H12009.

I suspect that a principal reason for inaction is the deep-seated conviction that public land ownership and disposal for urban development control purposes is somehow un-American, foreign to our experience, and incompatible with existing patterns of entrepreneurial activity. This belief is false, and it is to demonstrate that our tradition of public large-scale urban land management is not only extensive but also has lessons to teach our generation that I now turn.

EARLY HISTORY OF PUBLIC URBAN LAND MANAGEMENT

Two kinds of public urban land management activities of the past seem relevant to this inquiry. One involved public acquisition of sites for entirely new communities by purchase, exchange, condemnation, or reservation from the state or federal public domain. Literally dozens of towns and cities began in this way before the end of the nineteenth century. The other, which was less frequent but of at least equal importance, arose when certain cities came into ownership of very large tracts within their corporate boundaries and subsequently disposed of the land to private owners.

Planned New Communities

One does not usually think of George Washington and Thomas Jefferson as planning administrators and experts in urban land policy, but both played these roles in creating in the District of Columbia the largest and most impressive of America's new towns, a city planned on a site acquired for that purpose by a public agency. Both men were landed gentry themselves, and President Washington in an earlier day actively and successfully speculated in frontier land and town lots. Both knew of the speculative fever that gripped the landowners between the Potomac and Anacostia rivers early in 1791 when the president designated this area as the future site of the national capital. But both men agreed – and there is abundant evidence that neither considered any other possibility – that only if the entire tract of well over 5,000 acres passed into public ownership could a comprehensive plan be implemented for a city of unusual design and outstanding character.

The proprietors agreed to transfer to the president in trust all title to their property. He was to have a free hand in determining the plan of the new city. No payment was to be made for land used for streets, and owners were to receive compensation only for sites designated for public buildings. Half of the city lots would then be conveyed to the original landowners, while the federal government would retain the other half.

It was this arrangement that made possible Pierre L'Enfant's monumental plan for the city of Washington, an urban design concept unmatched in

America and surely ranking as one of the outstanding urban planning accomplishments in history. Public land ownership of the entire site, administrators
concerned with the public welfare, and a skillful planner all combined to
produce a unique urban community.[19]

The method employed, however, was far from unique; it was, in fact, the
prevailing technique used to create towns in colonial Virginia and Maryland,
with significant applications elsewhere in the English colonies. The colonial
capitals of these tidewater provinces originated in similar fashion. Annapolis
in 1694 and Williamsburg in 1699 were planned by government officials on
sites acquired by the public after the passage of appropriate legislation. Proceeds from sales of lots were used to reimburse the former owners of the
sites. With the opportunities afforded by ownership of the complete site, the
planner-administrator Francis Nicholson, who served as governor or deputy
governor of these and other colonies, succeeded in creating towns of unusual
beauty, interest, and functional utility.

Nicholson's lovely capital cities were but two among dozens of towns
founded by the Virginia and Maryland legislatures during the seventeenth and
eighteenth centuries. From 1680 to 1706 several new town acts were passed,
each designating a number of locations to be developed. These laws authorized purchase or condemnation of necessary property, directed county offi
cials to plan the towns, listed types of public uses for which sites were to be
reserved, specified the method of land sales, listed conditions to be imposed
on purchasers of building sites, and provided for compensation to proprietors
from proceeds of land sales. Norfolk, Virginia, came into being under one of
these statutes.

In the eighteenth century this policy of wholesale founding of towns was
modified somewhat, and the two legislatures created single towns as the need
arose. Baltimore and Georgetown were created in this fashion, as was Alex-
andria, which George Washington helped to survey in 1748 as a lad of seventeen learning his trade.

Public initiative in urban development was such a familiar activity to both
Washington and Jefferson that they regarded it as the normal procedure to
follow when they faced their responsibilities of creating a new national
capital.[20] They could have drawn on other colonial precedents. One was
Edenton, North Carolina, which the General Assembly of that colony created

[19] For a summary of the early development of Washington see John W. Reps, *Monumental Washington* (Princeton University Press, 1967), pp. 1–25. A more extended treatment of how the land was acquired can be found in William Tindall, *Standard History of
the City of Washington* (H. W. Crew and Co., 1914), pp. 37–112.

[20] Seven chapters of John W. Reps, *Tidewater Towns* (Colonial Williamburg, 1972)
describe in detail the public town-founding efforts of colonial Virginia and Maryland
briefly summarized above.

in 1712 on land acquired by public commissioners. Edenton shared with New Bern the status of colonial capital, and its design included ample sites for public buildings, wharfs and landings, and a broad mall leading from the waterfront to the church and courthouse.

Washington and Jefferson may have known also of the proposal made in 1730 by Governor Robert Johnson of South Carolina to create a series of new communities under governmental programs similar to those of Virginia and Maryland half a century earlier.[21] They may have been aware, as well, of the imaginative plan for George Town (later Hardwick), Georgia, intended in 1754 by Governor John Reynolds as a new capital for that colony. With its five civic squares, numerous sites for public buildings, surrounding common land, and ample reservations along the waterfront for maritime functions, this community also attested to the value of public land ownership in providing the city planner with opportunities for imaginative design. Brunswick, another Georgia town, had an even more unusual plan closely resembling that of Savannah, which is discussed in some detail later. This, too, was an example of public enterprise dating from 1771.[22]

One precedent for the founding and planning of Washington as a capital city was certainly familiar to the president. This was Columbia, designated in 1786 as the new capital of South Carolina. The legislature specified a site two miles square, and then appointed commissioners to acquire the site, prepare a plan with streets of generous widths and half-acre lots, reserve locations for the public buildings "as shall be most convenient and ornamental," offer one-fifth of the lots at auction, and stipulate that each purchaser should erect within three years a house at least eighteen by thirty feet of "frame, wood, stone, or brick . . . with brick or stone chimneys," or, on failure to comply with this covenant, to pay annually five percent of the purchase price.[23]

Columbia was the first of many planned territorial or state capitals for which the entire site was acquired by the public, surveyed into streets, blocks,

---

[21] Johnson's proposal, its modification by the Board of Trade, and the limited success of the program are described in Richard P. Sherman, *Robert Johnson: Proprietary and Royal Governor of South Carolina* (University of South Carolina Press, 1966), pp. 107–17, 149–51, and 173–83.

[22] For Brunswick see Allen D. Chandler, ed., *Colonial Records of Georgia* (Franklin Printing and Publishing Co., 1907), vol. 11, p. 383. A reproduction of a manuscript plan of George Town can be found in John W. Reps, *The Making of Urban America* (Princeton University Press, 1965), p. 197.

[23] The act appears in *North Carolina Statutes at Large*, vol. 4, pp. 751–52. For a summary of the legislation and a description of the founding and development of Columbia, see A. S. Salley, "Origin and Early Development," in Helen Kohn Hennig, ed., *Columbia: Capital City of South Carolina, 1786–1936* (Columbia Sesqui-Centennial Commission, 1936), pp. 1–12; and Edwin L. Green, *A History of Richland County* (R. L. Bryan Co., 1932), vol. 1, pp. 146–70.

and lots, and disposed of by auction or sale, often with conditions governing the use of the land. The procedure pioneered by South Carolina was followed elsewhere, although in many states the commissioners appointed to administer the project were given powers of site selection.

With some exceptions the capitals founded in this way were, like Columbia, superior in plan to those towns of the same period and in the same region originating as private speculations. The publicly planned communities usually had wider streets, more generous allocation of open spaces, more numerous sites for public and semipublic buildings, and greater emphasis on beauty. Proceeds from land sales were normally used for erecting public buildings or for other community improvements. In most cases the recreation, open space, market, and civic squares or other sites appearing in the original plan remained in public ownership for the use of future generations. In many of the privately promoted towns, such sites were held until they had served their purpose of attracting new residents, and were then disposed of for profit by the townsite promoter who had taken care not to dedicate them irrevocably for common use. Those who believe that superior planning and public enterprise in land development are incompatible should reexamine American urban planning history.

Raleigh, Louisville (Ga.), Milledgeville (Ga.), Tallahassee, Jackson, Indianapolis, Columbus, Jefferson City, Iowa City, Austin, and Lincoln were all planned capital cities; and Detroit was replanned in 1805-07 following the demolition by fire of the old French community.[24] But public enterprise in

[24]A full study of the extensive experience in acquiring and disposing of these planned urban domains would be a useful activity. Columbus, Jackson, and Indianapolis are treated briefly in Reps, *The Making of Urban America*, and reproductions of their early plans appear on pp. 227, 229, 272-75, and 321-23. The following references may prove useful to those wishing further information on some of these planned capital cities. Columbus, Ohio – Alfred J. Wright, "Joel Wright, City Planner," *Ohio Archeological and Historical Quarterly*, 56 (July 1947): 287-94; Detroit – John W. Reps, "Planning in the Wilderness: Detroit, 1805-1830," *Town Planning Review*, 25 (January 1955): 240-50; Lincoln – A. B. Hayes and Samuel D. Cox, *History of the City of Lincoln* (State Journal Co., 1889), and N. C. Abbott, "Lincoln: Name and Place," Nebraska State Historical Society, *Publications*, vol. 21 (1930), pp. 5-133; Austin – Ernest W. Winkler, "The Temporary Location of the Seat of Government," *Texas State Historical Association Quarterly*, vol. 10 (October 1906), pp. 140-71, and "The Permanent Location of the Seat of Government," ibid. (January 1907), pp. 185-245; Jefferson City – Perry S. Rader, "The Location of the Permanent Seat of Government," *Missouri Historical Review*, vol. 21 (October 1926), pp. 9-18; Iowa City – Margaret N. Keyes, *Nineteenth Century Home Architecture of Iowa City* (University of Iowa Press, 1966); Indianapolis – Donald F. Carmony, "Genesis and Early History of the Indianapolis Fund, 1816-1826," *Indiana Magazine of History*, vol. 38 (March 1942), pp. 17-30; Jackson – Dunbar Rowland, *History of Mississippi* (S. J. Clarke Publishing Co., 1925), vol. 1, pp. 516-22; Raleigh – Elizabeth Waugh, *North Carolina's Capital, Raleigh* (Junior League of Raleigh, 1967), pp. 3-5.

new town development was not confined to the creation of capital cities. At least three states actively participated in town founding in the years following the Revolution.

Pennsylvania used sites reserved from earlier sales or grants from its public domain. Allegheny, now part of Pittsburgh, was planned with a great central open space and a greenbelt of common land completely surrounding the city. Lot sales began in 1788.[25] Three years later the legislature authorized the governor to develop a second town on state land at the mouth of Beaver Creek on the Ohio River. Daniel Leet's plan, prepared under the direction of state commissioners, reserved four contiguous blocks at the center and one block at each of the four corners of the town for open space or public building sites, and these and seven lots set aside for public use were withheld from sale.[26]

In 1795 the Pennsylvania legislature authorized the governor to appoint two commissioners to survey 1,600 acres of state land on Lake Erie as a town and an adjoining 3,400 acres as outlots or farming tracts. General William Irvine and Andrew Ellicott prepared the plan for Erie, setting aside, as the act directed, 20 acres for public use of the city, and parcels of 30, 60, and 100 acres along the harbor for the federal government to use for dockyards, forts, and other installations.

The state conducted the first sales of land, but later one-third of the townsite and adjoining outlots, or more than 1,600 acres, was donated to the city, which in 1832 began to sell the land in 50-acre parcels. Further land sales by the city took place six years later when Erie's limits were extended beyond high water and a row of water lots was put up for sale. The city earmarked the proceeds of these sales for grading and paving of streets and for the construction of wharves, piers, and a canal basin.[27] In 1794 and 1795 three other towns in northwestern Pennsylvania were also planned under state supervision on public land: Franklin, Warren, and Waterford.[28]

Georgia has a similar nineteenth century history of town founding on public sites, continuing the colonial tradition in such places as George Town, Brunswick, and Savannah. Macon was laid out in 1823 with sites reserved for

[25] Pittsburgh Regional Planning Association and Pittsburgh City Planning Commission, *North Side Study* (1954), pp. 2–4; and Solon J. and Elizabeth Buck, *The Planting of Civilization in Western Pennsylvania* (University of Pittsburgh Press, 1939), p. 210.

[26] The basic act and some of the official correspondence and reports relating to the founding of Beaver may be found in Joseph H. Bausman, *History of Beaver County, Pennsylvania* (Knickerbocker Press, 1904), vol. 2, pp. 1236–43.

[27] *Nelson's Biographical Dictionary and Historical Reference Book of Erie County, Pennsylvania* (S. B. Nelson, 1895), pp. 387–90.

[28] Buck, *Planting of Civilization*, p. 220.

a courthouse, burial ground, and academy. Two principal boulevards 180 feet wide intersected at the central courthouse square. Other streets were platted a generous 120 feet in width, and along these thoroughfares the state commissioners arranged for the planting of shade trees.[29]

Five state commissioners in 1828 founded Columbus. They planned the town in half-acre lots fronting streets 99, 132, and 164 feet wide. In addition to common lands at the outskirts of the new city, the commissioners set aside several 4-acre blocks for public use: one for the courthouse, two for churches, and two for schools. In addition they provided a public promenade at the south end of the town from which the spectacular falls of the Chattahouchee River could be viewed. Georgians were quick to appreciate these unusual features made possible by public ownership of the site, and within two weeks from the beginning of land sales more than two-thirds of the 632 building lots were sold at auction, bringing the state the tidy sum of $131,000.[30]

In Illinois a larger and more important city originated from the activities of a state agency having jurisdiction over land in public ownership. At the request of the state legislature, Congress in 1827 granted Illinois title to alternate sections of land 5 miles on each side of a canal that was to be built to connect Lake Michigan with the Illinois River. Three years later the Canal Commissioners directed their engineer, James Thompson, to lay out as a town a portion of one of these sections of land at the mouth of the Chicago River.

About 240 acres in what is now Chicago's downtown were then platted in a gridiron of streets, square blocks, and rectangular lots. The balance of the 640-acre tract was subdivided shortly thereafter when speculative demand developed for town lots. Immediately to the south lay another square-mile section. This came into the ownership of school authorities under federal legislation governing surveys of the public domain. Despite some local opposition, this, too, was laid out in a great gridiron of 142 blocks, all but four of which were then sold. Chicago thus had its beginning as a town planned by state and local officials on land in public ownership.[31]

---

[29] John C. Butler, *Historical Record of Macon and Central Georgia* (J. W. Burke Co., 1958), p. 91.

[30] Nancy Telfair, *History of Columbus, Georgia, 1828-1928* (Historical Publishing Co., 1929), p. 33; and Etta B. Worsley, *Columbus of the Chattahouchee* (Columbus Office Supply Co., 1951), p. 75. The material on Columbus and Macon was brought to my attention by Joan Sears in an unpublished seminar paper, "Brunswick, Milledgeville, Macon, Columbus – Four Towns Founded by the State of Georgia," Department of City and Regional Planning, Cornell University, 1969.

[31] A Chicago historian writing in 1892 criticized the sale of the school section in the harshest possible words: "The sale of the school section was the greatest administrational blunder – or crime – in our annals. The tract . . . was . . . among the most valuable both for wharfing and building purposes in the present city. Suppose these to have been leased

To this list of new communities on public land can be added several towns
laid out by the federal government: Perrysburg, Ohio; Port Angeles, Washington; and many townsites in Oklahoma as former Indian reservations were
carved up for speculative purposes.[32] In addition, there must have been many
county seats whose founding, like that of Greensboro, North Carolina, followed an act of the legislature creating a new county and appointing a commission to select a site for its governmental seat on public land.[33]

Disposition of Municipal Land

I now turn to the second type of experience in urban public land management relevant to my subject — the disposition through sale or lease of large
tracts of land owned by municipalities. This topic has been strangely overlooked by scholars of public land policy whose work has largely focused on
the federal public domain.[34]

Cities whose experience should be investigated include San Antonio, Santa
Fe, San Diego, Los Angeles, Monterey, San Jose, Santa Cruz, and San Fran-

---

instead of sold (say upon fifty-year leases, in order that lessees should have proper
inducement to build upon them), they would now constitute an educational 'foundation' beside which Oxford, Edinburgh and Cambridge, Harvard, Yale, Cornell and
Columbia, all shrink to insignificance. At a rough guess the sum may be placed at
$100,000,000" (Joseph Kirkland, *The Story of Chicago* [Dibble Publishing Co., 1892],
p. 116). Kirkland states that the lots in the school tract brought $38,619.47 when they
were sold in 1832 or shortly thereafter (p. 117).

[32] For Port Angeles see G. M. Lauridsen and A. A. Smith, *The Story of Port Angeles*
(Lowman and Hanford Co., 1937), pp. 18–38. The role of federal surveyors in planning
many of the towns of Oklahoma has apparently never been studied. Plats prepared by
them can be found in the Cartographic Branch of the National Archives among the
Townsite Surveys of the General Land Office. They include such communities as
Chandler, Tecumseh, Enid, Lawton, Anadarko, Perry, Alva, and Woodward. Many existing Indian settlements were also replatted and extended by federal surveyors, including
Caddo, Vinita, and Tulsa. Oklahoma City and Guthrie, two of the earliest towns planned
in the former Indian Territory, resulted from private efforts.

[33] Ethel Stephens Arnett, *Greensboro, North Carolina* (University of North Carolina
Press, 1955), pp. 19–22. Circleville, Ohio was another such county seat established in
this manner. For the circumstances of its founding, its bizarre plan, and its subsequent
modification, see John W. Reps, "Urban Redevelopment in the Nineteenth Century: The
Squaring of Circleville," *Journal of the Society of Architectural Historians*, vol. 14
(December 1955), pp. 23–26.

[34] Studies of the management and disposition of the federal public domain are
numerous, including Benjamin Hibbard, *A History of Public Land Policies* (Macmillan,
1924, rev. ed., 1939); Roy Robbins, *Our Landed Heritage* (University of Nebraska Press,
1962); Payson Treat, *The National Land System, 1785–1820* (E. B. Treat, 1910);
Thomas C. Donaldson, *The Public Domain* (Government Printing Office, 1884); Paul
Gates, *Fifty Million Acres* (Cornell University Press, 1954); and Louise Peffer, *The
Closing of the Public Domain* (Stanford University Press, 1951). Town development on
the public lands is described in one chapter in Everett Dick, *The Lure of the Land*
(University of Nebraska Press, 1970), pp. 263–79.

cisco. All of these achieved municipal status under Spanish or Mexican administration and all received the customary land grant of 4 square leagues, a rectangular tract approximately 5¼ miles on each side embracing nearly 18,000 acres or some 28 square miles.[35]

After American occupation these enormous tracts were eventually surveyed more precisely, individual title claims were confirmed or rejected, and eventually municipal ownership was established over all land not legally sold or granted previously. Los Angeles may not be typical, but in 1853 the city owned approximately 80 percent of the original pueblo or municipal domain.[36] The policies followed in land sales in these cities of Spanish origin, the amount of revenues received, the purposes for which proceeds were used, and the ways in which land disposition may or may not have been employed to guide urban growth must someday be explored.

It would not be surprising to discover that many other cities found themselves with the same responsibilities and opportunities. At least two — New York City and Savannah — fall in this category. Both offer fascinating glimpses of past municipal land management and suggest at least a few directions for the future.

New York. The Dutch municipality of New Amsterdam owned some land within its boundaries, but its holdings were not extensive.[37] The first English governor, while extending the city boundaries to include all of the island of Manhattan in 1665, did not convey any additional land to the corporation.[38]

---

[35]The Los Angeles grant is described in J. M. Guinn, "The Plan of Old Los Angeles," *Historical Society of Southern California, Publications,* vol. 3, pt. 3 (1895), pp. 40–41. For the survey of this tract after American jurisdiction began and some information on land sales, see William W. Robinson, *Maps of Los Angeles from Ord's Survey of 1849 to the End of the Boom of the Eighties* (Dawson's Bookshop, 1966), pp. 15–31.

[36]Margaret Romer, "The Story of Los Angeles," pt. 3, *Journal of the West,* vol. 2 (April 1963), p. 171. For an exhaustive treatise on the legal conflicts involved in the final confirmation of San Francisco's claim to its municipal lands, see John W. Dwinelle, *The Colonial History of the City of San Francisco* (Towne and Bacon, 1866).

[37]George Ashton Black, *The History of Municipal Ownership on Manhattan Island to the Beginning of Sales by the Commissioners of the Sinking Fund in 1844.* Columbia College Studies in History, Economics and Public Law, vol. 1, no. 3 (1891), pp. 12–15 (hereafter cited as *Municipal Ownership*). Black's pioneering study is apparently the only systematic investigation of the topic. It has been extremely useful to me, although it does not deal with the period after 1844 when most of the public lands were alienated. Less useful because of its almost exclusive emphasis on the legal aspects of land titles in the city is Murray Hoffman, *Treatise Upon the Estate and Rights of the Corporation of the City of New York as Proprietors,* 2 vols. (McSpedon and Baker 2nd rev. ed., 1862). Another 19th century work containing some pertinent information is J. W. Gerard, *A Treatise on the Title of the Corporation and Others to the Streets, Wharves, Piers, Parks, Ferries, and Other Lands and Franchises in the City of New York* (Baker, Voorhis, 1873).

[38]Black, *Municipal Ownership,* pp. 15–16.

It was Governor Thomas Dongan who, in 1686, provided the city with its vast domain. For the sum of £324 Dongan issued a new city charter that granted to the municipality "all the waste, vacant, unpatented and unappropriated lands . . . within the . . . city . . . and on Manhattan's Island . . . extending and reaching to the low water mark . . . not heretofore given or granted."[39] The city promptly sold one tract of 16 acres on the Hudson River at the foot of Gansevoort Street and another group of fourteen lots on Dock Street to pay the governor's fee, thus beginning a long tradition of meeting municipal expenses through the sale or lease of public lands.[40]

The exact acreage of the city domain in 1686 is difficult to determine, but it was very large. Most of the land comprised the so-called "commons" north of what is now 23rd Street and between the Post Road running northeasterly to about the location of Third Avenue and the Bloomingdale Road, or Broadway, leading northwesterly to its crossings of present-day Sixth and Seventh avenues. This wide strip of what is now the central core of Manhattan continued to the north where it terminated at the common lands of Haarlem, a village with its own government although within the boundaries of the City of New York.

Some of these common lands were sold prior to their first detailed survey in 1785, but even so 1,300 acres remained in public ownership.[41] During the 99 years since the Dongan Charter the city had wisely refused to sell these lands and had, instead, leased some tracts while letting the rest simply lie idle.

Most of the lands disposed of during the eighteenth century were located below 23rd Street at the northern fringe of the city. Here and on city-owned tracts closer to the tip of Manhattan and now surrounded by private development the city followed a mixed policy of selling and leasing. There seems to be little evidence that the city used its public domain for development control purposes, but it did derive substantial revenues from its landed estate. Indeed, for many years of its colonial existence New York City managed to pay for most of its public improvements and municipal services through

[39] Marcus Benjamin, "Thomas Dongan and the Granting of the New-York Charter, 1682–1688," in James Grant Wilson, ed., *The Memorial History of the City of New-York* (New York History Co., 1892), vol. 1, p. 439. Benjamin gives the full text of the charter on pp. 437–46.

[40] Black, *Municipal Ownership*, p. 19. The municipal domain was enlarged in 1731 when Governor John Montgomerie conferred a new charter that extended public ownership 400 feet beyond low water mark around the southern tip of Manhattan, adding more than 200 acres to the area under city ownership (Gerard, *A Treatise on the Title*, p. 39). In 1807 the legislature extended this strip of public land under water four miles northwards along the Hudson and two miles along the East River (*An Act Relative to Improvements. . . , Laws of New York, 1807, Section XV*).

[41] Black, *Municipal Ownership*, p. 38.

income derived from leases and sales of lands, ferry and dock rentals, and miscellaneous fees rather than through taxation.[42]

One major sale of land in the northern part of Manhattan took place in 1701 when the city put up for auction 240 acres on the Hudson between what are now 107th and 125th streets. Receipts of £237 helped pay for the new city hall.[43] Some other and much smaller tracts and lots were sold in and near the built-up portion of the city, but much of the land was subdivided and leased. The town common of Dutch New Amsterdam, which began about 500 yards north of Wall Street, was one of the tracts made available for development in this manner. In 1759 fifty-nine lots were laid out on the western portion and leased for £2 to £4 a year. Three years later the city divided the eastern section into 61 lots and offered them on 21-year leases at £4 annually. In 1763 the city divided a 155-acre tract at the north of the old town common below 42nd Street and running west from 5th Avenue into 5-acre parcels and leased them at auction.[44]

Following the Revolution the city turned its attention to the 1,300-acre strip of common land stretching northwards from 23rd Street. In 1785 the city council ordered the city surveyors to lay out this land in plots of 5 acres so that they could be offered at auction to meet the increased cost of municipal services for the growing city.[45] The sale did not take place until 1789

[42] Writing in 1896, Durand concluded that "the rights and properties . . . acquired by New York over two hundred years ago have been down to the present day of immense financial importance, but, in view of the limited expenditures of the early town, they possessed far greater relative consequence then. Indeed, till the middle of the eighteenth century, the revenues from these sources were usually sufficient without taxation to meet the recurrent outlay for city purposes proper" (Edward D. Durand, *The Finances of New York City* [Macmillan, 1898], p. 19). Provincial and, later, state officials were reluctant to approve city requests for taxing powers in view of the potential revenues to be derived from the city domain. Thus, the state Council of Revision in 1785 vetoed a tax bill on the grounds that its passage would be "inconsistent with the public good to authorize the corporation to tax the citizens in order to raise moneys for the very purposes for which . . . the large estate they are allowed to hold was intended to provide, unless they show to the satisfaction of the Legislature that the increasing revenues arising from the public slips, docks and markets, and rent of corporation lands prove insufficient for the purpose" (N.Y. State Laws, 8 sess., Ap. 22, 1785, ch. 84, as quoted in Sidney I. Pomerantz, *New York: An American City, 1783-1803* [Columbia University Press, 1938], p. 359). While the legislature subsequently passed the bill over this veto, the passage quoted reflects the attitude that generally prevailed until after the Revolution.

[43] Black, *Municipal Ownership*, p. 23.

[44] Ibid., pp. 31–32.

[45] New York City, *Minutes of the Common Council, 1785-1831*, vol. 1, p. 145 (hereafter cited as *MCC*). The council also directed that a "middle road" be surveyed half way between Post and Bloomingdale Roads. This is the present Fifth Avenue. Its width was established at 66 feet in 1785 and later, in a subsequent council meeting widened to 100 feet (ibid., p. 199).

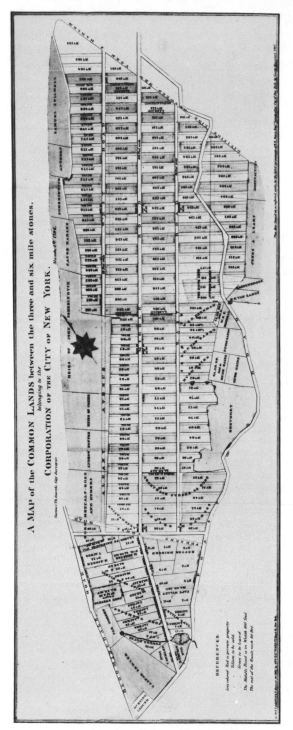

Figure 1. Survey of the Common Lands of New York City in 1796 north of 23rd Street. Alternating 5-acre parcels in the 1,100-acre tract were offered for sale and lease. (Olin Library, Cornell University.)

when nine purchasers bought not quite 200 acres of land for £5,400. Thus for an average price of about $70 an acre the city disposed of 105 acres bounded by Broadway, Lexington Avenue, 32nd and 42nd streets and 75 acres located between Third and Fifth avenues and 42nd and 48th streets. In 1792 the city sold another 50 acres between Third and Fourth avenues and 57th and 65th streets for about $30 an acre.[46]

Between 1790 and 1800 the city doubled its population to reach 60,000 and nearly quadrupled its assessed value, which at the beginning of the new century stood at $20 million.[47] These astounding rates of growth – and possibly criticism that the prices obtained for city land had been far too low – may have influenced the city council Committee on the Common Lands. In February 1796, the Committee recommended and received approval of a new policy of offering half of the remaining 1,100 acres for sale subject to an annual quit-rent and to put the other half up for 21-year lease. The 5-acre parcels of the 1785 survey were retained, and two additional north-south streets were surveyed on either side of Middle Road. These new streets established the location of what were to become Fourth and Sixth avenues. The 5-acre parcels were laid out in long rectangles with their narrow ends fronting the north-south thoroughfares. While no east-west streets were provided these eventually were surveyed along the north and south boundaries of the 5-acre plots to create the standardized blocks into which most of Manhattan Island is divided.[48] (The 1796 survey is shown in Figure 1.)

The report of the Committee on the Common Lands contained not a word about the use of public ownership to direct and guide urban growth but it was explicit about the financial advantages of its proposed policy:

> They are induced to recommend this Plan from a belief that it will tend to a speedy Improvement and that the one half which is to be leased will at the End of the Term be worth more than the whole now is. They further report that the Lots as they are now laid out be sold and leased under the management of a Committee who are to point out the Lots so to be sold and leased, and who are to be charged to sell and lease the same in such a manner as that the one half to be leased shall be best improved by that of the ones sold.[49]

[46]Black, *Municipal Ownership*, pp. 37–38; *MCC*, vol. 1, pp. 466–67, 470. Terms of sale specified a down payment of one-tenth within ten days of the auction, with the balance to be paid in five years in equal annual payments including 5% interest on the outstanding balance. *MCC*, vol. 1, p. 441.

[47]Black, *Municipal Ownership*, p. 38.

[48]Reproductions of the two surveys in 1785 and 1796 by Casimir Goerick are reproduced in my *The Making of Urban America*, p. 296. A redrawing with additional data can be found in Black, *Municipal Ownership*, maps V and VI.

[49]*MCC*, vol. 2, p. 216.

Alternate parcels were offered for sale and lease in June of 1796. Fifty-eight parcels, some of them less than 5 acres, were bought for £17,600, or about $165 an acre for the 266 acres sold. Most of the purchasers took the opportunity to lease an adjacent 5-acre tract, and in addition obligated themselves to pay the quit-rent of 4 bushels of wheat annually on the tract they bought.[50] Additional negotiated sales to existing landowners brought the total area then sold to 309 acres and the amount received to £18,850, a sum about 30 percent greater than the city's total bonded debt.[51] These properties were located between Third and Sixth avenues from 42nd to 65th streets and between Second and Seventh avenues from 65th to 85th streets.

Land disposition accelerated during the early years of the nineteenth century. In 1805 leases expired on six 5-acre parcels that had been leased in 1763. The northeasterly block in this group is now occupied by the New York Public Library at 42nd Street and Fifth Avenue. The city divided the land into 59 lots, auctioned them for $62,000, or more than $2,000 an acre, subject to an annual quit-rent of 20 bushels of wheat or its cash equivalent for each lot. Surrounding lands in 1789 had been sold at about $70 an acre.[52] The wisdom of the leasing policy should have been apparent, but two years later the city decided to sell outright 28 building lots on the Post Road at what is now bounded by Third and Fourth avenues and 65th and 69th streets. Total receipts were nearly $21,000, plus an annual quit-rent of 20 bushels of wheat per lot.[53]

The city council did make a rare effort to plan this tract in more than routine fashion. It directed the surveyor to reserve a public square 250 feet wide to be known as Hamilton Square. Two parcels 62 by 125 feet were set aside for "a Church and Academy." It further specified that lots should be sold subject to several conditions: all houses were to front the square and be set back exactly 20 feet from the street, and for a period of 20 years no more than one dwelling could occupy each lot.[54]

The financial benefits of public land ownership overshadowed potential advantages to be gained by disposing of the urban domain in such a way as to achieve a better planned city. In 1807 the mayor and the council virtually

---

[50]Black, *Municipal Ownership*, pp. 39–40; *MCC*, vol. 2, pp. 304–305.

[51]Black, *Municipal Ownership*, p. 40.

[52]Ibid., p. 42.

[53]Ibid., p. 43; *MCC*, vol. 7, p. 406.

[54]*MCC*, vol. 7, pp. 388–89, 622. These lots were known as the Dove Lots from the Dove Tavern on the Post Road. Black may be in error about their exact location. Stokes states that the area was bounded by Third and Fifth avenues and 66th and 68th streets (I. N. Phelps Stokes, *Iconography of Manhattan Island, 1498–1909* [R. H. Dodd, 1915], vol. 1, p. 404).

abdicated their authority to lay out new streets and requested the state legislature to assume this responsibility.[55] The legislature responded quickly with the passage of an act on April 3 naming three commissioners with "exclusive power to lay out streets, roads, and public squares, of such width, extent, and direction, as to them shall seem most conducive to public good." Their jurisdiction extended to all of Manhattan north of Houston Street, Astor Place, Greenwich Village, and Gansevoort Street. The mayor and council were authorized to purchase any land needed for these streets and squares or to acquire it by eminent domain. Benefit assessments could be levied to offset in whole or in part the cost of right-of-way acquisition.[56]

The commissioners did not complete their work until 1811 with the submission in March of their famous plan for a dozen north-south avenues and 155 cross streets linking the Hudson and East rivers. Historians and planners have criticized their lack of imagination in employing a rigid grid pattern, their failure to reserve sufficient open space and public building sites, and their disregard for topography. These critics, I among them, may have been unfair. The earlier surveys of the common lands in 1785 and 1796, the division of these lands into 5-acre parcels, and sale or lease of many of them had already stamped a pattern on the land that the commissioners could scarcely disregard. The three north-south roads of the 1796 survey were simply incorporated into the commissioners' lineal grid and became Fourth, Fifth, and Sixth avenues. The other avenues were laid out parallel to these earlier thoroughfares.

[55]The reasons for this action are stated in a memorial from the city to the legislature on February 16, 1807: "That the laying out of Streets and Roads in the city of New York form a branch of their duties highly interesting and important. The necessity of projecting them in such a manner as to unite regularity and order with the public convenience and benefit and in particular to promote the health of the City must be obvious in the prosecution of this subject however various and complicated difficulties and embarrasments exist. The first which naturally presents itself is a radical defect in the power of your memorialists any regulation however promotive of utility adopted by one Board unless carried fully into execution may be disregarded or annulled by its successors. There are others equally palpable and of very considerable magnitude. The diversity of Sentiments and opinions which has heretofore existed and probably will always exist among the members of the Common Council, the incessant remonstrances of proprietors against plans however well devised or beneficial wherein their individual Interests do not concur and the Impossibility of completing those plans thus opposed but by a tedious and expensive course of Law are obstacles of a serious and very perplexing nature" (*MCC*, vol. 4, p. 353).

[56]Acts of New York, 1807, Chapter 115. The full text of the statute is also given with the commissioners' report of 1811 in William Bridges, *Map of the City of New-York and Island of Manhattan; with Explanatory Remarks and References* (T. & J. Swords, 1811). The three commissioners were Simeon De Witt, Gouverneur Morris, and John Rutherford. The mayor and council had requested the legislature to name them in a resolution passed on March 4, 1807 (*MCC*, vol. 4, p. 368).

The width of the 5-acre parcels surveyed at the end of the eighteenth century suggested the approximate spacing of the east-west streets. For some unknown reason the commissioners used a slightly different module above 42nd Street, a decision that was to lead to almost endless confusion and difficulties in adjusting property boundaries and clearing city title to the land in streets when they were eventually opened.[57] It is also difficult to understand why the commissioners disregarded the street lines already established by the city in laying out certain tracts in lots, including those sold in 1807 on Hamilton Square.[58]

The report of the commissioners nowhere refers directly to municipal land ownership, and only indirectly is the subject suggested. In discussing their recommendation for the Grand Parade — a great open space to extend from 23rd to 34th streets between Third and Seventh avenues — they admit that its location seemed remote from the developed portion of the city. "It is to be lamented," they wrote, "that in this late day the Parade could not be brought further south, and made larger than it is, without incurring a frightful expense."[59]

One might take this as criticism of city officials who had not long before sold a substantial portion of this area in 5-acre tracts. The city council, in turn, expressed dissatisfaction with the commissioners because of the heavy expense of reacquiring land not only for the Parade but to create Union Place (now Union Square).[60] The mayor and council did succeed in eliminating the Grand Parade from the official map.[61] But many years later a new set of officials and the tax-paying citizens they served would have cause to regret this decision when they were forced to pay some $3,744,000 to acquire land

[57] Black, *Municipal Ownership*, pp. 58–59.

[58] The so-called Inclenberg Lots in the 30-acre tract running west from 42nd and Fifth Avenue mentioned earlier also had to be replatted. Black (p. 42) explains the procedure: "The purchasers generally accepted the city's offer to take back the lots and repay the money with interest, in bonds running two, three and four years from 1811." For the council's difficulties in resolving the problems with owners of the Hamilton Square development, see *MCC*, vol. 7, pp. 3, 41–42, 621–45.

[59] Bridges, *Map of the City of New York*, p. 27. The Commissioners added: "That it is too remote and too small, shall not be denied; but it is presumed, that those who may be inclined to criticism on that score, may feel somewhat mollified, when the Collector shall call for their proportion of the large and immediate tax which even this small and remote Parade will require."

[60] See the summary of a discussion that took place in executive session on Feb. 17, 1812 in *MCC*, vol. 7, pp. 40–43.

[61] For this and many other departures from and modifications of the Commissioners' plan to 1872, see the list and statutory citations in Gerard, *Treatise on the Title of the Corporation*, pp. 99–104.

Figure 2. New York in 1867 showing the city's development as planned in 1811. The common lands lay north of Union Square (the small circle near the center) and included the area that later had to be purchased for Central Park (the large rectangle near the top of the view). (Division of Geography and Maps, Library of Congress.)

for Central Park, most of which had once been in public ownership.[62] (See Figure 2 for a map of New York in 1867, showing the city's development as planned in 1811.)

While the commissioners were still at work on their plan, and immediately after their report, the city continued to sell individuals lots in the older part

[62]Land acquisition costs to Jan. 1, 1860 amounted to $5,406,193.74, offset in part by benefit assessments of $1,661,395.00 (New York City, Board of Commissioners of the Central Park, *Third Annual Report*, 1860, p. 23). Several blocks were later added to the park, extending its boundary to the north.

of New York. Several ponds and marshes were drained and reclaimed at this time, and the now buildable land was subdivided and put up for sale. One pond, when drained in 1809, yielded 20 lots sold for $25,000. In 1812, 34 other lots created by reclamation went for $22,000. Other lots sold during 1812 on Broad, Chambers, and Greenwich streets brought total land sales for that year to more than $100,000.[63]

The financial importance of the city's land program during this period can be appreciated by a look at the municipal budget for 1813. Total expenditures came to just over half a million dollars. Taxes provided slightly more than $200,000. Real estate receipts contributed more than $130,000 or one-fourth of all city revenues:[64]

Rents of docks and slips	$23,508
Rent & sales of common lands	85,476
Ground rent	14,667
Water lot rents	7,254

In the four years from 1816 to 1820 land sales totaled $226,000. Most of the revenues apparently came from lots in the built-up portion of the city, but some of the 5-acre parcels in the upper part of Manhattan were disposed of as well. In 1822 there still remained nearly 500 acres of this land in municipal ownership. Of the 93 parcels, 55 were leased, 12 or 13 remained idle, and another dozen were worked by the almshouse. During the 1820s another 14 were sold.[65]

Until 1844 the city pursued a general policy of leasing rather than selling land, wisely taking advantage of relatively short leases to capture increments in land values. A group of lots on Chatham Street that had been leased for $200 to $250 a year in 1806 each brought $400 to $450 when new leases were written in 1827.[66] Annual revenues from leases steadily increased during this period, rising from $41,000 in 1830 to $55,000 in 1840. Dock rents and fees rose from $44,000 to $68,000, while land sales were only $22,000 in 1830 and $21,000 in 1840.[67]

These were years of phenomenal increases in population and land values. From 1825 to 1835 population jumped from 166,000 to 270,000 while assessed value of real estate, including the city domain, soared from $52

---

[63] Black, *Municipal Ownership*, p. 45.
[64] *MCC*, vol. 7, pp. 662–63.
[65] Black, *Municipal Ownership*, p. 53.
[66] Ibid., p. 56.
[67] Durand, *Finances of New York City*, p. 223.

million to $142 million.[68] The urban fringe rapidly advanced northwards where the bulk of the city-owned lands were located. If the city had continued its policy of leasing these lands it might now be the wealthiest community in the nation. Instead, it abandoned that policy in 1844 and soon sold the bulk of these choice properties, electing to obtain immediate capital rather than wait for what surely would have been steadily and rapidly increasing leasehold payments in perpetuity. This shift in policy resulted from the need for funds to pay for public improvements and especially for the construction of the Croton Aqueduct, a project begun in 1835 and completed a decade later at a cost of some $13 million, which was well over twice the estimated figure.[69]

In an effort to reduce the city indebtedness the council in 1844 authorized and directed the Commissioners of the Sinking Fund "to sell and dispose of all real estate belonging to the corporation and not in use for or reserved for public purposes, at public auction, at such time and on such terms as they may deem most advantageous for the public interest."[70] The commissioners acted quickly. Sales amounted to $362,000 in 1844 and $358,000 in 1845. In mid-1843 the Comptroller reported the total value of Manhattan lots and common lands at $2,142,630, and by 1846 stated that this had been reduced to $1,429,500. By 1855 the value of the remaining common lands was put at $523,000, about half what it had been a decade earlier; but, as land values were rising, probably much more than half had been disposed of.[71]

It is instructive to compare the policy of selling the public lands in the interior of Manhattan with the city's policy of retaining ownership of land used for docks and of building and leasing docks on its own account. In 1830 real estate rents and rents received from docks were approximately the same, slightly more than $40,000. Dock rents steadily climbed during the remaining

[68] Black, *Municipal Ownership*, p. 58.

[69] Ibid., p. 59.

[70] The quotation is from section 17 of the ordinance as quoted in Black, ibid., pp. 60–61. The sinking fund had been established in 1813 (Durand, *Finances of New York City*, p. 34).

[71] David Valentine, *Manual of the Corporation of the City of New York* (New York City Common Council, 1859), p. 526; Black, *Municipal Ownership*, pp. 81–82; *Inventory of the Real and Personal Estate, Belonging to the Corporation*, Doc. No. 35, Board of Aldermen, Oct. 1, 1843, pp. 380–81; and *Annual Statement of Comptroller for Year Ending 1845*, New York (1846), p. 70. Even the substantially reduced urban public domain continued to produce revenues. The city realized $454,706 from the sale of land in 1862 and $228,000 in 1870. (*Annual Report of the Comptroller for 1862*, New York [1863], p. 124; and Durand, *Finances of New York City*, p. 223.) Despite the rapid liquidation of the capital base of publicly owned real estate, receipts from leases in 1890 were more than double those in 1840.

years of the century: 1840, $68,000; 1850, $108,000; 1860, $169,000; 1870, $249,000; 1880, $791,000; 1890, $1,492,531; and 1896, $2,000,000.[72]

The land policy pursued by New York City achieved only partial success. Even the very substantial sums realized from the sale of its domain were but a fraction of what might have been received from leases had the municipality retained ownership of the alternate 5-acre parcels surveyed in 1796. Moreover, these revenues would have increased when the time came to negotiate new leases, and the city would have captured the unearned increment of land values on which so many private fortunes were made. The city neither received the maximum possible income from its real estate nor did it use its vast holdings of land at the urban fringe to carry out a plan having any special merit. One or both of these objectives lay within its grasp; failure to achieve either of them is one of the tragedies of American urban planning and development.

Nevertheless, the New York experience demonstrates that large-scale municipal land ownership in America certainly was compatible with other cherished institutions of democratic capitalism, that it could be responsive to changing demands and needs, and that it did not seem to inhibit other components of the real estate and construction system. Furthermore, as the only serious investigator of the policy observed 80 years ago, "some stock arguments against municipal ownership are not borne out by the city's experience. Up to 1844 there had been neither a dishonest nor a fickle administration of the municipal estate."[73]

[72] Durand's summary of the city policy with respect to docks and wharves includes this passage: "Although the sale of the entire water front had been often advocated, and considerable parts had been actually disposed of before 1870, yet there remained a very large proportion belonging to the city when, in that year, a definite and comprehensive policy for a system of municipal docks was adopted. The city was even authorized to buy back wharf property held by private persons, and especially for the past three or four years considerable purchases of this sort have been made. . . . The dock revenues, moreover, have increased with great rapidity, multiplying more than eightfold since the new departure of 1870. Without attempting the impossible task of estimating the entire cost of the existing docks, a rough idea of the profitableness of this property may be formed by comparing the amount invested since 1870 with the income. The total expenditure under the new system (including cost of maintenance, which is, however, not over a fifth or sixth of the whole) to April 30, 1895, was $27,224,690. The dock revenue for the year ending that date was $1,940,079, or about 7½ per cent on the investment thus calculated" (ibid., pp. 227–28).

[73] Black (*Municipal Ownership*, p. 75) goes on to comment: "Governments, parties and officials changed, but there is a distinct continuity of fiscal policy, so far, at least as relates to corporation land. It would seem that underneath the tossing surface of politics there were deep economic interests of which political dynasties are the servants and not the masters, and which secure the retention to old age of not a few experienced officials, even under a system by which the spoils belong to the victors." Black, writing in 1891

Savannah. In sharp contrast to New York the City of Savannah used its ownership of land at the urban fringe to achieve planned development of a unique and highly satisfactory character. It did this while realizing impressive financial returns through land sales and at the same time almost totally eliminated sprawl or scattered growth with its attendant higher public costs for services and maintenance.

The original settlement design in 1733 was the work of General James Oglethorpe. He laid out the town in four wards to which he added two others in 1735 (see Figure 3). Each ward consisted of 40 house lots and 4 lots for public or semipublic uses grouped around an open square and served by streets whose various widths were proportioned to their expected importance and function. Some of the streets in the gridiron system were uninterrupted, while others passed by or terminated at the open squares. Scholars have speculated over the reasons why Oglethorpe adopted this unusual pattern, but the subject, while fascinating, is largely irrelevant to this paper.[74]

The town of Savannah was but part of a larger regional plan devised by Oglethorpe. South of the settlement he surveyed an area into a grid of squares, each consisting of 10 acres. Each square was in turn divided into two 5-acre parcels by a line connecting opposite corners of the squares. Each settler received one of the 60-by-90-foot house lots in the town, a 5-acre triangular garden lot, and a 45 acre rectangular farm in a much larger tract beyond the gardens.

Between the town proper and these agricultural lands Oglethorpe reserved about 250 acres as a common. His motives remain unclear. He may have visualized future growth of the town in this direction, he might have desired

---

and reviewing the city's experience with public land management to 1844, came to different conclusions than mine. In a final brief chapter he stated his belief that only if land were held in fee would it be devoted to its most productive use. "Municipal ownership and the leasehold system made necessary by it are relatively unprofitable, and unfavorable to improvements . . . . Improvements would hardly be undertaken on a shorter lease than twenty-one years, and on its twenty-one year leases as sold at auction the city got no fair return on the average selling value of its property for that time. Neither were the structures put up creditable. Nearly all were but two story and attic brick buildings, the minimum required by the leases." Black felt that benefit assessments and higher taxes on vacant land would bring in greater returns than leases while at the same time stimulating building and thus adding to the real property tax base (ibid., pp. 75–79).

[74] The principal studies of this aspect of the plan of Savannah are the following: Reps, *Making of Urban America*, pp. 185–203 and *Town Planning in Frontier America* (Princeton University Press, 1969), pp. 235–60; Frederick Doveton Nichols, *The Early Architecture of Georgia* (University of North Carolina Press, 1958); Turpin C. Bannister, "Oglethorpe's Sources for the Savannah Plan," *Journal of the Society of Architectural Historians*, vol. 20 (May 1961), pp. 47–62; and Laura Palmer Bell, "A New Theory on the Plan of Savannah," *Georgia Historical Quarterly*, vol. 48 (June 1964), pp. 146–165.

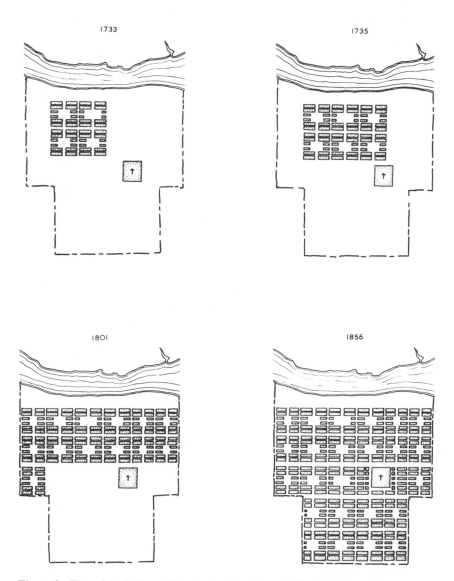

Figure 3. The original plan of Savannah, Georgia, established by James Oglethorpe in 1733 and its growth to 1856. The dashed line indicates the boundary of the common lands on which new wards were planned by the municipality.

to surround the community with a greenbelt of open land for reasons of health, or he may simply have followed European custom as had already been done in New England and such other colonial settlements as Annapolis or New Castle (Delaware), among many others. In any event, it was this common land that was to provide Savannah with the rare opportunity to plan its subsequent development.

Until after the Revolution the six wards or urban neighborhoods of Oglethorpe's day provided ample accommodations for the town's modest population. By that time title to the common had passed into the hands of the municipality.[75] When Savannah was incorporated as a city in 1790, it began its extraordinary program of planned development. Using its ownership of the common and employing a system of regulated sales and leases, the city for more than half a century guided growth to avoid sprawl and speculation, while at the same time creating a unique physical environment with considerable profit to the public treasury.

Two tiers of three wards each on the south bank of the Savannah River then comprised the town. Portions of the common lay to the east and west, while most of it extended to the south. In September 1790 the council passed an ordinance creating two new wards to the east and one to the west of the existing first tier of three wards fronting the river. Because all subsequent ordinances closely followed this initial enactment, an extended summary of its provisions seems essential.

Attached to the ordinance was a plat of the three new wards. Each was an almost exact duplicate of the Oglethorpe pattern with 40 house lots, 4 sites for civic or quasi-public use, and a central open square. A schedule annexed

[75] A statute approved on May 1, 1760 described the boundaries of the common and specified that it was "common property of the lot holders in the . . . town" and was not to be "aliened [sic] or granted away for any purpose, whatsoever, than by act of the General Assembly" (Ga. L. Dec. 1, 1760; M & C. Dig., 117; also in Edward G. Wilson [comp.], *A Digest of All the Ordinances of the City of Savannah* . . . [John M. Cooper, 1858], p. 505). (The title of the latter work on which I have drawn extensively is misleading. Pertinent statutes are also included, and virtually all of the acts and ordinances are given in full rather than in digest form.) Several subsequent statutes permitted minor adjustments or confirmed earlier sales or grants of a few lots within the boundaries of the common (ibid., pp. 505–509). On Feb. 10, 1787 the legislature authorized wardens elected annually by the lot owners "to let, lease, or rent at public sale, any lot or lots . . . of the said town of Savannah" (ibid., pp. 509–10). Two years later the legislature passed an act elevating Savannah to the status of an incorporated city, with the first elections for aldermen to be held on Mar. 1, 1790. The aldermen were to replace the wardens and to exercise their former powers (ibid., p. 510). The city then began sales of portions of the common. Apparently some doubts arose concerning the validity of titles to such property obtained in this manner. On Dec. 21, 1822 the legislature declared that all such conveyances were valid despite the provisions of the act of 1760 cited above (ibid., p. 512).

to the ordinance stated the minimum value of each lot, with prices ranging from £40 to £160. The ordinance specified that the lots were to be disposed of at auction with bidding starting at these figures. Any sum bid in excess of the minimum price was defined as "increase money," and the successful bidder was required to pay at least this much in cash. The purchaser then had the option of paying the balance in cash or taking the lot subject to an annual ground rent equal to 5 percent of the unpaid balance. Purchasers choosing the ground-rent option could later elect to pay off the balance and secure what the ordinance referred to as an "absolute estate." Until then, the estate was conditional, and the city reserved the right of reentry and resale if any quarterly ground-rent payment was not made within 15 days after the due date. Those taking conditional estates were also required to post a bond equal to four times the annual rent.[76]

The three new wards increased the size of the city by 50 percent. However, the introduction of Eli Whitney's cotton gin to Georgia's plantations and the development of Savannah as the principal cotton port of the South generated additional demand for building lots. The city created another three wards in 1799 and one in 1801, all on the same pattern and all located contiguous to one or more existing wards. The city then consisted of two tiers of six wards plus one ward at the southwestern corner of the now considerably expanded community.[77]

The continuation of this expansion policy to 1851 resulted in a total of twenty-four wards all planned on the novel pattern that Oglethorpe had established.[78] It was a city of remarkable beauty and charm. An English traveller and writer, James Silk Buckingham, visited Savannah in 1840 and commented favorably on its "eighteen large squares, with grass-plots and trees, in the very heart of the city, disposed at equal distances from each other in the greatest order; while every principal street is lined on each side with rows of trees, and some of the broader streets have also an avenue of trees running down their centre."[79] Fredericka Bremer, a Swedish writer, asserted "there cannot be in the whole world a more beautiful city than Savannah."[80] An English clergyman, Timothy Harley, wrote that while there were "far vaster and wealthier cities with much more commerce and culture than this city, . . . for architectural simplicity and natural beauty, for the indescribable

[76]"An Ordinance, for laying off into Lots certain parts of the Common appurtenant to this City, and for disposing of the same" (ibid., pp. 48–51).

[77]Ibid., pp. 52–57 for the ordinances creating these wards.

[78]Ibid., pp. 60–72 for the relevant ordinances.

[79]J. S. Buckingham, *The Slave States of America* (Paris, Fisher, Son and Co., 1842), vol. 1, p. 118.

[80]As quoted in Historic Savannah Foundation, *Historic Savannah* (1968), p. 12.

charm about its streets and buildings, its parks and squares . . . there is but one Savannah. Without a rival, without an equal, it stands unique."[81]

Almost no one who knows the modern city with its original and expanded pattern almost miraculously intact would take issue with these nineteenth century observers. Savannah's beauty and utility was enhanced by the city policy during this period of granting sites for institutional and religious purposes as the common land was gradually developed. The ordinances of the city record dozens of such grants to churches, schools, hospitals, state and federal governments, an orphan asylum, the Georgia Historical Society, and the Widows' Society as well as reservations of land for the city itself.[82] It was not long either before the numerous squares were embellished with landscaping, statues, monuments, and fountains. Forsyth Park was created in 1851 on one of the last portions of the common remaining in public ownership.[83] (See Figure 4, for a map of Savannah in 1856.)

This notable accomplishment was all the more outstanding because the city enriched itself in the process. The minimum price of lots in 1799 ranged from $200 to $600, and "increase money" determined at the auction was added to the base price. Lots auctioned in 1801 had a base price of $600 to $700. By 1803 prices ranged from $500 to $2,000, plus increase money. City records show that in 1837 Mathew Hopkins bid $935 for a lot valued at $800, paid down $187, and elected to pay ground rent of $42 annually at the 6 percent then established as the return to the city on the unpaid balance.[84]

By 1858, 639 lots in 22 wards had been sold subject to similar conditions, providing the city with annual revenues of nearly $28,000 from ground rents. The unpaid balance amounted to approximately $473,000, giving the city a return of 6 percent on its equity.[85] These revenues apparently went into the general fund, but in at least two cases proceeds from land sales were earmarked for special purposes: in 1803 for street lighting, and in 1841 for the retirement of bonds issued by the city to finance a railroad.[86]

---

[81] As quoted in ibid., p. 13.

[82] See the ordinances in Wilson, *A Digest of. . . Ordinances . . .* , pp. 246–56.

[83] Ibid., p. 75.

[84] This information is from a copy of an indenture in the city records furnished me in 1968 by Picot Floyd, City Manager of Savannah. I have not yet had an opportunity to make a detailed investigation of city records relating to the disposal of the common lands and therefore cannot judge if this was a typical transaction.

[85] These figures are derived from data in Wilson, *A Digest of. . . Ordinances . . .* , pp. 535, 537. Savannah received additional revenues from lands in Springfield Plantation, an area outside the boundaries of the common. This amounted to $1,621 on an unpaid balance of $23,174.

[86] Ibid., pp. 59, 67.

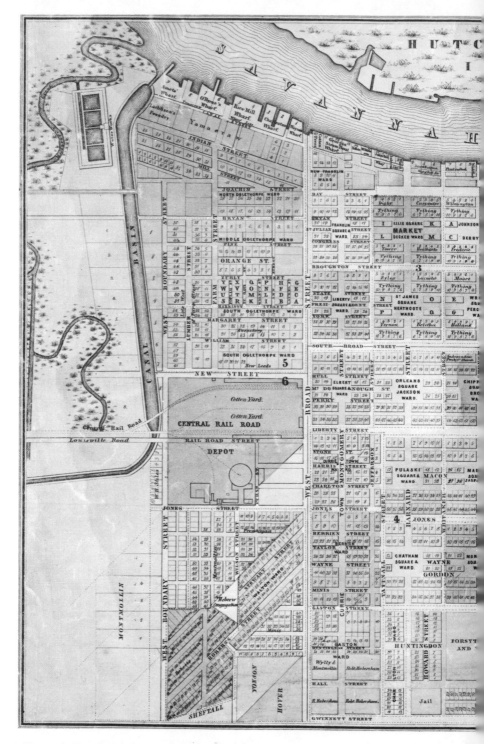

Figure 4. Savannah, Georgia, in 1856. The design of the 24 wards and squares created
through planned disposition of the public lands is in marked contrast to the crowded and

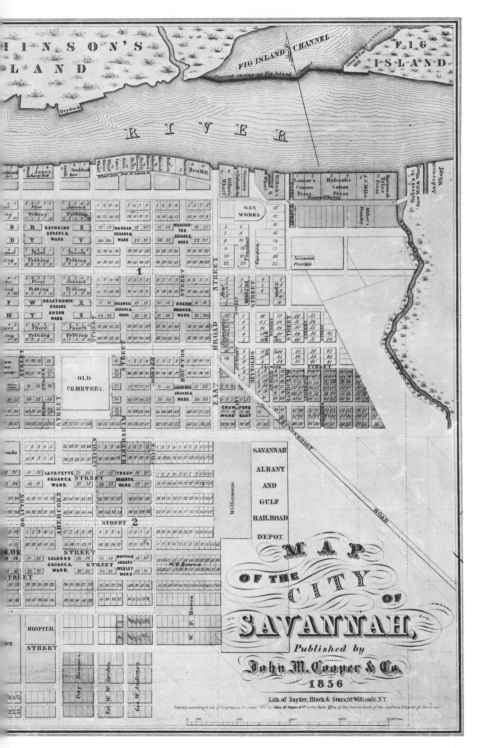

disorganized development on land held in private ownership beyond the boundaries of the old common. (Division of Geography and Maps, Library of Congress.)

By the middle of the nineteenth century the city had exhausted its supply of common land. Effective controls providing for the planned growth of Savannah could no longer be exercised. Initiative and decision-making powers now rested with private owners. Proprietors of the 5-acre triangular garden plots began to subdivide their property, in many cases using the peculiar diagonal field division as the alignment for new streets. These subdivisions were thoughtlessly attached to the well-planned and meticulously ordered portion of the city so carefully created out of the old common land. Even earlier, land owners nearer the river beyond the east and west boundaries of the common land had cut up their properties into a maze of narrow lanes and streets encompassing small lots and no open spaces.

There is no city in the United States whose physical pattern reflects so forcefully and clearly the results of two kinds of land policies applied to urban growth. One policy produced a community of unrivalled character; the other throttled it with a noose of mediocrity and blight. If the past has anything to teach, surely it can be read from successive maps of the city of Savannah and other well-planned towns founded on public land.

Justice Holmes once observed that a page of history may be worth more than a volume of logic. This historical summary of our own extensive experience with urban public land management may, I hope, anticipate and dispose of any argument that future programs of this kind are foreign to our tradition and therefore to be avoided.

We will need all the logic we can muster if we are to work out the details of a feasible program of massive urban land acquisition and planned disposal. But in approaching this challenging task we can take heart in the knowledge that the lesson of history at Savannah and elsewhere is not only clear but compelling, matching that of contemporary experience in Canada and northern Europe. In the years ahead we must reestablish this legacy of urban public land management, adapt it for modern needs, use it wisely, and begin to shape the future of our cities and metropolitan areas with the only planning implementation technique that has a chance of success.

HOUSING AND ASSOCIATED PROBLEMS OF MINORITIES

ROBERT C. WEAVER

In the context of land use, the principal issue for minorities is free access to shelter; and, when impediments to equal access of minorities to housing are mentioned, zoning immediately comes to mind. This is both pertinent and misleading. It is pertinent because zoning has become the most identifiable impediment to wider housing choices for minorities. It is misleading because zoning is not the only effective deterrent to such choices, nor does its modification or elimination assure more socially equitable patterns of land use. Interestingly enough, when communities have wanted to discourage or exclude minorities, they have resorted to other devices such as refusal of mortgage credit, obstructive real estate practices, neighborhood hostility, dedication of proposed sites to public use, and even threats of violence and destruction of property. These methods are also employed to complement or substitute for land use controls to exclude low- and moderate-income construction.

It is appropriate, nevertheless, to analyze how zoning is used — and why it is used — to discourage and prevent the construction of low- and moderate-income housing in suburban communities, thereby banning the production of

---

ROBERT C. WEAVER is distinguished professor of urban affairs at Hunter College. Mr. Weaver has served as Deputy Commissioner of Housing and Rent Administrator in New York State, as Administrator of the Housing and Home Finance Agency, and as Secretary of the Department of Housing and Urban Development. He is the author of four books and over one hundred articles in his areas of professional specialization — labor, housing, urban development, and minority problems. Born in 1907, Mr. Weaver received B.S., M.A. degrees and his Ph.D. in economics from Harvard University.

Author's note. I wish to express appreciation to Henry Schechter, of Congressional Research Service, The Library of Congress, and Donald G. Sullivan, Department of Urban Affairs, Hunter College, who read the manuscript and made valuable criticisms and suggestions for its improvement.

49

shelter that would meet the needs of most minority households. In the earlier phase of the urbanization of Negroes, the identifiable villain was the racial restrictive housing covenant, concentrated initially in the older, built-up section of the central city.[1] After the 1948 and subsequent decisions of the Supreme Court had "effectively eliminated the use of racial restrictive covenants as direct segregatory devices,"[2] land zoning became the new villain. Two factors were chiefly responsible. The first was legal, and the second reflected changes in the geographic distribution and economic characteristics of urban Negroes.

Obviously, the actions of the Supreme Court rendered racially restrictive covenants unenforceable in law, thereby significantly reducing their effectiveness. At the same time, the size of the urban black population in industrial and other urban centers was growing rapidly. With defense and war production, family income rose, and nonwhites developed an increased effective demand for shelter. Some sought housing in the suburbs. Past patterns in the housing industry, government policies, fear of alienating white customers, lack of ready mortgage finance, and community opposition discouraged or prevented minorities from participating in the new housing that was concentrated in the suburbs. In some urban communities, largely in the South, racially segregated suburbs developed.[3] But most of the expansion of nonwhite areas of occupancy occurred in the central cities as whites fled beyond their borders.

As the outlying areas grew, they began to attract industry and generate white-collar and service jobs. Lower-income families wanting to move nearer the new source of employment found that their attempts to secure shelter were quickly resisted on economic and racial grounds. Soon the desire to exclude minorities and the opposition to low- and moderate-income groups merged.[4] The major instrument was zoning which, by banning construction of lower-income housing, barred most minority families. Its real potential for this objective was not generally recognized until wartime and postwar developments had occasioned a growing interest in suburban housing on the part of a significant number of racial minority and low- and moderate-income households.

[1] Robert C. Weaver, *The Negro Ghetto* (Harcourt, Brace, 1948; reprinted by Russell and Russell, 1967), chap. 13.

[2] Loren Miller, *The Petitioners: The Story of the Supreme Court of the United States and the Negro* (Pantheon, 1966), p. 331.

[3] Robert C. Weaver, *The Urban Complex* (Doubleday, 1964), pp. 227–28. In the North, too, Negroes were sometimes concentrated in the older, already decaying, first generation inner-ring suburbs.

[4] For an interesting set of case studies that illustrate this merger, see Raymond and May Associates, *Zoning Controversies in the Suburbs: Three Case Studies*, Research Report No. 11 (The National Commission on Urban Problems, 1968).

Zoning has been aptly described as responding to the desire of local residents to maintain the status quo. The president of Levitt and Sons observed that, where school districts are small, there is apprehension that new housing construction will mean acceleration of the growth of schools and large increases in taxes. "As a result, various forms of prohibitive codes and zoning are established which exclude any sizable or any moderate-cost housing production."[5]

The principal ways in which restrictive zoning contributes to the exclusion of low- and moderate-income families from the market for new housing are:

(1) by increasing the cost of new housing,
(2) by significantly limiting the volume of construction in metropolitan areas,
(3) by preventing the construction of low tax-paying residential facilities,
(4) by preventing the construction of lower-cost housing, such as mobile home and lower-rental multifamily units, and
(5) by significantly increasing the cost of new land and site improvements.[6]

One of the technical studies for the President's Committee on Urban Housing noted that the "rise in the cost of land improvements has been due in no small part to land use policies that are designed to increase per-lot investment to encourage the production of high-valuation (and high tax-yield) housing. Indeed, fiscally motivated zoning and subdivision actions are responsible for much of the increase in site costs in one-family housing since the middle 1950's."[7] The study summarized the operation of zoning in restricting housing opportunities for the poor and nonwhite:

> The adoption of restrictive zoning policies, including large lot sizes and high minimum house sizes, by suburban communities has rendered it most difficult to undertake substantial subdivision activity, whether for middle-income households, or for low- and moderate-income households. Moreover, zoning for upper-middle-income housing is accompanied by prohibitions against other than single-family housing, and, to a lesser extent, high-rise luxury housing . . . as a result of these developments in suburban zoning . . . , the residences permitted to be built are beyond the financial reach of most families living in substandard housing, and indeed of low- and moderate-income families generally . . . and finally, the resultant imbalances in intrametropolitan housing markets between land-poor cen-

[5] *The Report of the President's Committee on Urban Housing* (1968), vol. 2, p. 70.

[6] "The Relationship of Zoning to Adequate Housing for Low- and Moderate-Income Families and Negro Families" mimeographed (Urban Research Center, Hunter College, June 19, 1968), p. 9.

[7] Neil N. Gold and Paul Davidoff, "The Supply and Availability of Land for Housing for Low- and Moderate-Income Families," *The Report of the President's Committee on Urban Housing*, vol. 2, p. 375.

tral cities, which contain substantial unsound housing, and land-rich suburbs, which exclude low- and moderate-cost housing, are likely to vitiate
the Nation's goal of constructing six million low- and moderate-cost housing units in the next decade, unless something is done to change policies
which have brought us to our current impasse.[8]

Thus, of all the current impediments to freedom of movement among
minorities, two stand out. The first is an external control: restrictions on land
use — primarily zoning and subdivision regulations. The second is an internal
condition: the high incidence of absolute and relative poverty among minorities.[9] I deal with the first of these at this point and return to the second
subsequently.

Those who seek the villain in the piece generally assert that exclusionary
zoning is *the* reason why nonwhites and low-income households find it so
difficult to secure shelter in the suburbs. Those who assert or imply that
abolishing zoning would destroy the impediments to free movement to the
suburbs overlook the fact that zoning is only one type of land use control,
and that it is not impregnable.

During the late 1940s I found that the racial restrictive covenants were
often no match for market forces. "Once there are widespread vacancies in
neighborhoods that lie in the path of the geographic expansion of the Black
Belt, values decline, income from properties shrinks, and the Negro occupants
suddenly become attractive to owners and investors . . . . Profits, even in real
estate, are usually color blind."[10] The covenants were a more lasting impediment to Negro occupancy in more remote new subdivisions and districts, but
many areas closer to the then existing Black Belt were occupied by blacks
before the covenants against them had run out.[11]

Today zoning is sometimes equally ineffectual in prohibiting types of land
use that it purports to ban. A recent study for the National Committee
Against Discrimination in Housing revealed that in several counties of New
Jersey where a minuscule proportion of buildable land is zoned for multifamily use the preponderance of construction during the 1960s was multifamily.[12] There is strong evidence that this occurred not only because

[8]Ibid., p. 347.

[9]See Marion Clawson, *Suburban Land Conversion in the United States: An Economic
and Governmental Process* (Johns Hopkins University Press for Resources for the Future,
1971), pp. 363–64. For a more comprehensive treatment of the significance of relative
poverty, see Lee Rainwater, *Behind Ghetto Walls* (Aldine, 1970), chap. 14.

[10]Weaver, *The Negro Ghetto*, pp. 236–37.

[11]Ibid., pp. 236–38.

[12]Ernest Erber, "Jobs and Housing," Final Summary Report on the Housing Component of the Study of Employment and Housing for Racial Minorities in the Suburban

builders and developers used almost all the vacant land zoned for this purpose but primarily because they followed another course. In response to the strong demand for rental housing in the 1960s, builders scouted around for sites; secured parcels for multifamily construction in the older communities, where nonwhite families were already in residence; and sometimes resorted to demolition. This resulted in increasing stratification by race and income and contributed to overcrowding. The other, and more prevalent, approach was for developers and builders to secure rezoning through negotiation with local public officials.[13]

This is not to imply that zoning is no longer a significant impediment to apartment construction in the suburbs. It does suggest, however, that zoning, like racial restrictive covenants, responds to market forces under certain circumstances even though it is still a strong force for delay and frequently a barrier that cannot be surmounted.

Perhaps the most insidious aspect of zoning is that it can be perverted to accomplish questionable ends. Initiated as a land use tool much needed to accelerate orderly growth and development of urban and urbanizing areas, zoning can, and frequently does, achieve unstated and undemocratic objectives, such as exclusion.

Yet, as insidious as zoning can be, it is by no means the sole or most direct instrument for eliminating low-income shelter in the suburbs. For example, a political jurisdiction that does not want public housing can kill it by many other devices. The simplest way is not to create a public housing authority or enter into a cooperative agreement with the federal government. California took an additional step, requiring a referendum before low-income subsidized housing could be built in a community. In April 1971, the Supreme Court in *James* v. *Valtierra* upheld the right of California to stipulate such a referendum.

Currently, new approaches for economic and ethnic exclusion are emerging. Wrapping themselves in the popular bunting of concern for ecology, opponents of multifamily and lower-income housing speak of the attendant problems of water and sewers, waste disposal, and high densities. Others raise the issues of overcrowding in schools and traffic congestion. These views are already finding expression in the refusal of localities to provide adequate public services. In Charles City, Maryland, for example, the Department of Housing and Urban Development (HUD) recently approved a project in which about 80 percent of the one-family units would enjoy direct subsidies. The

---

Areas of the New York Metropolitan Region, mimeographed (National Committee Against Discrimination in Housing, March 1972), pp. 33-37.

[13]Ibid.

county government protested and refused to provide necessary local facilities. The project could not be built.

Regardless of whether zoning or some other tool is used in attempts to limit housing choices or exclude minorities, the effects are the same. Not only does such action impose economic costs on those restricted, but it also serves to perpetuate and symbolize second-class status for nonwhites. Clearly, the restriction of choices to a segmented market limits and perverts the efficient operation of the housing market.

The most frequently articulated justification for screening out low- and moderate-income families from suburbs is the notion that these families do not pay their share of local service costs. It is an argument that appears rational and respectable to local residents and officials, particularly since the localities have to raise 60 to 70 percent of the costs of local services.[14] One study of the problem observes that exclusion of low- and moderate-income families rests upon the assertion that their entrance would result in less tax revenue (than the permitted land uses yield), give rise to greater costs, and threaten the homogeneous cultural and value patterns of the suburbs. "Add to these three reasons the latent racism in most Americans and it is not difficult to understand the continued resistance of suburban areas to the presence of low-income families generally, and to blacks in particular."[15]

Several ways of dealing with exclusionary practices come to mind. The first is to abolish zoning, which has so frequently been perverted to achieve what many (including the writer) believe to be antisocial ends. That approach, like most simplistic ones, leaves much to be desired. As others will indicate, zoning offers many positive benefits, and its destruction would be a step backward in the process of orderly land use and development. Therefore, even those who may be ambivalent about having an economic and racial mixture in their communities should have a real interest in advocating a cessation of financially exlcusive zoning.

Litigation is the most likely method for challenging this type of restrictive zoning, but it has two principal limitations: it can be time-consuming, and it usually is applicable only to the most obvious and extreme abuses. Favorable decisions, at best, ban certain actions; they do not establish affirmative programs that can offset or compensate for the rational economic and the popular ecological opposition to lower-income residents in the suburbs. Without such programs, the racist elements will constantly gain support from a broad segment of the community.

[14] Morton J. Schussheim, "National Goals and Local Practices: Joining Ends and Means in Housing," *Papers Submitted to Subcommittee on Housing Panels*, Committee on Banking and Currency, 92 Cong. 1 sess. (1971), Pt. 1, p. 153.

[15] Joel L. Fleishman, "Goals and Strategies of a National Housing and Urban Growth Policy," *Papers Submitted to Subcommittee on Housing Panels*, Pt. 2, p. 719.

It is extremely difficult to differentiate between class and color aspects of suburban exclusiveness, but this much is clear: there is opposition to low- and moderate-income families of all ethnic backgounds in suburbia, and this becomes accentuated when the element of color is introduced.[16] The problems confronting minorities who can afford suburban housing are of a different order from those harassing poor people. Zoning and associated land use controls are less significant barriers, and there is no scarcity of shelter within their purchasing power. The traditional paucity of mortgage finance is less oppressive, although many financial institutions hesitate to provide minority applicants with mortgage financing in areas removed from centers of minority concentration or racially transitional neighborhoods. The actual (if not the anticipated) economic impact is minimal; the basic challenge to dominant values is slight; there is no need to make a frontal attack upon existing economic land use patterns; and no subsidies are needed. All that is required are (1) the willingness of owners to rent or sell to minorities, and (2) access to mortgage finance. In a word, the solution is primarily a matter of enforcing the Fair Housing Title of the Civil Rights Act of 1968, demonstrating again that civil rights legislation is relevant primarily for those who have achieved middle-class economic status.

THE IMPACT OF RECENT FEDERAL LEGISLATION

In 1968 two pieces of legislation offered new hope to low- and moderate-income households interested in moving to the suburbs. The first was the Housing and Urban Development Act of that year, which included new programs for moderate-income housing, FHA sections 235 and 236. By using an interest rate subsidy, these two new sections translated the need for such housing into an effective demand, and developers were encouraged to build for income groups that usually could not afford new or rehabilitated housing. The second new ingredient was the Fair Housing Title of the Civil Rights Law of 1968. It extended prohibitions of discrimination in the sale or rental of all tract housing and a large proportion of single-family, individually owned units, covering about 80 percent of the housing supply.[17]

[16] Robert C. Weaver, "Class, Race, and Urban Renewal," *Land Economics*, vol. 36, no. 3 (August 1960), pp. 235–51. See also Morton Grodzins, *The Metropolitan Area as a Racial Problem* (University of Pittsburgh Press, 1958).

[17] Subsequently, the Supreme Court held "that an 1866 civil rights law, enacted under the authority of the 13th amendment, prohibited racial discrimination in all housing, private as well as public." (U.S. Commission on Civil Rights, *Home Ownership for Lower Income Families: A Report on the Racial And Ethnic Impact of the Section 235 Program*, June 1971, p. vii.)

Because of the chronic shortage of standard low-rent and low-cost housing in the nation, federal programs designed to upgrade the quality of shelter for low-income households have been directed at increasing the production of such shelter. Thus, housing subsidies for the poor, first in the form of public housing, have been attached to the housing unit rather than the occupant. When the first federal program for moderate-income housing – FHA section 221 (d) (3) – was initiated in 1961, it followed this established approach. Its method of financing was to provide a de facto federal direct, below-the-market interest rate program. Since government financing of the entire mortgage occurred at the time of the loan closing, the total amount of the mortgage was included in the budget for the then current year. The consequence was that budgetary considerations greatly limited the volume of the 221 program.

Rent supplements, enacted in 1965, were designed to spread out the budget impact. Instead of a single capital cost budget item reflecting the total mortgage cost, rent supplements involved annual subsidies and were spread out over the duration of the mortgage. FHA sections 235 (ownership) and 236 (rental and cooperative) followed a similar pattern. The subsidy, again, is tied to the housing unit and its amount varies with the occupant's income (representing the difference between mortgage payments or the fair market rental and 20 or 25 percent of the household's income). The maximum amount of the subsidy is the difference between the market rate of interest and one percent. In both rent supplements and the 235 and 236 programs the subsidies are in the form of federal payments to the developer.

Experience under section 221 (d) (3) had indicated that, when it became profitable, some builders were ready to undertake subsidized rental and cooperative projects. Often the inducement, in addition to the demand support and income tax advantages, was the opportunity for builders to use optioned or owned sites that did not justify luxury rentals but were much more desirable than any previously available locations for moderate-income housing. When section 235 provided for sales units and an interest subsidy to supplement low incomes (this was the first program to offer direct subsidies for home purchase), rendering a new economic group able to purchase housing, the program was much more attractive to developers than 221 (d) (3) had been. Then, too, it and the rental and cooperative section 236 sibling got under way when mortgage funds were scarce, interest rates high, and the volume of construction low. The new moderate-income housing programs were sweetened in 1969 by the FNMA-GNMA tandem plan (Federal National Mortgage Association and Government National Mortgage Association). In essence this guaranteed federally financed mortgages at favorable rates to rent-supplement developments, nonprofit-sponsored section 236 projects, and section 235 one-family houses. In the first two programs, mortgages were purchased at par; in the one-family section 235 programs, at 96 percent.

The net result was that the new approach attracted many developer participants, so that the percentage of directly subsidized units[18] in the volume of housing starts grew from 4.2 percent in 1962 to 10.8 in 1968 and 13.3 percent in 1969. It was 29.5 percent in 1970 and projected at 21.4 for 1971.[19]

In 1968, for the first time, there was a program of direct subsidies that provided sales housing at prices attractive to, and possible for, lower-income families. Developers find the program profitable and are building in the suburbs; realtors are pushing the programs in the used housing markets of the central cities. High building costs in relation to maximum mortgage limits permitted under the section 235 program have resulted in concentration of construction in the southern and border states; only 6 percent of the units had been built in the heavily populated Northeast region, as of the end of 1970.[20]

A distinctive feature of both the rental and cooperative section 236 program and the section 235 sales program was the omission of the requirement that a "workable program for community improvement" be adopted as a condition for initiation of the programs. This departure from federal practice was of great significance. Few urbanizing suburban areas needed or wanted urban renewal, and thus few had or needed workable programs. In practice, the requirement was a de facto veto power to local communities that did not welcome low- and moderate-income housing. Today the workable program is no longer required for section 221 (d) (3) and public housing.[21] Its removal will probably accelerate the utilization of restrictive zoning and other devices to accomplish the same results.

Despite the abuses and scandals incident to the section 235 program (primarily in more generous application to used central city units, unanticipated

[18] In this paper the term "directly subsidized" is used advisedly, since the largest aggregate subsidies are received by middle-and higher-income groups through preferential income tax treatment. Henry Aaron, "Income Taxes and Housing," *The American Economic Review*, vol. 60, no. 5 (December 1970), pp. 789–806; and J. B. Shelton, "The Cost of Renting Versus Owning A Home," *Land Economics*, vol. 44, no. 1 (February 1968), pp. 59–72.

[19] HUD table "U.S. Housing Starts, 1961–70, by Categories," December 29, 1971, and HUD table as of February 8, 1972.

[20] U.S. Commission on Civil Rights, *Home Ownership for Lower Income Families*, p. viii.

[21] Since, however, where section 236 housing is combined with rent supplements, formal local approval is still required, there remain serious limitations upon maximum subsidies for low-income families, especially in the suburbs.

by its sponsors), there is every reason to believe that the program will continue, although perhaps at a lower level of funding. Even if the used housing component championed by the real estate industry is increased (as is now proposed), the national commitment to home ownership *per se* and its real economic benefits (outlined below) suggest that the section 235 program will survive. (My concern is lest we assume that the problems of the slums and racial conflict are solved once we graft a middle-class institution – home ownership – on those who have neither middle-class opportunities nor goals.) As has repeatedly been pointed out, home ownership is possible for low- and moderate-income households that have reasonably certain incomes and the motivation to move up. This means that both careful selection of participants and effective counseling services are needed. The first of these requirements negates the notion that through home ownership alone the problems of poverty, uncertainty of income, or social pathology can or will be solved. The second requires that we learn – and learn quickly – how to counsel this new universe of home owners and that we be prepared to pay for this service.

To date, the section 235 program in the suburbs has been primarily for white families. The U.S. Commission on Civil Rights is highly critical of these results. In light of the geographic concentration of the program in the South and border states and the high concentration of minority involvement in used housing in central cities, the commission seems justified in recommending more aggressive enforcement of the fair housing provisions of the Civil Rights Act of 1968 and a higher mortgage ceiling.

In a June 1971 report on the impact of the section 235 program, the Commission drew attention to the difficulties posed by local authorities:

> Local laws and policies on land use have limited the choice of sites for 235 housing. Because of restrictive zoning laws, such as minimum lot size requirements, builders who seek to construct new 235 housing in suburban sections of metropolitan areas often have been prevented from doing so.[22]

As the administration of the section 235 program corrects past deficiencies and the pressure engendered by the U.S. Commission on Civil Rights becomes effective, the demand for minority participation in the suburban sector of the lower-income ownership program will rise. Unless the suburbs have a sudden change of heart, they will turn to local governments for action, and accelerated utilization of zoning and other land use restrictions will be the most probable instrument. This move, however, may be opposed by the building industry.

Should the supply of mortgage money continue to be abundant at interest rates that buyers not benefiting from direct subsidies will pay, a smaller

[22]U.S. Commission on Civil Rights, *Home Ownership for Lower Income Families*, p. viii.

number of home builders will be committed to section 235 housing. But many builders have lived through periodic shortages of mortgage credit and will hesitate, even under the most favorable credit conditions, to abandon programs such as section 235 and section 236 that almost assure a market and a supply of mortgage credit. Some will continue to use the programs, at least until they develop marginal sites, either owned or optioned. Enough builders will decide to stick with the programs, as either a major or restricted part of their operations, to utilize the direct and indirect subsidies available. Some will take an active role in challenging restrictive zoning, as they opposed local referendums for public housing once they could participate profitably in that activity under the "turnkey program," where they built public housing and sold it to local housing authorities.[23] More significant will be the role of home builders in dealing with local zoning boards. The two groups are not strangers to each other, and the expertise that the builders have developed in dealing with the zoning boards may present a new challenge to the type of zoning that would destroy sections 235 and 236 housing in the suburbs.

The challenge to zoning in the courts may be stepped up now that there is a goal-oriented national housing policy. No longer is zoning an issue of concern primarily to poor people and only a few builders. It negates the purpose of a federal housing program and a national housing policy at the same time that it endangers the profits of many builders and developers who want to participate in programs under sections 235 and 236. And, regardless of the legislative fate of these two programs, existing allocations and commitments will assure a high volume of construction of this type of subsidized units over the next few years.

A recent development in New Jersey may be a straw in the wind on the litigation front. In Madison Township, a court case was brought on behalf of black, white, and Spanish-speaking people of low- and moderate-income who were denied housing opportunities as a result of the zoning ordinance. In addition to the fact that the suit was initiated on behalf of all persons in the class identified above, it was the first exclusionary zoning litigation to recognize the right of persons residing outside a community to challenge that community's zoning ordinance in the courts. The judge struck down the entire zoning ordinance on the ground that it prohibited as much as 90 percent of the population from obtaining housing in the township. The judge further found that "such economic discrimination was not in the general

[23]John Herbers, "16 Groups Urge Court to Upset Coast Low-Cost Housing Curb," *New York Times*, October 27, 1971, p. 19.

The most recent manifestation of homebuilders' concern about land use controls was the action at their 1972 convention in Houston. Among the policies adopted was one stating: "Zoning and other land use controls not legitimately based on health, safety and welfare of the public as a whole must be vigorously challenged." (*Housing Affairs Letter*, February 4, 1972, p. 3.)

welfare of the citizens of the State of New Jersey and, therefore, violated the constitutional standards for zoning embodied in the New Jersey Zoning Enabling Act."[24]

Subsequently the scope of judicial assault on restrictive zoning was enlarged. A suit on behalf of all minority oppressed persons has been filed against a number of communities in Bergen County, New Jersey in an attempt to seek a coordinated regional approach to low-income housing. This has been identified as the first legal attack against restrictive local zoning ordinances that named the defendants on a regional basis.[25]

Many large builders are already diversifying and creating a variety of dwellings for the new middle class. Their efforts are concentrated in large, master-planned communities — including new communities — with a mix of residential and commercial uses. Modular units and high-grade mobile homes are included, as well as high-rise condominiums and other types of apartments, townhouses, cluster housing, and fourplexes.[26] In all probability these larger producers of shelter will lead the way in seeking modifications in restrictive zoning.

The struggle for removal of restrictions on the construction of multifamily and lower-income housing beyond the central cities is creating strange bedfellows. Largely because of direct and indirect subsidies in this market, developers are increasingly becoming advocates of fewer restrictions on land use. The rise of new and unexpected alliances in housing is not novel. A quarter of a century ago a property owners' association in Chicago, which had long vehemently opposed Negro occupancy in its community, joined with elements of the black community to champion occupancy standards as a substitute for racially restrictive covenants. At that time I identified this as a collaboration of the lion and the lamb.[27] Perhaps there is a current analogy.

EFFECT OF ENFORCED RESIDENTIAL SEGREGATION ON EMPLOYMENT OPPORTUNITIES AND HOUSING COSTS

Before discussing the economic consequences of enforced residential segregation, I want to comment briefly on some of the philosophical and political issues of ethnic residential concentration or dispersion. The housing problems

---

[24]"Zoning Ordinance Invalidated," *American Society of Planning Officials, Planning*, vol. 38, no. 1 (January 1972), p. 19.

[25]"4 Bergen Towns Sued on Housing," *New York Times*, February 18, 1972, p. 24.

[26]Shirley L. Benzer, "New Dimensions in Home Building," *New York Times*, January 2, 1972, Section 3, p. 3.

[27]Weaver, *The Negro Ghetto*, pp. 354–58.

of minorities are often presented in terms of rehabilitation of the black ghetto versus opening the suburbs to low- and moderate-income households, of which a large proportion are nonwhite. But this "either or" approach ignores the fact that *both processes can occur simultaneously and both are necessary.*[28] Also there is controversy about the role of the upwardly mobile and the established middle-class blacks in the development of the ghetto. The extreme rhetoric seems to say that all blacks should remain in the ghetto, that moving to the suburbs means copping out.

A much more sophisticated approach is one that recognizes the intrinsic locational and real estate value of many black ghettos,[29] urging that blacks control, occupy, and develop them.[30] This position does not necessarily imply that all blacks are to remain in the central city. Some who articulate it would recognize the economic and psychological costs of exclusion from the suburbs where new housing and new jobs are concentrated. They would agree with Congressman Parren J. Mitchell when he said, "Let's get the record straight. I'm not at all sure that most blacks want integration . . . I am sure that we want equal access to the housing market. . . ."[31]

Obviously, these are matters worthy of a paper specifically addressed to them. As tempting as such a discussion is, I limit myself here to a consideration of how *enforced* residential segregation affects employment opportunities and price of shelter.

Employment

An imposing body of literature asserts or documents that the current development of employment opportunities outside the central cities and the concurrent restriction of housing opportunities for most nonwhites in the suburbs result in a significant reduction of nonwhite employment.[32] The principal elements involved are:

[28] Robert C. Weaver, *Dilemmas of Urban America* (Harvard University Press, 1965), chap. 4; and Anthony Downs, "Alternative Futures for the American Ghetto," Martin Meyerson (ed.), *The Conscience of the City* (Braziller, 1970), pp. 259–306.

[29] Robert C. Weaver, "Beyond the Ghetto," *Ebony*, vol. 25, no. 10 (August 1970), pp. 148–51.

[30] "Let's Keep the Inner City Black," *Ebony*, vol. 27, no. 3 (January 1972), p. 108.

[31] Parren J. Mitchell, "Address to NAHRO 33rd Annual Conference," October 5, 1971, Kansas City, Missouri, *Journal of Housing*, vol. 28, no. 11 (December 1971), p. 589.

[32] For a detailed analysis of this, see John F. Kain, *The Effects of the Ghetto on the Distribution and Level of Non-White Employment in Urban Areas* (Rand Corporation, 1965), and "Housing Segregation, Negro Employment, and Metropolitan Decentralization," *Quarterly Journal of Economics*, vol. 82, no. 2 (May 1968), pp. 175–97; Richard W. Epps, "Suburban Jobs and Black Workers," *Business Review*, Federal Reserve Bank

(1) Distance and difficulty (including costs) of reaching job opportunities from ghetto residential areas.
(2) Lack of information on job opportunities.
(3) Fear on the part of employers that hiring nonwhites may create local resentment if the community regards this move as a step toward open housing.

Kain, in analyzing the situation in Chicago and Detroit, concluded that the pronounced racial residential segregation in Chicago had an adverse impact upon the distribution of Negro employment. He also asserted, and correctly in my opinion, that his data suggest that housing segregation may significantly affect the level of Negro employment in metropolitan areas. It seems, therefore, that a part of what is usually attributed to employment discrimination may well be an indirect effect of housing discrimination.[33]

In a later paper involving a more intensive analysis of employment and racial residential data in Chicago, Kain concluded: "the empirical findings do suggest that postwar suburbanization of metropolitan employment may be further undermining the position of the Negro, and that the continued high levels of Negro unemployment in a full employment economy may be partially attributable to the rapid and adverse (for the Negro) shifts in the location of jobs."[34] Of course, this finding implies that the location of white-collar, service, and industrial jobs in the suburbs adversely affects blacks largely because of their lack of access to shelter outside central cities. All of these findings take on greater significance in light of current trends in the location of industry and the geographic concentration of white-collar and service jobs. These trends strongly suggest that the growth of employment opportunities in these categories will be concentrated increasingly in the urbanizing areas outside the central cities.

Since it is recognized that the significant underrepresentation of blacks in employment zones distant from the ghetto militates against their job opportunities, it was inevitable that alternative compensatory strategies would develop. One of these, of course, is black capitalism in the central cities. But

---

of Philadelphia, October 1969; E. Sherman Adams, "Coping with Ghetto Unemployment," *The Conference Board Record*, vol. 7, no. 5 (May 1970), pp. 41–45; National Committee Against Discrimination in Housing, *The Impact of Housing Patterns on Job Opportunities* (1968); and Regina Belz Armstrong, *Linking Skills, Jobs and Housing in the New York Urban Region* (Regional Plan Association, March 1972, mimeo.). This matter is also analyzed in detail by Wilbur A. Steger in his paper in this book.

[33] Kain, *The Effects of the Ghetto on the Distribution and Level of Non-White Employment in Urban Areas.*

[34] Kain, "Housing Segregation, Negro Employment, and Metropolitan Decentralization," p. 197.

such an approach, aside from its fringe psychological and real entrepreneurial development potential, hardly begins to provide the volume of employment needed by blacks.[35] Even some of the more articulate black nationalists have begun to realize this.[36]

Housing

Until a decade ago, housing studies generally concluded that residential segregation forced Negro households to pay more than whites for identical facilities.[37] Recently more exact tools have been addressed to the problem and more and better quantitative data have been collected and processed. What had formerly been accepted as conventional wisdom is now challenged by some,[38] but the preponderance of evidence and opinion supports the conclusion that "there is reason to believe that poor people, especially blacks, pay more to rent housing in relation to what they get for their money, than do higher-income people."[39] Similarly, in the purchase of housing, the dollar in a black hand seldom buys as much as the dollar in a white hand. Even if there were no quantitative studies to support this conclusion, it might be deduced from the fact that the price of any commodity is inflated if the purchase is restricted to a segment of the total market. A well-documented analysis, which also reviews the literature pro and con, stated, "Evaluation of the diverse empirical studies leads us to conclude that blacks may pay between 5 and 10 percent more than whites in most urban areas for comparable housing."[40] As Steger delineates in the following paper, such a mark-up occasions a high annual aggregate of discrimination cost.

[35] Andrew Brimmer and Henry S. Terrell, "The Economic Potential of Black Capitalism" (paper presented to the 82nd Meeting of the American Economic Association, December 29, 1969); and Adams, "Coping with Ghetto Unemployment."

[36] Clarence Funnye, *Black Power and Desegregation: A Retreat To Reality* (National Committee Against Discrimination in Housing, New York, 1969).

[37] See, for example, Corienne K. Robinson, "Relationship Between Condition of Dwelling Units and Rentals by Race," *Journal of Land and Public Utility Economics*, vol. 22, no. 3 (August 1946), pp. 296–302; Weaver, *The Negro Ghetto*; Charles Abrams, *Forbidden Neighbors* (Harper, 1955); and Davis McEntire, *Residence and Race* (University of California Press, 1960).

[38] Included are M. J. Bailey, "Effects of Race and Other Demographic Factors on the Value of Single-Family Homes," *Land Economics*, vol. 42, no. 2 (May 1966), pp. 215–20; and Richard F. Muth, *Cities and Housing: The Spatial Pattern of Residential Land Use* (University of Chicago Press, 1969).

[39] Marion Clawson, *Suburban Land Conversion in the United States*, pp. 114–15.

[40] John F. Kain and John Quigley, "Housing Market Discrimination, Home Ownership, and Savings Behavior," *American Economic Review*, vol. 62, no. 3 (June 1972), p. 263. The authors also contend that "researchers, in their concern about estimating the magnitude of price discrimination, have overlooked a far more serious consequence of

For the same number of rooms, at the same rent, Negroes obtain a substantially greater proportion of substandard housing units.[41] The degree to which this is operative reflects the existence of a tight housing market. While the low-income black suffers most from residential segregation in terms of employment opportunities and substandard housing, the upwardly mobile low- and moderate-income and middle-income black family is also adversely affected by the mark-up and artificially limited choices in a segregated housing market.[42] Frequently involved are both higher prices and the limitation of the middle-income black purchaser to properties on the periphery of the ghetto — which in a racially segregated market is sure to expand.

In a recent study Kain and Quigley wrote:

> Persistence, a thick skin, and a willingness to spend enormous amounts of time housing-hunting are minimum requirements for nonwhites who wish to move into white neighborhoods. These psychic and transaction costs may be far more significant than out-of-pocket costs to Negroes considering a move out of the ghetto. Most blacks limit their search for housing to the ghetto; this limitation is more than geographic. There is less variety of housing services available inside the ghetto than outside; indeed, many bundles of housing services are unavailable in the ghetto at any price.[43]

In the same study Kain and Quigley gave detailed attention to the different propensities of Negro and white households to purchase homes and the resulting costs to the deprived group. Their findings suggest, with significant documentation, that housing discrimination has reduced Negro opportunities for home ownership, and they conclude that this may in large part explain the lesser assets owned by Negro households at each income level.[44]

The relative incidence of home ownership in 1960 is shown in Table 1.

Not owning a home occasions severe economic losses because it means losing out on the many economic benefits of home ownership: favorable

---

housing market discrimination. In asking whether blacks pay more than whites for the *same* kind of housing, they have failed to consider adequately the way in which housing discrimination has affected the kind of housing consumed by Negro households." (Ibid., pp. 263–64.)

[41] Chester Rapkin, "Price Discrimination Against Negroes in the Rental Housing Market," *Essays in Urban Land Economics* (Real Estate Research Program, University of California, Los Angeles, 1966), pp. 333–45.

[42] Robert Schafer, "Slum Formation, Race and Income Strategy," *Journal of the American Institute of Planners*, vol. 37, no. 5 (September 1971), p. 350.

[43] Kain and Quigley, "Housing Market Discrimination, Home Ownership, and Savings Behavior," p. 264.

[44] Ibid., p. 274. The authors "conclude that the 'supply restrictions' on Negro residential choice and on the kind of housing available to black households may be largely responsible for the wide discrepancy between ownership rates for otherwise identical black and white households." (Ibid., p. 270.)

Table 1. Percentage of Homeownership within Income Groups, 1960

Income groups	All homeowners	Nonwhite homeowners
Under $3,000 per year	43%	33%
$3,000 to $6,000 per year	50%	36%
Over $6,000 per year	67%	55%
Over $8,000 per year	80%	67%

Source: U.S. Commission on Civil Rights, *Home Ownership for Lower Income Families: A Report on the Racial and Ethnic Impact of the Section 235 Program,* June 1971, p. 3.

federal income tax treatment, especially for a higher-income household; an important hedge against inflation; an often involuntary, or at least unconscious, form of savings; low interest rates because of federal mortgage insurance and special advantages provided to mortgage-lending thrift institutions; and do-it-yourself savings in annual maintenance costs.[45] Today one could add the benefits of below-the-market interest rates on section 235 sales housing and homes financed under the Farmers Home Administration rural housing programs. Again Steger's paper quantifies the economic loss suffered by blacks.

Factors other than economic costs are also involved. The current controversy over school busing emphasizes the social costs of residential segregation. And there is the ever-present matter of freedom of choice in the selection of a place to live. Issues of this nature are of utmost significance and have been repeatedly discussed in the literature on housing and race. As one writer expressed it, "The ghetto reinforces the inferiority and discrimination which is produced elsewhere. It adds discrimination, exploitation, and destruction of its own. And it then concentrates those who are discriminated and embittered together."[46]

SUBSIDIES FOR THE HOUSING UNIT OR THE INDIVIDUAL?

If lower-income and black households are to have greater housing choices, there must be a supply of housing within their economic reach; the supply must be located throughout the metropolitan area; and owners must be willing to rent or sell to them.

For the first condition to be met, there will have to be both enough standard housing and substantial programs of income maintenance and hous-

[45] Ibid., pp. 273–74.
[46] Stephen D. Berger, *The Social Consequences of Residential Segregation of the Urban American Negro* (Metropolitan Applied Research Center, New York, 1970), p. 34.

ing subsidies. Even if new technology were developed and applied, land costs materially reduced, and real estate taxes appreciably cut, a large number of low- and moderate-income households would still require some form of subsidy.[47]

The nature of the subsidy is a matter of great dispute. The main issue is whether to subsidize the housing unit, as is done in major existing programs, or to grant subsidies directly to the tenant or purchaser. The first type, which is obviously designed to increase the production of housing available to poorer people, is said to be outmoded at a time when there is a surplus of decent housing in low- and moderate-income central city areas and abandoned units are creating problems. Subsidies to individuals might ease the abandonment problem, be more equitable (if they are extended to *all* in given income ranges), and cost less per household.[48] Some assert that they would also be less difficult to administer in that less federal bureaucracy would be involved. However, since local building departments are often envisioned as the inspection agents, there is a question of the efficacy of such substitution.[49]

The benefits and costs of each approach cannot be discussed in detail in this paper, but certain observations are relevant. As a tool for providing housing for lower-income groups outside the central city, the housing subsidy to individuals leaves much to be desired. Although we do not yet know the exact production response to greater effective demand in this segment of the market, there is significant support for the position that for several years increased purchasing power will produce higher rents or prices for all consumers with little upgrading in the quality of shelter except in very loose housing markets. But the suburban locations from which lower-income families have long been excluded have neither loose markets nor a supply of

[47]For an excellent resumé of the cost factors in the price of housing, see Schussheim, "National Goals and Local Practices," pp. 146–52.

[48]There is a great deal written on this. A series of excellent articles appeared in Part 2 of the *Papers Submitted to Subcommittee on Housing Panels.* They include Morton L. Isler, "The Goals of Housing Subsidy Programs"; Lester C. Thurow, "Goals of a Housing Program"; Donald D. Kummerfeld, "The Housing Subsidy System"; Ira S. Lowry, "Housing Assistance for Low-Income Urban Families: A Fresh Approach"; Frank deLeeuw, "The Housing Allowance Approach."

For a more recent analysis, see Irving Welfeld, "That 'Housing Problem': the American vs. the European Experience," *The Public Interest*, no. 27 (Spring 1972), pp. 78–95. While there is great economic validity in Welfeld's advocacy of European models that involve substantial initial subsidies, he ignores the politically adverse budgetary impact that such subsidies would have in this country owing to the absence of a capital budget concept.

[49]For an interesting case history of an individual and a building department, see Charles Kichuche, "A Brownstone Is A Home Symbol," *New York Times*, February 13, 1971, sec. 8, pp. 1 and 9.

housing that the less affluent could afford even with reasonably liberal sub-sidies.

If we are really committed, as I am, to the ultimate goal of opening the suburbs to lower-income groups and blacks, I believe that housing subsidies should be attached to the dwelling unit and directed to builders who will rent and sell to those families. As noted earlier, the profit motive attracted builders to exploit the new low- and moderate-income housing need that was translated into an effective demand by sections 221 (d) (3), 235, and 236. Once attracted, builders who either owned or obtained sites outside the central city used their expertise and contacts to secure zoning modifications. I doubt if housing subsidies to individuals would evoke such effective responses. As Thurow put it, "Subsidies to the renters will do little good since the desired housing is not available in the right areas and since the [would be] occupiers may not rent or purchase in the areas that would accomplish the social objectives."[50]

In the central cities and some of the more modest suburbs built immediately after World War II, housing subsidies to individuals would facilitate greater choices in loose housing markets. But restricting the blacks, the poor, and the moderate income to shoddier suburbs is hardly a viable approach in the 1970s. Furthermore the volume of shelter in the suburbs resulting from subsidies to individuals would not appreciably ease the employment consequences of racial and economic exclusion beyond the limits of the central city. The results, even with effective enforcement of fair housing legislation, would be too little and too late.

In central city localities where used housing is available and abandonments are prevalent, housing subsidies to individuals may prove to be more effective and economical than subsidies to housing units, which are designed not to effect transfers but to encourage production of housing. The matter is quite different in Model Cities, where the emphasis is on upgrading or producing low- and moderate-income shelter, and in urban renewal areas, where federal regulations now encourage (and at times require) low- and moderate-income housing in redevelopment. Eliminating production-oriented subsidies would delay and endanger these vital central city programs.

It is my guess that we shall discover that each type of subsidy has a role to play and that the mix will depend upon the composition of the particular housing market and its vacancy rates by price and size categories.

Without neglecting new construction, national housing goals should be reformulated to reflect the objectives of improving the current quality of housing services, preventing physical deterioration, and minimizing the

[50]Lester C. Thurow, "Goals of a Housing Program," p. 445.

tragic kind of stock loss exemplified by abandonment. . . . Such commitment should not be interpreted as a substitute for new construction. . . . Long-term construction and short-term housing service goals can and should coexist.[51]

ACCESS TO SUBURBAN COMMUNITIES: APPROACHES AND LIMITATIONS

In the fall of 1971, the Banking and Currency Committee of the House of Representatives held hearings on a bill, HR-9688, introduced by the Chairman for himself and sixteen of the other twenty-one Democratic members of the Committee. Incorporated in the proposed legislation (and in the Report and Recommendations of the Three Study Panels upon which the legislation was based[52] and the *Papers Submitted to Subcommittee on Housing Panels*) were certain ideas set forth by Anthony Downs in "Alternative Futures of the American Ghetto,"[53] especially the concept of incentives to suburban communities for encouraging acceptance of lower-income housing.

The basic thrust of the report and the accompanying proposed legislation is to facilitate areawide housing programs by making community development block grants contingent on the formulation of a program that, as described in the report, would include "activities designed to provide an adequate supply of standard housing, particularly for low- and moderate-income families and individuals, within reasonable proximity to their places of employment."[54] The language in the bill itself is somewhat ambiguous,[55] but the intent of the report is clear: to use the leverage of community development grants — covering urban renewal, neighborhood facilities, rehabilitation assistance, code enforcement, programs to counter abandonments, certain types of Model Cities activities, relocation payments, open space acquisition and development, and basic water and sewer facilities — as an inducement for metropolitan approaches to low- and moderate-income housing.

The report stresses the importance of making the housing demands of the lowest income groups more effective and the geographical distribution of

---

[51] Isler, "The Goals of Housing Subsidy Programs," p. 425.

[52] *Housing and the Urban Environment*, Report and Recommendations of the Three Study Panels of the Subcommittee on Housing, Committee on Banking and Currency, House of Representatives, 92 Cong. 1 sess. (1971).

[53] In Meyerson (ed.), *The Conscience of the City*, pp. 259–306.

[54] *Housing and the Urban Environment*, p. 33.

[55] *Housing and Urban Development Legislation — 1971*, Hearings Before the Subcommittee on Housing, Committee on Banking and Currency, House of Representatives, 92 Cong. 1 sess. (1971), Pt. 1, p. 337.

housing more equitable. To achieve increased access to employment opportunities and reduced concentration of lower-income families in the central city, the report suggests that housing block grants be made to state and metropolitan housing agencies so that housing assistance programs could be carried out on a metropolitan or areawide basis. To encourage this areawide approach, it suggests: (1) the payment of up to $3,000 per unit over a decade to cover part of the cost to the jurisdiction providing the housing facilities and services, and (2) the elimination of local tax exemptions for public housing. The actual amount of the incentive payment would vary from community to community in accordance with the need for additional services and the fiscal condition of the community.

Each metropolitan housing agency would be required to develop three-year programs, including specific amounts of low- and moderate-income housing. In approving such proposals, HUD would evaluate the amount and geographic distribution of lower-income housing in the area. Although there would be no requirement that every community must have some subsidized housing during the three-year program, the report makes it clear that the basic intent of the proposal is "to provide housing for low- and moderate-income families in a manner that *equitably and efficiently* promotes greater access to job opportunities throughout the metropolitan area."[56]

The possibility of losing grant funds for water and sewer and open space might induce some local governments to reassess their position and participate in an areawide approach to housing. All the components in community development grants are sweetened by increasing the federal share to 90 percent. This makes them especially attractive to the suburbs where there is scant opportunity for grant-in-aid credits, which are generated primarily by urban renewal.

Federal grants would also be made to states for the purpose of developing a master plan for the modernization of state and local governments. The plans would include a timetable of proposed actions of implementation. Included among state actions designed to strengthen local government in metropolitan areas are:

(1) authorizing the municipalities to exercise extra-territorial planning, zoning, and subdivision control over unincorporated areas;
(2) restricting zoning authority in metropolitan areas to metropolitan units, to larger municipalities, to counties, or to the state, in order to prevent zoning by smaller municipalities that exclude housing for lower-income families;

[56]*Housing and the Urban Environment*, p. 30.

(3) authorizing the formation of metropolitan planning agencies to make recommendations to local governments concerning such matters as land use, zoning, building regulations, and capital improvements;
(4) furnishing state financial and technical assistance to metropolitan areas for such matters as planning, building codes, urban renewal, consolidation, and local government and finance.

The report and proposed legislation are significant for two reasons. First, they indicate types of federal inducements and programs that can sometimes encourage the provision of low- and moderate-income housing outside the central cities. Second, they reflect the changes that are occurring in the analysis of housing problems and public policy formulation. As of this writing, it seems improbable that HR-9688 will be enacted this session of Congress. But five years ago no such bill would have been developed by the Banking and Currency Committee in either house of the Congress.

The first significant step toward a new sophistication in housing and land use policy in the United States was the establishment in 1968 of a timetable of national housing goals. That was followed by provisions for development of a national urban growth policy in 1970 — an event that was more significant than the contents of the first *Report on National Growth*, which devoted more space to state and local action than to federal action.[57] HR-9688, with its areawide approaches to housing and community development grants and its incentives to localities for the construction of lower-priced shelter, suggests we may be moving away from a system of control over the allocation of urban land that depends entirely on autonomous, and often self-serving, local units of government. More and more recognition is being given to the impact of zoning and associated devices upon land costs, and there are proposals before Congress that would render land use policies more sensitive to housing goals and national growth policy.

The proposals included in HR-9688 do not exhaust the principal legislative tools for modifying the restrictive nature of zoning and associated instruments. As Mason Gaffney indicates, taxation can be used effectively for this purpose. Another device is advance public acquisition of land for urban use. Interestingly enough, when I called attention to the omission of reference to a national urban land policy at the hearings on the legislation, one of the principal sponsors of the panels, Congressman Thomas L. Ashley, agreed that advance land acquisition by public bodies is essential, and he observed that

[57]Executive Office of the President, Domestic Council, *Report on National Growth*, *1972.*

the new communities legislation (of which he was the principal sponsor) does actually involve advance land acquisition.[58]

New Communities

Our limited experience with new communities has already demonstrated how they can influence zoning and control land use in large developments. Their impact upon ethnic and economic mix could be equally significant. Planning decisions affecting unprecedented large areas of land are in the hands of a developer or a single development corporation. Because the project is large and usually to some degree self-contained, it basically creates its own environment and is less responsive to outside attitudes or actions. Many who move into new communities see certain advantages in them. These may include better services and facilities, improved site planning, greater open space, and associated physical facilities. Then, too, there is often a high degree of satisfaction with the small neighborhood environment in new communities.[59]

At this stage of development, there is evidence at Columbia, in Maryland, and perhaps at Reston, in Virginia, of a feeling on the part of some residents that they are establishing a new way of life as well as a new community. Included, of course, is acceptance of a limited amount of economic mix in housing. Also the residents of some of these new communities usually know that nonwhites will be welcomed; thus there is some elimination of whites who completely reject minority neighbors. This last circumstance, combined with the intrinsic appeal that new communities have for some people, may lead to greater stability of racially mixed housing patterns than is generally the case.

On the other hand, since most new communities in the near future will probably be developed by private enterprise, market response to economic or ethnic living patterns will have a significant impact upon the kind of communities that emerge. Conventional business wisdom and past practices suggest that it may be difficult to merchandise highly heterogeneous developments. At the same time, more and more developers of new communities seek federal assistance. If there is significant public financial support there is sure to be pressure for low- and moderate-income housing, and there is unquestionable responsibility for compliance with the Fair Housing Title of the Civil Rights Law of 1968.

[58] *Housing and Urban Development Legislation – 1971*, pp. 337–40.

[59] Robert B. Zehner, "Research Report: Neighborhood and Community Satisfaction in New Towns and Less Planned Suburbs," *Journal of the American Institute of Planners*, vol. 37, no. 6 (November 1971), pp. 379–85.

Out of all this, I hazard the prophecy that, to the extent federal aid is utilized, new communities removed from existing centers of urban concentration will have a higher proportion of lower-income and minority residents than traditional suburban developments. It is, I believe, highly improbable that most developments (exclusive of those predominantly nonwhite or designed primarily for low- and moderate-income occupancy),[60] will house a significant number or proportion of very low-income families. Much depends, of course, upon the degree of federal assistance, the vigor with which antidiscrimination legislation is administered, and the interpretation and enforcement of HUD regulations. The draft regulations for the Urban Growth and New Community Development Act of 1970 require that new communities "be designed to increase the available choices for living and working for the fullest possible range of people and families of different compositions and incomes (including a substantial provision for housing for persons and families of low and moderate income) and must be open to all, regardless of race, creed, color, or national origin."[61]

In determining the sufficiency of ethnic and economic housing mix, the draft regulations stipulate that consideration be given to:

(1) existing and projected distribution of families for the region in which a project is located,
(2) existing and projected housing supply and demand, with special attention to lower-income groups, in the project region and market area, and
(3) income and family characteristics of those likely to be employed in the new community.

Also, it is stipulated that construction of low- and moderate-income housing be provided at every major residential development stage of the community.[62]

---

[60]And there are such proposed: Soul City in North Carolina and the broader New Communities Family Mobility System which includes a demonstration project in the Louisville Urban Region. For a description of the latter proposal, see *Newcom: Summary* (Urban Studies Center, University of Louisville, 1971).

[61]*Draft Regulations: Urban Growth and New Community Development Act of 1970. Federal Register*, 36 F.R. 14 205–14 (July 31, 1971).

[62]Ibid. In the winter of 1972, an eighth new community was conditionally approved by HUD — San Antonio Ranch, 20 miles from the city of San Antonio. *HUD Newsletter* (March 13, 1972) reported that, of the same 28,000 dwelling units contemplated, one-fourth were designed for low-income families.

Jonathan, Minnesota, is the first new community to receive HUD federal support under the 1968–70 new communities acts. It is paired with Cedar-Riverside, a new town/in town located in Minneapolis. Both are planned to be balanced communities. In Jonathan the pattern would mean that about 20 percent of the residents would have incomes less than $7,200 a year, with half of them earning less than $4,800. Half of all

New communities developed with federal financial support should prove to be effective tools for widening the housing choices for lower-income and minority households. But their total impact over the next five years or more will be limited because most of the expansion in housing will be concentrated in more conventional suburban communities and because of the length of time required to plan, initiate, and complete a new community.

Housing Troubled Households

If the above evaluation is sound, it highlights a chronic problem — housing the most troubled elements in our population. It can be anticipated that even the new communities designed predominantly for low- and moderate-income families will seek the upwardly mobile elements among the poor. And logic suggests that traditional suburban developments, if they house lower-income occupants, will be equally or more selective in seeking the "respectable poor."

The methods for dealing with abandonment that are incorporated in the proposed HR-9688 indicate that the new small-scale indigenous owners in the ghetto will resort to careful tenant selection. Sponsors of 221 (d) (3) and 236 rental developments, limited profit developments, and, to a lesser degree, nonprofit ones will all seek tenants who will not be expected to create management problems. Public housing, in an understandable effort to become more attractive to the "respectable poor," will often do likewise.[63] When public housing breaks out of ghetto locations, there is a tendency to assure reluctant locales that carefully selected families and the elderly will be chosen for occupancy. But what of families and individuals who present serious problems to neighbors and management alike? Are they to be concentrated in public housing where they can be inundated with services and special assistance? Or are they to be widely dispersed so that they will not feed on each others' problems?[64]

Since most landlords are rapidly moving toward more careful tenant selection, occupants who present serious management problems are the undesirables in the housing market. In New York City, private landlords who accept

---

families would have incomes of $10,500 and up. In Cedar-Riverside most of the housing would be for low- and moderate-income households. The site already has a 600-unit high-rise public housing project built for the elderly in 1963. Under construction are 117 units of turnkey public housing and 552 units of section 236 housing. See "New Town/ Out of Town: Jonathan," and "New Town/In Town: Cedar-Riverside," *Journal of Housing*, vol. 29, no. 3 (March 31, 1972), pp. 120-31.

[63] Roger Starr, "Which of the Poor Shall Live in Public Housing?," *The Public Interest*, no. 23 (Spring 1971), pp. 116-24.

[64] *Housing and Urban Development Legislation — 1971*, pp. 281-82.

welfare tenants have been found to charge exorbitant rents or provide minimal services, or both. *The problems of those who are poverty stricken, alienated, and often least able to participate effectively in the urban labor market, cannot be solved by housing alone.*

If Rainwater is correct, the most single important need of poor families is more money. This is probably true in an absolute sense, in that they need more and better goods and services. It is probably also true in a relative sense, in that their relative poverty needs to be made less striking.[65] Housing subsidies, of whatever nature, are ill-equipped to meet the total need. A return on the part of public housing to careful selection of middle-class–oriented poor may make the program more viable, but it will only complicate the status of the rejects. We must either develop effective programs for the dependents of our society or adapt public housing to include them, with recognition that the resulting shelter is only a small element in the approach to the overall problem. Either route is expensive. But we cannot ignore the human beings involved, and we should cease the pretense that our housing programs do, or will, meet their needs. To a significant degree, the original concept and the legislation for Model Cities recognized these truths.

It is misleading, of course, to identify low-income or welfare households with "undesirable" tenants. A recent study of the management of federally assisted housing in New York City, while recognizing the impact of tenant selection upon occupants, management, and the community, found "no necessary relationship [among subsidized tenants involved] between income levels and the incidence of rent delinquencies, vandalism, crime, tenant-management conflict, or turnover."[66] It did identify drug addiction among tenants or in the neighborhood as the most serious social factor leading to maintenance and management problems. And it found that the tenants of these projects, like tenants of public housing, often complain about the presence of addicts. Although families with large numbers of children also cause maintenance and management problems, the latter are frequently avoidable if the development is properly designed and the management skillful.[67]

These and associated findings seem to indicate that private, semi-private, and public developments with effective and dedicated management can successfully house most of the urban poor, but not those with deep-seated social and psychological problems.

The social policy and human resources required to rehabilitate multiproblem families and individuals will seldom be forthcoming in suburbia. Their

[65] Lee Rainwater, *Behind Ghetto Walls*, chap. 14.

[66] *The Management of Federally Assisted Housing in New York City* (The Center for Community Change, Washington, 1970), pp. 179 and 186.

[67] Ibid., pp. 186–88.

problems must be met, as Model Cities recognized, at the locale where most of them live and will continue to live. Involved are drugs, crime, and fear, which, in turn, occasion maintenance, housing management, and community problems of unprecedented magnitude. Their situation is largely an inescapable heritage and the most ugly manifestation of the black experience in America.

Over the short run, all the housing problems of minorities will not be solved by providing free access to shelter outside the central city. In the long run, such action may ease the pressures that go far in creating social pathology.[68] A much larger aspect of the matter relates to the human, physical, and economic rehabilitation of the ghetto. And, as Steger stresses, a major element is the low incomes of nonwhites. All these elements must be recognized, and all of them need to be dealt with simultaneously. The fact that this paper concentrates upon the issue of free access is due to the circumstance that it is presented under the rubric of land use problems. It does not imply inclusiveness or a priority judgment.

FUTURE ECONOMIC AND RACIAL PATTERNS IN SUBURBIA

If there is a diversified cost pattern of suburban shelter and effective enforcement of the fair housing provisions of the Civil Rights Law of 1968, a larger amount of shelter for minorities will be available outside central cities. Modification of economically exclusive zoning would, of course, facilitate the process, but several issues remain. Will lower-income shelter be in separate developments or dispersed? Will the newer nonwhite resident of all income levels be housed in ghettos or in racially integrated neighborhoods? And to what extent will minorities avail themselves of suburban housing? Currently, there is little consensus on any of these matters, and matters of economic and ethnic exclusion are often confused.

Economic Patterns

Since economic patterns of shelter often limit the degree of ethnic diversification, especially for lower-income households, economic mixture merits priority in a discussion of racial residential patterns. Thus, from the point of view of public policy and efficient utilization of resources, it is pertinent to consider the potential advantages of greater economic mixture in neighbor-

[68]There are those who would challenge this; see Edward C. Banfield, *The Unheavenly City* (Little-Brown, 1970). A concise rebuttal is in Robert C. Wood, *The Necessary Majority: Middle America and the Urban Crisis* (Columbia University Press, 1972), chap. 2.

hoods. Obviously such living areas provide an opportunity for greater social contacts between different income groups. We know, of course, that proximity does not necessarily lead to meaningful relationships, but there is some evidence that these do develop among children. With or without busing, more economic mixture occurs in the public schools.

Economic diversification in housing also permits families to move up and down the socioeconomic ladder without shifting neighorhoods. Such results require a continuum of housing types with no wide cost gaps, a situation that has the added advantage of making housing turnover more effective. Then, too, opportunity is provided for partial subsidization of the less affluent by the more affluent in a given development. Lower-income households can share facilities not usually available to them, providing types and quality of retail services that are generally inaccessible to lower-income households. (Although some would counter that there would be a paucity of services designed to meet the special needs of the less affluent.) Finally, as the new community of Columbia recognizes, economically and socially mixed housing enables the wide variety of workers who are needed by the community to live near their jobs.[69]

For decades planners and other professionals have advocated economic mix on the grounds that variety in housing types was desirable. Recently, however, the feasibility of such mixture has been challenged. A report to the Department of Housing and Urban Development by the National Research Council's Social Science Panel, while recognizing increasing acceptance of racially mixed shelter,[70] asserts that there is a trend among both blacks and whites toward narrower economic and social groupings. The study warns that simultaneous efforts to reduce racial segregation and class stratification in housing may in fact be counter productive.[71]

As to whether or not economic and social mixture is feasible probably depends upon a series of circumstances. The most significant of these are the central control of planning and sales policies, greater market expertise, and opportunities to establish patterns and precedents − all of which are in the hands of the sponsor of a large development or new community. Also impor-

[69]Warren Boeschenstein, "Design of Socially Mixed Housing," *Journal of the American Institute of Planners*, vol. 37, no. 5 (September 1971), pp. 317–18.

[70]As recently as 1970, according to the findings of the National Opinion Research Center, slightly less than half of the white Americans indicated acceptance of racially integrated neighborhoods; seven years earlier about 42 percent so reacted. See Andrew M. Greeley and Paul B. Sheatsley, "Attitudes Toward Racial Integration," *Scientific American*, vol. 225, no. 6 (December 1971), p. 14.

[71]National Research Council, *Freedom of Choice in Housing: Opportunities and Constraints*, Report of the Social Science Panel of the Advisory Committee to the Department of Housing and Urban Development (undated), pp. 49 and 55.

tant are the quality and uniqueness of the development. If it offers a better environment (from the point of view of those who elect to live in it) and if the purchaser or renter is satisfied that he gets more for his housing dollar, a socioeconomic mixture is much more palatable. And, in addition, if the residents find the development – or much more likely the new community – a challenging and exciting way of life, experiment, or commitment, their acceptance of new patterns is heightened, and they may even accept economic mix.

But alas, one has to be realistic. Under the most favorable circumstances, it is doubtful that even the larger development or the much larger new community located some distance from a city will even try to include a large proportion of low-income occupants, unless forced to do so by federal policy. New York State Urban Development Corporation has adopted a minimum 10-20-70 formula, which provides for 10 percent low-income elderly, 20 percent low-income family, and 70 percent moderate- and middle-income distribution. This may well be the maximum income mix that is currently feasible (from the point of view of current market response) in some parts of the state. For the foreseeable future there is a limit to the degree to which suburbia will absorb poor people.

Racial Patterns

For middle-class blacks greater dispersion seems probable. In the first place, in moving to the suburbs they are seldom interested in transferring from one racial ghetto to another, and few cities have enough black upper-income families to support a separate suburb. The entry of a limited number of black, relatively affluent families is unlikely to cause their white neighbors to flee from a suburban community. As successful Negroes gain access to more suburban locations, the chances of new Negro middle-class suburbs decline. If the fair housing provisions of the Civil Rights Act are vigorously enforced, the result should be much wider opportunity for the dispersion of middle-class nonwhites. This will be self-sustaining because the white suburbanite will have no safe place to hide from his black prototype in many sections of the country.

Where low- and moderate-income households are involved, the situation will differ. Resistance to low-income families in the suburbs (and to a large degree in central cities) reflects in part an identification of the urban poor with blacks, Puerto Ricans, Mexican-Americans, welfare recipients, and associated groups and individuals considered undesirable. In the suburbs, as in the central city, the white poor will probably eschew residence with large numbers of poor blacks. Vast low-income housing developments with a large component of blacks will appeal to few whites, and will become mini-ghettos. Despite the greater economic opportunities they offer, these large suburban complexes may soon develop some of the pathology of the urban ghetto, and they therefore have real limitations as a long-term solution to minority status. A better approach would be to scatter public and other low-income housing throughout the suburbs where land is available. This would certainly serve to reduce ethnic concentration, and perhaps economic concentration as well.

Moderate-income blacks and other minorities are in a better position than the poor, partly because they represent a smaller proportion of the total number in their income group. Both they and their white prototypes frequently need subsidies to afford decent housing, as do the poor, but there is much less possibility (if not apprehension) that a new suburban development will be inundated by moderate-income minorities. The farther the housing is removed from existing concentrations of minorities, the more remote the possibility. Where directly subsidized housing provides real bargains and attractive developments, the possibility of stable biracial shelter is increased. Actually, it is this segment of the nonwhite community – the employed blue-collar, clerical, and lower professional worker – that will find the suburbs attractive both in terms of job opportunities and escape from the ghetto. In my opinion, both society as a whole and minority people would be benefited if the new pattern of moderate-income housing were biracial. I believe this to be feasible as well as desirable in a democracy.

Finally, if and when minorities have access to a larger supply of shelter in the suburbs, will they take advantage of it? Here there is a host of speculations and a few relevant analyses. Studies of limited coverage in the Boston area (1964) and the Chicago area (1971) found that most of the blacks who first moved into integrated housing in the suburbs were young professional men and women, many of whom were employed in industries and research plants outside the central cities.[72] These studies provided provocative leads, since earlier studies had indicated the impediments to movement outside the ghetto of established middle-class professional and business people.[73] The rise of new job opportunities for highly trained blacks and their frequent achievement of jobs (as a result of active recruitment by industry) before housing, resulted in the fact that a large proportion had lived but a short time in the

[72] Lewis G. Watts, Howard E. Freeman, Helen M. Hughes, Robert Morris, and Thomas F. Pettigrew, *The Middle-Income Negro Family Faces Urban Renewal* (Brandeis University, 1964); and Leadership Council for Metropolitan Open Communities, "Factors Affecting Housing Choices for Black Families in Chicago," mimeographed (Chicago, 1971).

[73] Robert C. Weaver, "The Effect of Anti-Discrimination Legislation upon the FHA- and VA-Insured Housing Market of New York State," *Land Economics*, vol. 31, no. 4 (November 1955), pp. 306, 313.

two cities.[74] No doubt their employer sometimes took a role in finding housing and assuring mortgage financing. And, too, because many of those involved are primarily middle-class Americans, they find the middle-class values and institutions of the suburbs compatible and attractive.

This, of course, is not a new phenomenon. In a few urban areas where Negroes had steady incomes and could secure mortgage financing, a small number moved to the suburbs many years ago. The areas they pioneered were usually within the city limits and could be reached by streetcar. With a growth in the Negro middle class, a larger number moved to these suburbs. The few areas available were eventually inundated by minorities who had few, if any, comparable alternatives.[75]

The growth of the black middle-class, more employment in integrated industries, plants, and offices (often in the suburbs), and the support of the fair housing provisions of the Civil Rights Act of 1968 should result in an accelerated trek to the suburbs. There are long-standing circumstances which still deter many professionals and businessmen from leaving the ghetto, as will the current controversy over the role of the black middle class. Many of the younger, better-trained, and occupationally integrated minority households may find suburbia both accessible and attractive. Other young blacks, especially in the North, are today questioning the advantages of racially integrated neighborhoods. Greater and easier access will encourage wider participation, but, as always, some middle-class blacks — for the present, a larger proportion than in the past — may elect not to move out of black communities; and others will prefer integrated neighborhoods in the central cities to suburban life.

What of the low- and moderate-income urban black? Such fragmentary data as we have suggest that their hesitancy to move to the suburbs is based primarily upon fear of personal violence and isolation. In a small sample in Chicago, almost three-quarters of the 145 moderate-income households interviewed had never seriously considered moving out of the black community. Interestingly, the same proportion had lived in an integrated community and experienced its not remaining stable because the whites moved out.[76] This strongly suggests that they had lived in transitional city neighborhoods from

---

[74]In contrast to the findings for Boston and Chicago, the black families that pioneered into white neighborhoods in Seattle seemed to be established residents; they were more prosperous and better educated than the average nonwhite in the city as well as their white neighbors. See L. K. Northwood and Ernest A. T. Barth, *Urban Desegregation: Negro Pioneers and Their White Neighbors* (University of Washington Press, 1965), pp. 25-29.

[75]Weaver, "Class, Race, and Urban Renewal," footnote 29, p. 243.

[76]"Factors Affecting Housing Choices for Black Families in Chicago."

which whites had fled when there was a sizable influx of blacks. Also there was evidence of an unrealistic fear of high cost and unavailability of mortgage finance.

Clearly, the degree to which nonwhites avail themselves of housing outside the ghetto is responsive to a series of circumstances. In a situation where there has been little or no housing for low- and moderate-income minorities outside the ghetto, any announced change is bound to be greeted with skepticism. One's experience with market limitation establishes conventional wisdom and creates conforming market behavior. Here, as in a few other aspects of housing, supply can generate demand, but as Downs observes, "merely providing the *opportunity* for Negroes to move out of the ghettos would, at least in the short run, not result in many moving."[77]

One way of creating greater housing opportunities for minorities in the suburbs is a matter of administration. If and when there is affirmative action to achieve the Fair Housing Title of the Civil Rights Law of 1968, minority people will be advised of the availability of suburban property, builders and real estate agents will be required to take action to attract them, lenders will be required to make loans to them on the same basis as others, and HUD will be responsible for seeing that this comes to pass. Clearly, such a positive approach will accelerate the dispersal of nonwhites and their greater movement to the suburbs.

A second approach would be aimed at requiring greater economic mixture, especially outside the central cities, and lessening the opposition to lower-income families in the suburbs. It would attack the economic base of this opposition through federal grants to receiving communities. Provisions to this effect should augment the opportunities for lower-income households, including blacks, to find housing in suburbia.

If the nation wants to move toward reducing the impediments to access of minorities to housing in the suburbs, more than revision of housing and community development legislation is required. This follows because many areas outside the central cities are prepared to do without water and sewer and open space grants (the two HUD programs that are attractive to most suburbs) if this is the price that must be paid for their exclusionary housing practices. Nor will they respond affirmatively to the types of financial assistance proposed in HR-9688.

If we are serious about lower-income households' having access to shelter in the suburbs and about fair housing provisions as well as constitutional mandates of equal protection, the federal government must use *all* its tools to achieve the desired goals. Fiscal policy, highway support, HEW grants, sup-

[77]Downs, "Alternative Futures of the American Ghetto," p. 279.

port for mass transit and associated activities, as well as HUD programs, should all be directed toward these specific objectives. Consideration should be given to the findings of agencies such as the Advisory Commission on Intergovernmental Relations and to the reports of the U.S. Commission on Civil Rights. Also, since employment is becoming even more closely related to shelter, the Equal Employment Opportunity Commission should concern itself with equal housing opportunities.

This issue obviously transcends zoning and other devices that directly affect land use. If minorities are to compete with equity in the housing market, irrational actions and conflicts between programs and agency goals must be eradicated.

ECONOMIC AND SOCIAL COSTS
OF RESIDENTIAL SEGREGATION

WILBUR A. STEGER

It is difficult for an economic futurist like me not to dismiss many of the problems of this conference as trivial in the sense that they are "bound to vanish" someday. At the same time, I cannot forget Lord Keynes's admonition that "in the long run, we are all dead." Therefore, while attempting to satisfy that part of each of us that dreams of the delights of the future world, I shall be pessimistic or realistic enough to keep one eye on the present. Recent headlines prevent me from straying too far from the present, anyway:

"Busing: Next Stop, Suburbia"
(*Wall Street Journal*)

"Washington Panel Adopts Plan to Disperse Lowcost Housing in Suburbs"
(*New York Times*)

"Lack of 'Open' Housing Hurts City and Suburbs"
(*Pittsburgh Post-Gazette*)

"High School Rezoning for Bronx and Manhattan Is Proposed to Cut Racial Imbalance" (*New York Times*)

"Subsidized Housing Rise in Suburbs Alarms Cities"
(*New York Times*)

"Big Crime Gains Exodus from City to Suburb"
(*Pittsburgh Press*)

"HUD to Give Poor Funds for Homes"
(*New York Times*)

WILBUR A. STEGER is president of CONSAD Research Corporation, Pittsburgh, and was formerly with the Rand Corporation. He is interested in the economics and social impacts of methods for addressing complex urban and regional issues in the fields of transportation, housing, health, finance, and quality of life, and is the author of more than fifty publications on these subjects. Mr. Steger received his B.S. from Yale University in 1946 and his M.A. and Ph.D. (economics) from Harvard University.

These potential inroads on "undesirable residential segregation" are likely to produce short-run psychological fallout. Counterreaction, backlash, and even local panic may result. The incidence of residential desegregation is bound to be spotty and uneven geographically, socioeconomically, and by type of neighborhood. I do not minimize the strength of the resistance of current residents of suburban neighborhoods to the entry of "lower-class" households. For the purposes of this discussion, I assume that the short-run consequences of attempts to desegregate schools and to open up suburbs to low-income groups and to members of racial minorities will sporadically increase the integration of residential suburbs. Authors of other papers in this book forecast the speed and mode of this short-term phenomenon, citing legal and social pressures. This I leave to them.

My interest is in neither such short-term influences and changes nor examinations and analyses that seek to discover whether or not certain of today's "social problems" are likely to disappear or to become much less significant by the year 2000 or later. Those of us who are attempting to find solutions to urban housing, transportation, employment, health, and related socioeconomic problems find little solace in the thought that by the year 2000 the median income will have more than doubled (in real terms) and that "poverty" as we know it in absolute terms today will have become a mere shadow of itself.[1] The following statement about the year 2000 will surely be largely true for some cities and regions of the United States:

- Gains in real income, broadened antidiscrimination laws, significant aging and some deterioration of housing in the suburbs as we know them today, considerable nationalization in welfare programs, the emergence of a black middle class, and subsidized housing for the poor, taken together, will afford the poor a much wider choice of residential locations. In certain metropolitan areas, racial discrimination in housing will virtually disappear. In almost all areas, the poor white family will be afforded a wider choice of residential locations.

Reflections about *long-run* possibilities (those of 2000 and later) provide too little useful information about the next five, ten, or fifteen years to be of

---

[1] Of course, there are those who believe that, so long as the lowest two deciles of income recipients continue to receive less than 8 percent of total personal income, poverty will not have been eradicated. And, since there are no structural changes contemplated in long-run income distribution, there will continue to be relative poverty, which is poverty in its most meaningful sense. In *Suburban Land Conversion in the United States* (Johns Hopkins University Press for Resources for the Future, 1971, p. 7), Marion Clawson notes that rising *absolute* income of the poor will not solve their housing problems, and that *new* housing (suburban or center city) is unlikely to be the total solution to racial residential disparities.

much help in policy guidance today. Moreover, such reflections may lull some of us into a false complacency because the beneficent long-range trends will come about only *if* the right actions are taken now and during the next several years. Such actions must recognize the basic sociopsychological problems and the economic implications of our current and prospective actions. These are the underlying structural realities with which any set of programs and policies will have to cope, and they are the basis of this paper.

In the next section of this paper I present some basic data on income and earnings according to the race and location of the recipients. In the following three sections I present more detailed information and conclusions about the social costs of residential segregation: those due to increased housing costs, those due to poor income opportunities and resultant insufficient earnings, and those due to substandard social and environmental conditions. In the concluding section I summarize the analysis and suggest directions for the kinds of further research needed to guide policy.

INCOME AND EARNINGS, BY RACE AND LOCATION

The observation that "the principal reason for slum housing is the low income of its inhabitants" is one with which I agree.[2] To the extent that the private market reacts to rising personal aggregate income by upgrading housing quality, efforts to raise the incomes of lower-income groups (through housing allowance programs, for example), may offer the best single prospect for solving the problems of low-quality and slum housing. The following data indicate the tremendous scale of the problem.

The segment of the U.S. population characterized as "low income" was 22.4 percent in 1959 but only 12.6 percent in 1970, or a decrease of 35 percent in absolute numbers of low-income people over this period, during which total population rose by 26 million.[3] Blacks were 27 percent of the

[2] Richard F. Muth, "Urban Residential Land and Housing Markets," in Harvey S. Perloff and Lowdon Wingo (eds.), *Issues in Urban Economics* (Johns Hopkins University Press for Resources for the Future, 1968), p. 312. I do not agree completely with Muth's emphasis on the role of market forces in explaining urban residential and housing phenomena, including decentralization and segregation. See Richard F. Muth, *Cities and Housing* (University of Chicago Press, 1969).

[3] The data in this paragraph come from U.S. Bureau of the Census, "Characteristics of the Low-Income Population, 1970," *Current Population Reports*, Series P-60, No. 81, November 1971. The "low-income" (poverty) statistics in this report are based on a definition adopted by a federal Interagency Committee in 1969. The low-income threshold for a nonfarm family of four was $3,968 in 1970, $3,743 in 1969, and $2,973 in 1959.

low-income total in 1959 and 30 percent in 1970;[4] 55 percent of all blacks
had low incomes in 1959 and 34 percent in 1970; 18 percent of all whites
had low incomes in 1959 and 10 percent in 1970. The total number of poor
people declined rather steadily from 1960 to 1969, but in 1970 it rose by 1.2
million — the number of whites increasing by 4.9 percent and the number of
blacks by 6.0 percent. Metropolitan areas accounted for 90 percent of the
one-year increase,[5] the poverty numbers in the central cities growing by 4.0
percent to 8.2 million persons, and the poverty numbers in the suburbs
growing by a surprising 12.5 percent to 5.2 million persons.

Other general data of relevance for the 1960–70 decade include:

- A moderate growth in central cities as a whole of less than 1 million
persons;

- The black population (which in total increased 4.4 million persons in the
decade) increased 3.2 million in central cities as a whole, but decreased by
nearly a quarter of a million in the nonmetropolitan areas; central city
white population declined by 2.6 million persons over the decade;[6]

- Growth of black population in both center city and suburbs was due more
to natural increase than to net inmigration;

- While the proportion of black families living in poverty areas in large
central cities has declined in the last decade, white families are leaving
these areas at a considerably faster rate — perhaps three to four times
faster.[7]

Changes in the racial composition of the low-income population in metropolitan areas both inside and outside central cities and in nonmetropolitan
areas are indicative of significant underlying structural patterns.

The significance of these structural patterns is not that poverty is vanish-
ing, but that it is declining in the United States. The increase in 1970 is
probably only a temporary one reflecting the state of the economy at that
time. Inflation, unemployment, and underemployment all affect the size of
the poverty segment of the population and its difficulty in "making do."

My own beliefs about the future low-income situation are as follows. First,
as we approach the twenty-first century the poverty class will probably in-

---

[4] The proportion of blacks was approximately constant between 1968 and 1970.

[5] Only 32 percent of the nation's poor now live in central cities, and 52 percent in
metropolitan areas including central cities.

[6] The data in this paragraph come from U.S. Bureau of the Census, "Social and
Economic Characteristics of the Population in Metropolitan and Nonmetropolitan Areas:
1970 and 1960," *Current Population Reports*, Series P-23, No. 37, June 1971.

[7] Data in the foregoing two paragraphs come from *HUD Newsletter*, Office of Public
Affairs, U.S. Department of Housing and Urban Development, vol. 3, numbers 1, 2, and
9.

clude at least 3.25-3.5 million families. My forecast is slightly higher than Martin Gainsborough's estimate (for the White House Conference on the Industrial World Ahead, February 7-9, 1972, Washington, D.C.) that by 1990 the number of poor would be about 55 percent of the number today, which would mean a poverty class of 2.5-3 million families. Since Gainsborough's estimate is based on optimistic assumptions about declining unemployment and rising employment and increasing labor force participation, I regard the estimate itself as somewhat optimistic. Perhaps 4 percent of the nation's families and 5-6 percent of the population will be unable to move out of the poverty class, unless significantly different assistance is made available to low-income families with a female head and children under 18 years of age and to the increasing numbers who because of age or physical or mental disabilities cannot obtain sufficient income in the labor market. Second, part of the poverty problem is relative, not absolute; so long as less than 5 percent of the total personal income of all blacks accrues to the lowest fifth and approximately 45 percent to the top fifth, *substantial residential segregation will continue. No significant structural change appears to be forthcoming.* [8]

INCREASED HOUSING COSTS DUE TO RESIDENTIAL SEGREGATION

Within the Standard Metropolitan Statistical Areas (SMSAs), the center cities have both the largest number and the largest share of crowded dwelling units of poorer quality (measured by rental value for bundles of similar housing and environmental attributes). These units are occupied by households with larger than average numbers of members, with less than average wealth and permanent income, with a high proportion of female heads, and with a higher proportion of unrelated individuals and adult members. It is not surprising that numerous studies of both low-income and black populations have discovered that the same bundle of housing attributes commands a significantly higher effective or real price in segregated areas. [9] According to

[8] There is a little more inequality, measured this way, in black than in white income distribution. During 1970 there was an increase in the ratio of top fifth to bottom fifth income for both white and black. (U.S. Bureau of the Census, "Income in 1970 of Families and Persons in the United States," *Current Population Reports*, Series P-60, No. 80, October 4, 1971, tables 14 and 15.)

[9] B. Duncan and P. Hauser, *Housing a Metropolis – Chicago* (The Free Press, 1960); John F. Kain, "The Commuting and Residential Decisions of Central Business District Workers," in *Transportation Economics*, A Conference of the Universities and the National Bureau Committee for Economic Research (National Bureau of Economic Research, distributed by Columbia University Press, 1965), pp. 245-74; John F. Kain and

Muth's estimates in *Cities and Housing*, which are at the lower end of the spectrum, blacks may pay 2 to 5 percent more than whites (p. 239), but he attributes the difference to increased operating and maintenance costs for comparable dwelling units (p. 303).[10] Ridker's and Henning's study in St. Louis indicates a 5-8 percent difference (favoring whites) for identical single-family homes. Kain and Quigley found that "the average ghetto unit would rent for about two percent less in all-white city neighborhoods" (i.e., blacks were paying 2 percent more for such housing), while "the average nonghetto unit would rent for ten percent more in the ghetto."[11]

The difference in cost of housing for blacks, as compared with that for whites, is only part of the story. In addition, blacks find it more difficult to buy a home; and since home ownership includes substantial economic advantages in terms of tax relief, hedge against inflation, and the like, this works to the disadvantage of blacks. Kain and Quigley estimate that the likelihood of buying a home is at least 9 percent less for a black than for a white and may be as much as 12 percent less; in each case, all factors other than race are assumed to be equal.[12] This lesser propensity for home purchases is attributed by these authors to two factors: first, the greater difficulty, again all else being equal, for blacks to move past the institutional and psychological constraints; and, second, the influence of past discrimination, which makes blacks less likely to become homeowners than whites. They estimate that, by limiting homeownership, discrimination raises monthly housing costs for blacks by at least 18 percent in a nonappreciating market and by as much as 50 percent in a rising housing market, in addition to excluding them from the tax advantages of homeownership.

J. M. Quigley, "Measuring the Quality and Cost of Housing Services," Harvard University Program on Regional and Urban Economics Discussion Paper No. 54, July 1969; Davis McEntire, *Residence and Race* (University of California Press, 1960); Richard F. Muth, *Cities and Housing* (University of Chicago Press, 1969); Chester Rapkin, "Price Discrimination Against Negroes in the Rental Housing Market," in *Essays in Urban Land Economics* (University of California Press, 1960); R. G. Ridker and J. A. Henning, "The Determinants of Residential Property Values with Special Reference to Air Pollution," *Review of Economics and Statistics*, May 1967, pp. 246-57; Chester Rapkin and W. Grigsby, *The Demand for Housing in Racially Mixed Areas* (University of California Press, 1960).

[10] Muth and others, particularly Lapham, are not convinced that blacks pay higher housing prices, ceteris paribus, due to involuntary segregation. See Victoria Lapham, "Do Blacks Pay More for Housing?," *Journal of Political Economy*, November–December 1971. While the final evidence is not yet in, I remain more convinced by the opposing views and analysis, which cite sufficiently valid statistical evidence of this real and significant difference.

[11] John F. Kain and John M. Quigley, "Measuring the Value of Housing Quality," *Journal of American Statistical Association*, June 1970, p. 540.

[12] John F. Kain and John M. Quigley, "Housing Market Discrimination, Homeownership, and Savings Behavior," *American Economic Review*, June 1972.

Present and previous homeownership are highly correlated variables. A family that has been able to buy a home in the past is in a much stronger position to buy a new home than is a family that has never accumulated the down payment for a home. The intercorrelation of these variables makes it difficult to be sure of the effect of various socioeconomic variables upon present homeownership. A number of explanations have been offered for lower black homeownership — differences in tastes, self-imposed black segregation, and lowered permanency of income for blacks.[13] Kain and Quigley largely dispose of these arguments. Given the widely quoted and stable findings of the Tauebers, Pascal, Shelling, Duncan and Hauser, Kain, McEntire, and others, the existence of a dual housing market seems proven beyond a reasonable doubt.[14] I conclude that the Kain-Quigley findings are largely a product of the residential owner's *anti-black discrimination.*

Blacks tend to move more often than whites, presumably in search of a more satisfactory place in which to live. While residential moving for both races is related to changes in such factors as family size, family income, social status, and others, the higher incidence of moving by blacks is attributable largely to racial discrimination and not to socioeconomic differences.[15] The various segregation indices — all of which measure the difference between completely proportional dispersal of each race by small areas and the actual distribution — are well explained by Schelling, who argues that the strength of *attitudes* about segregation is not necessarily equal to the *perceived* levels:

[There] is no evidence that [people] prefer segregation, only that, if segregation exists and they have to choose between exclusive associations, people elect like rather than unlike environments.

Arithmetic plays a role. If blacks are a tenth of the population we cannot have the whole country integrated except in nine-to-one ratio; if that ratio makes blacks uncomfortable and they withdraw in the interest of less extreme "integration," the mechanism of withdrawal may or may not be compatible with mixed living. If it is, arithmetic determines what fraction of the whites must stay away so that the black-white ratio in the mixed environment can remain within comfortable limits. If blacks are willing to be the minority but not smaller than one quarter, and whites willing to mix equally but not in minority status, the limits are 3:1 and 1:1, and in a

[13] Margaret G. Reid, *Housing and Income* (University of Chicago Press, 1962).

[14] Karl F. and A. F. Taueber, *Negroes in Cities* (Aldine Publishing Co., 1965); A. Pascal, "The Economics of Housing Segregation," Rand Corporation, P-3095, March 1965; T. C. Shelling, "On the Ecology of Micromotives," *The Public Interest*, Fall 1971. Also see references in note 9.

[15] Jeanne C. Biggar, "Racial Differentials in the Determinants of Prospective Mobility," American Statistical Association, *Proceedings* of the Social Statistics Division, 1971.

population 90 per cent white, two thirds of the whites have to stay apart or they swamp the whole arrangement.

The dynamics are not always transparent to cursory analysis. There are chain reactions, exaggerated perceptions, lagged responses, speculation on the future, and organized efforts that may succeed or fail.[16]

Nevertheless, given the basic "arithmetic" of the situation and the fact that behavioral changes lag behind attitudinal change by several years if not decades, it is likely that low-income blacks will find it difficult to move out of the inner-city ghettos *even if* their incomes rise substantially. Furthermore, the irreducible U.S. poor — perhaps 3.25–3.5 million families, or more than 4 million households, or 16 million people — are likely to be found increasingly in center cities. The percentage of low-income individuals living in center cities will probably rise over the next decade from 30 percent to perhaps 35 or 40 percent of the total low-income group and the percentage of the total inner-city poor who are black will rise from the current 40 percent to 45 or 50 percent or more over the next decade.

Housing (or residential) discrimination causes much more than price discrimination. For poor, low-income blacks, however, I estimate that 15 percent of their total housing expenditures represent an overpayment due to the dual (or segregated) residential market.[17] Since poor people spend 30 to 40 percent of their total income on housing services, this discrimination of 15 percent in real terms amounts to a 5 to 6 percent *real income* loss to low-income black people. At an average income of $2,530 (1970) for low-income black families, this means a yearly loss of $125 to $150 per family. For the approximately 600,000 low-income black families living in inner cities today, the aggregate real income loss is between $75 million and $90 million. This assumes that all or most of these families are either living in, or directly affected by, the dual market. For the approximately 190,000 low-income black families currently living in metropolitan areas but outside central cities, the annual real income loss (calculated as above) ranges from $23.8 million to $29.0 million.[18] The annual social toll for segregated housing almost surely exceeds $100 million, in addition to other costs described in later sections.

[16]"On the Ecology of Micromotives," p. 82. This finding confirms the generally accepted conclusion that the American public is significantly changing and loosening its attitudes toward racial integration, uninterrupted by the racial strife of the 1960s. See A. M. Greeley and P. B. Sheatsley, "Attitudes toward Racial Integration," *Scientific American*, December 1971; M. W. Karmen, " 'Elitism': How Much is Enough?," *Wall Street Journal*, February 2, 1972.

[17]I use 7.5 percent as the midpoint of the 5 to 10 percent markup shown in several of the studies cited, and another 7.5 percent because of the homeownership discrimination.

[18]There is, perhaps, a compensating factor in central cities, in that housing for remaining blacks is in larger supply due to the rapid exodus of whites and the reduced

INSUFFICIENT EARNINGS AND INCOME OPPORTUNITIES

Continuing on the assumption that low-income blacks find it considerably more difficult to move from center city residences to suburban residences where job opportunities are expanding at a rate at least five or six times that of the center city, it is not surprising to find that:

- The people in the United States "most dissatisfied with their jobs" are black workers under 30 years of age (Survey Research Center, Survey for the U.S. Department of Labor, 1972).

- When white worker unemployment is 5.4 percent (as in December 1971), the black percentage is almost double this (10.3 percent); for teen-agers, the mean rate of 17.5 percent unemployment indicates a 25 percent rate for blacks, minimally.

These distinctions are even sharper when labor force participation rates and unemployment data for low-income individuals inside and outside center cities are compared for blacks and whites in 1960 and 1970. Table 1 reveals the following points:

(1) Labor force participation fell slightly from 1960 to 1970 for all categories of male workers, due largely to the impact of the 1969 recession. But the drastic decline of nearly thirty percent for central city low-income black males and the less severe decline of under twenty percent for low-income black males outside the central cities point to increased demoralization of these groups.
(2) While the unemployment rate for all males declined slightly during the 1960s, the rate for both black center city and black outside center city changed dramatically for the worse, the latter changing more relatively (but remaining absolutely smaller than the former).
(3) While labor force participation is always lower for low-income males than for all males (even more so in 1970 than in 1960), low-income black males had higher labor force participation than low-income white males.
(4) Labor force participation of low-income black females declined only 3 percentage points in the 1960s compared with the decline of more than 11

---

rate of inmigration of both whites and blacks. This has the effect of moving the demand function for housing downward or to the left. It is difficult to estimate whether the Kain-Quigley (or other) findings will still be applicable in 1975, for instance. See Peter Marcuse, "Social Indicators and Housing Policy," *Urban Affairs Quarterly*, December 1971, p. 200. I have not compensated for this effect, anticipating both supply and demand functions will be affected, in somewhat compensating and offsetting degrees. While there are lower segregation indices in "outside central city" metropolitan areas, the anti-homeownership discrimination is considerably more significant and amounts to more of a real loss in these areas.

percent

Table 1. Labor Force Participation and Unemployment Rates for Males and Females 16 Years of Age and Over, by General Metropolitan Location and Race, 1970 and 1960

General location	1970				1960			
	Total population		Low-income people		Total population		Low-income people	
	Labor force participation	Unemployment	Labor force participation	Unemployment	Labor force participation	Unemployment	Labor force participation	Unemployment
Males								
All races	76.2	4.1	48.7	9.5	78.6	5.1	55.1	11.0
Inside central city	75.6	4.6	42.8	11.2	79.7	5.9	51.2	17.1
Outside central city	79.1	3.6	49.4	10.2	81.7	4.1	50.8	10.2
Nonmetropolitan	73.8	4.2	51.6	6.9	75.1	5.2	58.2	8.2
Whites	76.8	3.8	48.1	8.1	79.1	4.7	53.1	10.5
Inside central city	75.7	4.1	43.1	8.2	79.8	5.1	46.9	9.0
Outside central city	79.7	3.5	48.5	12.1	82.0	4.0	48.1	12.2
Nonmetropolitan	74.7	4.0	50.3	16.1	76.0	4.9	57.1	15.0
Blacks	72.0	6.8	51.1	13.6	74.5	9.6	62.5	12.4
Inside central city	76.0	7.5	43.7	22.6	79.2	10.6	61.2	18.9
Outside central city	71.8	6.1	53.8	16.7	73.9	7.8	63.7	7.4
Nonmetropolitan	64.8	5.6	55.6	7.9	67.3	8.5	63.1	9.5

Females

All races	42.6	5.3	24.3	11.2	35.5	5.7	23.3	10.8
Inside central city	44.9	5.0	24.4	9.0	40.6	5.7	27.8	12.2
Outside central city	42.1	5.2	27.8	10.3	34.4	5.2	23.0	8.5
Nonmetropolitan	41.1	5.6	22.7	9.5	31.6	5.2	20.9	9.1
Whites	41.9	4.9	21.9	8.6	34.7	5.2	20.0	10.3
Inside central city	43.3	4.3	20.9	6.4	39.4	4.6	24.0	10.9
Outside central city	41.6	5.0	26.1	9.2	33.9	5.1	20.3	8.5
Nonmetropolitan	41.1	5.2	20.6	8.3	31.1	5.9	18.0	8.9
Blacks	49.1	8.5	31.6	16.9	43.0	9.6	34.6	11.9
Inside central city	51.8	7.8	31.2	17.6	46.6	10.8	36.5	14.6
Outside central city	52.2	9.9	38.9	20.2	45.0	6.3	39.5	10.0
Nonmetropolitan	42.1	9.1	30.7	15.4	36.6	8.8	31.8	9.9

Source: U.S. Bureau of the Census, "Social and Economic Characteristics of the Population in Metropolitan and Nonmetropolitan Areas: 1970 and 1960," *Current Population Reports*, Series P-23, No. 37, June 24, 1971, tables 13 and 22.

93

percentage points for low-income black males; however, labor force participation of low-income white females actually rose slightly during the decade.

(5) Low-income black females also had significant increases in unemployment over the decade, in contrast to low-income white females. Unlike the case of low-income black males, however, inside central city unemployment rates grew less rapidly over the decade than rates outside the center city.

(6) For females of both races, as for males, labor force participation is lower for low-income workers than for all workers. For both sexes, the difference was greater in 1970 than in 1960. Labor force participation of black females considerably exceeds that of white females, both for "all" and for "low-income" females.

Trends in earnings are another often-cited symptom of discrimination attributed to residential segregation and its concomitant attributes (Table 2). The trends of primary interest for our purpose are:

(1) The disparity in earnings of black males relative to white males changed relatively little from 1959 to 1969; inside the central city it declined slightly, partially offsetting increases elsewhere. In sharp contrast, the disparity in median incomes of black females relative to white females decreased sharply for each location and in total, by amounts ranging from over $300 to over $700.

(2) The tendency for earnings of males of both races located outside the central city to accelerate faster than those for inside central city.

(3) The increasing disparity of black worker earnings (both sexes) between nonmetropolitan and inside central city locations continues to provide an income incentive for black migration to central cities, even though other factors may be mitigating this incentive.

(4) Median incomes of both whites and blacks, of both sexes and in all locations, have long been lower in the South than in other regions, and the gap between the races has been widest there. The gap between median incomes of blacks and of whites in central cities of the South has been decreasing, both absolutely and relatively. The South is advancing economically quite rapidly, but it is not clear how much this may close the gap between the races.[19]

Data on median earnings of low-income individuals and families, particularly central city blacks, show how poor their income opportunities are, but

[19] Andrew Brimmer, "Regional Growth, Migration, and Economic Progress in the Black Community," paper presented at Bishop College, Dallas, Texas, September 1971.

Table 2. Median Earnings and Comparisons, Workers 14 Years of Age and Older, Non-agricultural Occupations (for Those Working 50–52 Weeks), 1969 and 1959

1969 dollars

	1969			1959		
	All	Black	White	All	Black	White
	Median earnings per worker					
Males						
All locations	$8,376	$5,881	$8,641	$6,718	$4,143	$6,870
Inside central city	7,963	6,425	8,466	6,637	4,731	6,881
Outside central city	9,604	6,448	9,729	7,485	4,375	7,568
Nonmetropolitan	7,415	3,991	7,593	6,005	2,911	6,140
Females						
All locations	4,517	3,468	4,662	3,843	2,066	3,986
Inside central city	4,801	3,854	5,051	4,050	2,618	4,279
Outside central city	4,904	3,777	4,959	4,199	2,350	4,276
Nonmetropolitan	4,033	2,129	4,141	3,211	1,010	3,374

	Difference between white and black median earnings per worker			
	1969		1959	
	Males	Females	Males	Females
All locations	2,760	1,194	2,727	1,920
Inside central city	2,041	1,197	2,150	1,661
Outside central city	3,281	1,182	3,193	1,926
Nonmetropolitan	3,602	2,012	3,329	2,364

	Difference between 1969 and 1959 median earnings per worker			
	Males		Females	
	Blacks	Whites	Blacks	Whites
All locations	1,738	1,771	1,402	676
Inside central city	1,694	1,585	1,236	772
Outside central city	2,073	2,161	1,427	683
Nonmetropolitan	1,080	1,453	1,119	767

	Difference between median earnings of "inside central city" and "nonmetropolitan" workers	
	1969	1959
Black males	2,434	1,820
Black females	1,725	1,608

Source: U.S. Bureau of the Census, "Social and Economic Characteristics of the Population in Metropolitan and Nonmetropolitan Areas: 1970 and 1960," *Current Population Reports*, Series P-23, No. 37, June 24, 1971, table 17.

the following are better indicators of why: A significantly lower percentage of families with male heads; a high percentage with no earnings at all (as opposed to income from other sources); a large percentage of total jobs in unskilled categories; a low number of weeks worked; longer-than-average durations of unemployment; and a lower percentage of labor union membership and of self-employed.

Economists and other social scientists have placed partial or full responsibility for the low labor force participation, high unemployment, and low earnings of blacks (particularly low-income blacks, both male and female) upon segregation and discrimination of various types. Residential segregation, poorer educational systems in ghettos, more limited access to suburban job opportunities, and inferior ghetto social environmental and health conditions are offered as causal factors.

A crude estimate of the social costs of this environment and the associated lower-income opportunities for low-income blacks can be approximated by any of several methods. One method uses the concept of income deficit or poverty gap, defined as the "difference between the total income of the families (and unrelated individuals) below the poverty level, and their respective poverty thresholds." The mean income deficit, the number of families experiencing these deficits, and the total deficit is shown for 1959 and 1969 (in constant 1969 dollars) in Table 3, by race and sex of head of family, and by residence inside and outside central cities.

Quite obviously, it is not good economic analysis to attribute the full income deficiency of low-income blacks, whether inside or outside central cities, to residential segregation; I attempt to develop some attribution indicators below. But the almost $800 million annual deficit for central city black males and females at least represents an upper limit of the sum needed to reach a poverty level income ($3,743 for a family of four in 1969) for center city blacks. Moreover, this sum declined 32 percent (in real terms) over the decade for the central city blacks as compared with the 42 percent decline for white low-income residents of the center city.

Using conservative estimates for the "n.a." entries in Table 3, another $180 million of income deficit for low-income blacks outside central cities is the maximum sum required for restoration to a poverty level, or a total approximating $1 billion annually for blacks in all locations. (Similar 1970 statistics would have exceeded $1 billion.) These gaps compare with an income deficit of less than $2 billion for all low-income white families, both inside and outside central cities. The deficit for blacks was over one-third of the total although they are less than one-third of the low-income population.

Time and space constraints do not justify a complete examination of the relationship between residential segregation and family income opportunities

Table 3. Mean and Total Income Deficits (in Constant 1969 Dollars) for Low-Income Families, by Race and Sex of Head, Inside and Outside the Central City, 1969 and 1959

	1969			1959		
	All	Black	White	All	Black	White
	Families with a male head					
Inside central city:						
Mean income deficit ($)	1,139	1,285	1,087	1,346	1,495	1,281
Number of families (1,000)	746	192	535	1,428	451	962
Total deficit ($ million)	849.7	246.7	581.5	1,922.1	674.2	1,232.3
Outside central city:						
Mean income deficit ($)	1,129	n.a.	1,146	1,483	1,867	1,408
Number of families (1,000)	558	66	481	1,053	159	882
Total deficit ($ million)	630.0	–	551.2	1,561.6	296.8	1,241.8
	Families with a female head					
Inside central city:						
Mean income deficit ($)	1,301	1,399	1,178	1,590	1,746	1,450
Number of families (1,000)	738	390	337	585	278	303
Total deficit ($ million)	960.1	545.6	397.0	930.1	485.4	439.3
Outside central city:						
Mean income deficit ($)	1,507	n.a.	1,460	1,617	n.a.	1,556
Number of families (1,000)	373	72	297	276	52	222
Total deficit ($ million)	562.1	–	433.6	446.3	–	345.4

Source: U.S. Bureau of the Census, "Social and Economic Characteristics of the Population in Metropolitan and Nonmetropolitan Areas: 1970 and 1960," *Current Population Reports*, Series P-23, No. 37, June 24, 1971, table 27.

Note: The income statistics refer to receipts during the calendar years 1969 and 1959; the characteristics of the person and the composition of families refer to the time of the enumeration (March 1970 and April 1960).

n.a. = not available.

and realization. There is quite obviously an interdependence between lower black earnings and income and the extent of black-white residential segregation. One is not completely the cause of the other. Furthermore, and even more important, a number of other variables — particularly those involving the provision and use of other social services — are related to both lower income and residential segregation. Difficulties of estimating the separate effects of correlated variables have prevented all but a scattering of findings. Some sound and reliable quantitative studies, however, indicate the ways in which real income, particularly earnings, is affected by racial residential segregation.

A 1965 study reported that as many as 40,000 nonwhite workers in Detroit and 112,000 in Chicago might have moved from central ghettos to outlying residential areas if racial barriers to nonwhite housing choices were removed.[20] In 1960 these workers represented approximately one-third of Detroit's nonwhite work force and over 40 percent of Chicago's (or over 4 percent of Detroit's work force and 7 percent of Chicago's). The primary effects of such moves, particularly for black males (employment discrimination aside), would involve higher earnings outside central cities.

Other estimates, also for Detroit and Chicago, of black job loss "caused by housing segregation," are based primarily on worsening access of blacks to areas where employment is growing.[21] Estimates based on both access and racial-mix variables indicate in a statistically sound fashion that an additional 9 percent of Chicago's working blacks would have found viable employment opportunities, and similarly a maximum of 7 percent of Detroit's working blacks (1960), if black workers were proportionately allocated to all residential areas. Increasing "access gaps" between residential and changing (primarily suburban) job locations have occurred over the decade, probably increasing the impacts attributable to residential segregation and job access.

Access discrimination, based on increasing distances to jobs (and relatively poorer transportation), causes an additional social cost. All else being equal, blacks travel longer distances to their places of work and incur increased costs of transportation.[22] Studies, based on existing residential segregation patterns and on white and nonwhite work-travel patterns, indicate an effective wage reduction for center city blacks of 5 percent and for outside center city blacks of 1 percent.

Another important indicator of the loss in income opportunity due to residential segregation is the number of people of working age who are not in the labor force (neither working nor looking for work in the week preceding interviewing) but who want to work. A 1968–69 survey in the poverty areas

[20] John Meyer, John Kain, and Martin Wohl, *The Urban Transportation Problem* (Harvard University Press, 1965), pp. 163–66.

[21] John F. Kain, "Housing Segregation, Negro Employment and Metropolitan Decentralization," *Quarterly Journal of Economics*, May 1968, pp. 189–90. Detroit's lesser impacts can be attributed to a lower residential segregation index, a smaller black labor force, and a lower percentage of the total labor force being black. Joseph D. Mooney ("Housing Segregation, Negro Employment, and Metropolitan Decentralization," *Quarterly Journal of Economics*, May 1969, pp. 299–311) partially disputes Kain's findings, attributing low employment of central city blacks more to aggregate demand factors; however, Mooney agrees that central city male blacks face increasing difficulties with respect to job opportunities. Furthermore, if macro (aggregative) factors affect central city employment (because of its industry structure) more than they affect suburban employment, central city residential segregation continues to impose a harsher, employment-oriented discrimination against center city blacks, both males and females.

[22] David Greytak, "Residential Segregation, Metropolitan Decentralization, and the Journey to Work," Syracuse University, Urban Transportation Institute, 1970.

of six major cities discovered that, while these areas had approximately the same labor force participation rate as the nation as a whole, the proportion of poverty area nonparticipants wanting a job was significantly larger than the comparable proportion nationally.[23] Twenty-eight percent of nonparticipants in these sampled areas wanted "a regular job now, either full or part time," contrasted to less than ten percent of the nonparticipants nationally. While it is not proper to ascribe these differences entirely to the ghetto area location, many of the reasons given for nonparticipation can be related directly to poverty, poor health conditions, lack of access, and lack of employment references.[24] A slightly higher rate of "discouraged workers" (not in the labor force because of lack of success) exists in these areas also.

Migration into and out of ghetto areas plays a substantial role in the reduction in income opportunity due to residential segregation. To benefit substantially from an expanding economy, the black inner city would have to undergo a radical change in employment mix. Black inmigrants would have to be those capable of seeking and acquiring higher-skilled city jobs while black outmigrants would have to be those in lower skilled jobs. The converse, in reality, has been true.[25] While the rate of black migration to center cities has decreased, there has been an increased outflow of better trained blacks — due partly to public policy programs such as inner city manpower development programs. If suburban segregation becomes less severe, the ironical impact may very well be that inner-city residential segregation may become even worse, given the greater outflow of better-trained, higher-paid individuals.

A larger number of studies have analyzed the reasons for lower earnings of blacks, ceteris paribus, relative to whites. Basic differences in earnings have been attributed to: the different industrial mix of employment for blacks relative to whites; the skill levels to which black educational levels lead in the world of work; regional differences in earnings (e.g., lower earnings in the South, with the concentration of black workers greater in these regions); more irregular employment as reflected in lesser number of quarters worked per year;[26] racial discrimination in employment due to attitudes and practices of fellow employees, consumers and employers;[27] alleged differences in "in-

---

[23]Harvey J. Hilaski, "Unutilized Manpower in Poverty Areas of Six U.S. Cities," *Monthly Labor Review*, December 1967, p. 45.

[24]Ibid., pp. 47–48.

[25]David E. Kaun and William Lentz, "Occupational Migration, Discrimination, and the Central City Labor Force," *Monthly Labor Review*, December 1971, pp. 57–61.

[26]Arnold Strasser, "Differentials and Overlaps in Earnings of Blacks and Whites," *Monthly Labor Review*, December 1971, pp. 16–26.

[27]Gary Becker, *The Economics of Discrimination* (University of Chicago Press, 1957).

nate ability," preference for leisure, the quality and quantity of education received;[28] and the lesser quantities of "capital stock per worker" in black worker dominated industries.[29]

The "lower innate ability" argument may be dismissed on the grounds that ability is randomly and equally distributed among all races. All other factors adduced for lower black earnings are relatable to residential segregation, particularly those where blighted, ghetto conditions prevail:

(1) "Increased desire for leisure" (higher quit rates and lower intensity of job search) is partly, if not totally, ascribable to real or imagined employer discrimination and to lack of knowledge about increasingly diffused job opportunities.

(2) "Lower capital/worker" ratios in inner city areas, or in jobs for those living in inner cities, is due to an increase in service and white-collar jobs, the extremely high cost of inner city "land value/worker," and obsolescent but still present (and tax-reducing) capital present in center city industrial establishments.

(3) The average AFQT (Armed Forces Qualification Test) results and other measures of educational achievement are significantly higher for schools outside the inner city areas; furthermore, AFQT, ceteris paribus, is related monotonically and relatively linearly to earnings.[30]

(4) If discrimination among employees is a function of a lack of day-to-day familiarity of adults with persons of other races, residential segregation is a contributing factor. Similarly, employer discrimination due to hesitation to utilize black employees in contact situations with white customers would be substantially reduced if adult interaction, spurred by residential desegregation, would be considerably accelerated.

(5) Both black and white consumers of a variety of commercial services tend to favor white providers, for price as well as social reasons. Furthermore, while residential segregation may promote larger markets for black firms in some cases, the higher costs of performing certain services in inner cities tend to reduce this possible advantage.

(6) Self-employment, which is one way of reducing the impact of racially motivated discrimination by employers, is unlikely to increase substan-

[28] David W. Rasmussen, "Discrimination and the Income of Non-White Males," *American Journal of Economics and Sociology*, October 1971, pp. 377–82.

[29] Becker, *Economics of Discrimination*, p. 20.

[30] W. C. Hansen, B. Weisbrod, and W. Scanlon, "Schooling and Earnings of Low Achievers," *American Economic Review*, June 1970, pp. 409–18; B. D. Karpinos, "The Mental Test Qualification of American Youths for Military Service and Its Relationship to Educational Achievement," *Proceedings of the American Statistical Association, Social Science Section*, 1966, pp. 92–111.

tially in inner city areas, since professional blacks are leaving these areas and the costs of starting up small businesses are high. Residential segregation is again an important factor in reducing income opportunities.

These are only some of the impacts on earnings ascribable directly or indirectly to residential segregation. Some authors hold that these factors, *taken separately*, account for 10–50 percent of the difference between white and black earnings.[31] Their combined effect may be different; no one has attempted to weld all these factors and ask: What differences would exist *today* if there were no residential segregation? *Or* how soon would *all* earnings' differences disappear?

The evidence is difficult to combine in a single quantitative index. Quite obviously, substantial residential desegregation would tend to increase income opportunities in the following ways:

· Black head-of-household families would move closer to areas with more job opportunities, particularly for black males.

· Employee and employer discrimination, arising from infrequent adult interpersonal communication, would considerably diminish.

· Blacks would discover better job opportunities, and have work for a greater number of weeks.

· Blacks would spend less time traveling to and from work.

· Black representation would increase in most occupations, but certain occupations (e.g., secretarial in northern cities) would continue to have more white representation.

· Labor force participation rates of nonparticipating blacks would rise.

· Migration of higher-skilled blacks from the ghetto would increase.

· Black mean earnings would increase.

It would be unrealistic to estimate that all black poverty would be eradicated by these changes; aging, infirmity, temporary unemployment, and family disintegration would still create problems for blacks as well as whites. But the *rate of decrease* in black poverty would be stepped up considerably — certainly to at least the same rate as whites, and, in fact, probably more rapidly. More rapid decrease, I believe, would stem from the larger base, and the fact that much of the present "poverty" base today derives from the

---

[31] For example, labor force participation of nonparticipating low-income blacks would more than double (Hilaski, "Unutilized Manpower in Poverty Areas," pp. 45–46); black mean earnings would rise by 17 percent in northern cities and 45 percent in southern (Rasmussen, "Discrimination and the Income of Non-White Males," p. 376).

Table 4. Percentage Distribution of Earnings of All Workers, 1969 and 1959, by Race, Sex, and Urban Location

Annual earnings in 1969 dollars	Inner city							
	1969				1959			
	Females		Males		Females		Males	
	Black	White	Black	White	Black	White	Black	White
Under $1,000	25.9	21.5	14.0	9.6	33.7	23.2	11.5	8.1
$ 1,000–$ 1,999	15.2	13.0	5.9	6.0	24.5	14.1	10.0	6.4
$ 2,000–$ 2,999	14.8	10.7	6.4	4.7	17.9	13.7	12.7	5.0
$ 3,000–$ 3,999	14.9	12.8	9.4	5.0	10.8	15.3	18.9	7.9
$ 4,000–$ 4,999	9.4	11.9	10.5	5.6	5.9	12.6	12.1	8.0
$ 5,000–$ 5,999	7.5	10.5	12.1	7.6	4.3	10.1	15.0	12.7
$ 6,000–$ 6,999	5.5	7.3	10.9	8.8	1.9	5.8	12.6	15.9
$ 7,000–$ 7,999	3.2	4.7	12.4	9.8	.7	2.1	3.5	10.6
$ 8,000–$ 8,999	1.6	2.9	7.3	8.4	.1	1.2	1.6	7.3
$ 9,000–$ 9,999	.6	1.3	4.6	7.4	–	.5	.5	4.3
$10,000–$11,999	1.1	1.8	3.3	10.6	.1	.6	1.2	5.7
$12,000–$14,999	.3	1.1	2.1	7.7	–	.3	.1	3.5
$15,000 and over	–	.4	1.0	8.6	.1	.3	.1	4.6
Nonoverlap[a]	12.8	12.7	24.6	24.5	25.1	24.9	32.1	32.2
Overlap[b]	87.3		75.4		75.0		67.8	

Source: U.S. Bureau of the Census, "Social and Economic Characteristics of the Population in Metropolitan and Nonmetropolitan Areas: 1970 and 1960," *Current Population Reports*, Series P-23, No. 37, June 24, 1971.

[a]The differences in percentage distribution between the two races at each income level are calculated for each sex, date, and location, and summed; minor differences be-

"earnings opportunity strangulation" of the black earners described above. If the $1 billion annual "poverty gap" for blacks inside and outside central cities were reduced at a decadal rate of 50 percent rather than the current 25 percent rate, the annual social gain would be $125 million in 1975, $250 million in 1980, almost $300 million in 1985, and more than $300 million by 1990. The present discounted value of this more rapid decrement in the income gap exceeds $1 billion most conservatively, for most assumed discount rates, and closer to $2 billion for reasonable ones. This value, it must be remembered, assumes that a poverty population continues to exist – consistent with the observations made above (page xx) about the slowing rate of poverty eradication – but also assumes that a more favorable economic climate can put a significantly large number of black low-income earners and potential earners on a more rapid track to reaching and exceeding the poverty income level.

To estimate the impact of residential segregation, as it is now, and residential desegregation as it could be, on the incomes and earnings of blacks who

Table 4. (Continued)

Annual earnings in 1969 dollars	Outside central cities							
	1969				1959			
	Females		Males		Females		Males	
	Black	White	Black	White	Black	White	Black	White
Under $1,000	29.2	28.8	14.6	10.6	47.3	27.5	17.1	8.5
$ 1,000-$ 1,999	17.1	13.6	9.0	5.2	19.9	15.9	16.6	5.1
$ 2,000-$ 2,999	13.2	10.4	5.5	3.6	12.8	12.6	13.4	4.3
$ 3,000-$ 3,999	14.0	10.6	10.3	3.2	9.0	14.3	14.9	5.9
$ 4,000-$ 4,999	8.7	10.2	8.5	3.6	5.0	11.0	8.6	6.0
$ 5,000-$ 5,999	6.3	9.2	12.5	5.4	2.4	9.1	13.3	10.7
$ 6,000-$ 6,999	4.4	6.4	10.5	6.8	2.6	5.1	7.6	15.3
$ 7,000-$ 7,999	1.9	4.1	9.8	8.7	.8	1.9	5.5	11.2
$ 8,000-$ 8,999	1.3	2.5	6.4	9.1	–	1.0	1.8	8.7
$ 9,000-$ 9,999	.4	1.4	3.1	7.4	–	.6	.4	5.2
$10,000-$11,999	1.4	1.4	5.3	13.5	–	.4	.6	8.2
$12,000-$14,999	1.5	.9	2.6	10.3	.3	.2	–	4.4
$15,000 and over	.3	.3	1.9	12.5	–	.4	.2	6.5
Nonoverlap[a]	10.7	10.8	33.6	33.5	24.1	24.0	43.4	43.4
Overlap[b]	89.2		66.4		76.0		56.6	

tween columns for races, for same sex, year, and location are due to the fact that published Census percentages do not, in fact, add to 100.0 percent although published tables so state.
[b]Difference between nonoverlap and 100.0 percent.

are not in the poverty population, I first calculated the nonoverlap and overlap of the percentile distribution of 1959 and 1969 black and white earnings, male and female earners, inner and outer central city (Table 4); the greater the overlap, the more nearly the income distributions were identical, and hence the smaller the effect of segregation. I then computed the rate at which the overlap had approached unity over this last decade as follows:

	Inside central city		Outside central city	
	Males	Females	Males	Females
1969 overlap	75.4%	87.3%	66.4%	89.2%
1959 overlap	67.8	75.0	56.6	76.0
1959–69 change	11.2	16.4	17.3	17.3

The black-white earnings overlap, or the degree to which the income distributions were identical, is greater for females than for males. The rate at which the black and white income distributions came together was lowest for the inner-city males, because inner-city blacks made less headway in overcoming their disparity in income distribution than did any other group. Nor is it surprising that the overlap is less for males outside the center city than for males in the inner city; more high-income whites than high-income blacks live in the suburbs. This latter difference decreased somewhat over the decade, however.

Were residential segregation substantially decreased, permitting considerably freer access to expanding income opportunities throughout our metropolitan areas, I estimate that the degree of overlap would increase at a rate of about 34 percent per decade,[32] substantially exceeding the rates of change in each of the preceding decades. The impact would be a trebling of the rate of change of inner-city black males, and an approximate doubling of the rate of change for each of the other three groups. To estimate the total impact of such accelerated rates (of black-white similarity) on black worker earnings over a decade, I applied these decadal "acceleration" indices to the relative increase in mean earnings of black males and females, inner and outer center city, as these changed over this decade.[33] The decadal increase in *mean* earnings (in 1969 dollars) would have been approximately $3,600 (instead of $1,200) for black inner-city males; about $3,500 (instead of $1,770) for black outer center-city males; nearly $1,800 (instead of $890) for black inner-city females; and about $2,200 (instead of $1,120) for black outer-city females. On an annual basis in 1969 these total differences (in 1969 dollars) would have amounted to approximately $9.66 billion annually – $5.28 billion for black inner-city males, $0.97 billion for outside central-city black males, $2.98 billion for inner-city black females, and $0.43 billion for outer center-city black females. Remedying the discrepancy in annual earnings due to residential discrimination is worth more than $90 billion at any given point in time, if a reasonable public sector rate of discount is applied.[34]

Together, the poverty and nonpoverty aspects of black income opportunity deprivation due to residential segregation are estimated to exceed $10

[32] My reasoning is that with no residential discrimination the lowest overlap should approximate the highest. In 1969 the lowest overlap was 66.4 and the highest was 89.2; in 1959 the corresponding figures were 56.6 and 76.0. In each case the highest overlap was 134.3 percent of the lowest.

[33] U.S. Bureau of the Census, "Social and Economic Characteristics of the Population in Metropolitan and Nonmetropolitan Areas: 1970 and 1960," table 18.

[34] Throughout, I assume that increased incomes and earnings for blacks would *not* (necessarily) be at the expense of white earners. Some (e.g., Joseph D. Mooney, "Housing Segregation. . .") would claim this begs the question. In my opinion, the type of income and earnings deprivation depicted here is of the underemployment type; the correction of this condition (at least partially) carries with it certain aggregate demand-expanding features, at the same time the shares of a given total are changing. I believe the total pie changes with the correction of human capital deprivation, similar to that of correcting certain regional "income gap" disparities.

billion annually. This estimate is felt to be a conservative one. Removing this social cost is worth a commensurate expenditure of public and private resources, about which more is said below.

While the reasoning of this section may seem to contradict Keynesian economics somewhat, and be more supportive of Say's Law that supply creates its own demand, the statement holds, I believe, in the longer run. The movement of considerable numbers of semiskilled and skilled black males to the suburbs, I believe, will alter labor supply functions and, simultaneously, production functions, in a way that will reduce the *productivity-enervating forces of the dual labor market.* I have not decided, in my own mind, the importance of the manpower training and retraining programs that must accompany a rapid suburban black migration. Many black males are in less productive jobs simply because of the dual labor market. Others could not find significantly different work even if there were no dual market; they suffer a "skills gap" wherever they live. Studies of the New York labor market suggest that the latter category is by far the larger of the two, and thus emphasize a joint retraining and labor market assimilation action. My own feeling is that evidence points to a very large number in *both* categories. I believe that my estimates of closing the income gap by considerably more rapid desegregation are *not* dependent on significantly larger retraining programs; I also believe these programs may require refocusing to become more attuned to the larger regional labor market to which freer access and relocation should give rise.

EXPOSURE TO SUBSTANDARD
SOCIAL/ENVIRONMENTAL CONDITIONS

Having considered in the two foregoing sections the social costs that residential segregation imposes on its victims by reason of increased housing costs and decreased earnings, I now come to some social/environmental considerations. These are often related to the qualitative functional areas typically reserved for "social indicator" measurements, and require less extensive documentation than housing and earnings. For one thing, my estimates of housing and earnings impacts have probably encompassed the implications of many of these social factors, such as poor health and education, deprivation of income, poor physical neighborhood environmental conditions, and inadequate opportunities of all types. To an extent, an attempt to quantify these factors would involve having to make a large number of heroic assumptions, and possibly a substantial amount of double counting.

Assessments of the psychological effects of residential segregation range from statements attributing residential segregation to conditions brought about by high levels of anomie and societal noninvolvement to assertions that ghetto conditions lead to a certain physical and spiritual hardness and to character building of young people.

While I do not entirely dismiss the latter type of argument, I feel that it is generally defensive and patronizing in nature. Clearly, there are many ways to buy a character-building environment. A number of studies have attempted to connect various socializing factors to benefits from improved housing, but most of the differences found under controlled tests have been either small or statistically insignificant. Correlating superior housing with decreased demand for health services and changes in worker productivity,[35] income increase,[36] reduced morbidity rates and better mental health,[37] and increased self-respect and less anomie[38] is based on flimsy evidence at best. The Douglas Commission[39] and the Kaiser Committee[40] also attempted to combine the best evidence, but found weak scientific evidence at best. The status of social indicators is partly responsible, as Peter Marcuse describes:

> No such indicators are now on the horizon, nor has the search for them even begun in earnest. Until they are found, we must use existing indicators, crude, input-oriented, inaccurate, physically biased and incomplete as they are. Politically, negative criticism of the value of present indicators will have policy consequences probably adverse to greater housing production. A more constructive approach would seek supplementation of existing indicators with better measures of the desired outputs of a national housing policy. Much work remains to be done in defining these outputs in other than physical terms, but the job is tremendously important. Without it we are in danger of shaping our national policy to achieve measurable goals solely because they are measurable while ignoring the much more important if less measurable goals of decent social, economic, aesthetic, and human environment that we really want. The paradox of present housing indicators is that they serve well and are perhaps indispensable in telling us whether we are moving forward in solving some of our housing problems, but they do not tell us whether the road we are moving

[35] L. S. Burns, *Housing: Symbol and Shelter*, University of California, Los Angeles, 1970.

[36] National Capital Housing Authority, *Large Family Rent Subsidy, Demonstration Program*, Washington, D.C., 1966.

[37] Daniel Wilner et al., *The Housing Environment and Family Life* (Johns Hopkins University Press, 1962).

[38] Peter Marris, "The Social Implications of Urban Redevelopment," *Journal of the American Institute of Planners*, August 1962.

[39] National Commission on Urban Problems, *Building the American City*, Washington, 1968.

[40] President's Committee on Urban Housing, *Report of the President's Committee on Urban Housing: A Decent Home*, Washington, 1969.

on leads us to the ultimate destination we want to reach. It is time we found out. The search for adequate housing indicators may help.[41]

Technical problems of assigning causality and its direction, and the interrelationship of compounding and confusing variables, are at least equally responsible. What are we searching for in these studies and analyses of housing policy impacts? What estimates of social impact should we seek, and how should we use them? To these issues, I now turn.

BENEFITS, PROGRAMS, AND FURTHER RESEARCH

Benefits

I have been searching for a reasonable assessment of the social benefits that would result if substantial residential segregation *attributable directly and/or indirectly* to public and private actions were somehow removed — and removed at a cost significantly less than the social and private benefits. In developing and implementing residential desegregation policies, it is important to assess the benefits that would result from raising social and environmental factors to at least the level of nonsegregated communities if: (1) estimates of already quantified social benefits were insufficient to justify the social costs involved; and/or (2) the social and environmental factors were themselves independent variables in promoting the same or greater social benefits and could be utilized as policy levers.

Examining the first possibility: if the social benefits from substantial residential desegregation (estimated above at over $11 billion annually) were to be applied to the 6 million subsidized housing units for low-income groups recommended by the Kaiser Committee Report,[42] they would provide an annual subsidy of more than $1,800 per unit, or $150 per month per unit, making it possible for 25 million people (6 million families) to be substantially better housed than they are today.[43] This amount, although less than the cost of public housing units,[44] would be significant as a housing allowance; it would certainly equal or exceed the standard of 25 percent of monthly income that low-income families are expected to pay for housing.

[41]Peter Marcuse, "Social Indicators and Housing Policy," *Urban Affairs*, vol. 7 (December 1971), pp. 215–16.

[42]President's Committee on Urban Housing, *Report of the President's Committee on Urban Housing: A Decent Home.*

[43]Or 20 million people (5 million families) if the subsidization program costs 20 percent to administer.

[44]Variously estimated from $25,000 to $125,000 per unit, depending upon the costs considered in the estimate.

Some may deny the appropriateness of utilizing all the estimated annual benefits as a housing incentive subsidy. Actually, I do not propose this, but have only set an upper limit to these expenditures. In reality, additional considerations should apply in developing a rationale for subsidizing residential desegregation: (1) the costs of incentives should not be equal to the total housing allowances paid but should be limited to the opportunity costs of the resources consumed in the administration of the program; (2) a mix of manpower training and residential desegregation incentive programs is needed; (3) it is possible, and desirable, to calculate the tax requirements and implications of alternative public programs, using an econometric model that considers SMSAs and the productivity, production function, supply function, and taxable income consequences.

Programs

The current HUD Housing Allowance Experimental Program, like other HUD demand-oriented projects and programs, is designed to assess the impacts of a housing allowance on housing supply, housing prices, aggregate consumption of housing services, changes in tenure relationships, etc. Another objective is to see whether such a program can work administratively and economically.

My own belief is that the demand-oriented programs have *at least* the same potential, per dollar spent, for reducing residential segregation as the supply-oriented housing programs of recent decades. In fact, I believe they have a greater potential. For example, I have great doubts about the viability of proposals that require a given percentage of new, subsidized units to be allocated to low-income groups. I doubt, on both economic and community opposition grounds, that such forced seeding will work in enough localities to substantially reduce housing segregation practices.

My enthusiasm for substantial experimentation and demonstration, followed by sizable, full-scale housing allowance and/or modified negative income-tax programs, rests on the following grounds. First, opposition to more than a certain percentage of blacks in a neighborhood varies considerably by neighborhood, region, and metropolitan area. Given the current trend toward local option in so many functional activities, the degree and method of residential desegregation are likely to reflect the personality and character of each locality.[45] The rather gentle nudging of the housing allowance, made

---

[45] See W. A. Steger, "Inventing Economic Institutions for Urban Survival," Carnegie-Mellon Conference on Advanced Urban Transportation Systems, May 1970; Charles M. Tiebout, "Intra-Urban Location Problem: An Evaluation," *American Economic Review*, May 1961.

up as it will be in each metropolitan area of thousands and thousands of micro decisions, will permit communities and neighborhoods to avoid the large-scale, binary decisions on subsidized housing projects that have polarized so many neighborhoods. Second, current and proposed anti-inflation policies and programs — which I believe will be national policy, in some form, for a long time — should lessen the inflationary impact on housing prices that a housing allowance program would otherwise have. Housing allowances, however, permit the property owner to charge a higher rent in return for more services provided. If the allowance program is accompanied by a counseling program, as is currently planned, the profit-maximizing property owner outside the central city may find rational ways to tap the newly developed market and still remain within anti-inflation guidelines. Given the substantial blighting trends in certain suburban neighborhoods, a coalescence of interests may well be given just the necessary push by the housing allowance program, and lead to substantial residential desegregation. Third, the housing allowance program is designed to minimize the impact of large-scale decisions by the real estate industry. This will tend, in my opinion, to control or inhibit those parts of the industry which have been held wholly or partly responsible for tragic neighborhood "tipping" whereby large areas shifted wholly from white to black. In my belief, the industry cannot and should not be held responsible for results stemming from basic attitudes, but it is often the unwitting agent of change and a sufficient force to turn a potentially neutral situation into an "overshoot" condition.

Others in this symposium are measuring the potential of a variety of legal devices, planning actions, and economic pressures for desegregating our residential environment. I leave to them the judgments about the relative efficacy of these forces in achieving racial desegregation. And I leave the moral judgments about desegregation to those who specialize in these. I have, instead, emphasized the economic arguments, which amount in conservative terms to more than one percent of U.S. personal income, and to still larger sums if the employment rate for low-income workers increases. Furthermore, while it would require significantly more speculation and consideration, I would seek the approval — pending the favorable outcome of the housing allowance experiments and demonstrations — of housing allowances *in the billions of dollars* annually (with or without significant changes in housing supply programs). Significant expansion of income opportunity would accompany the substantial residential desegregation that a properly utilized and designed housing allowance would promote. The cost effectiveness of such a program might, in fact, exceed that of a negative income tax or a manpower training program where these did not lead to the same pressures for residential desegregation.

Quite obviously, the research and evaluation efforts accompanying the various demand-stimulating programs of the federal government — the negative income tax, the housing allowance programs, and others currently contemplated — will be most helpful here. However, the relative transience of these experiments and demonstrations may serve to minimize their potential impact: families may not move readily if continuance of the programs is in doubt. Nevertheless, these programs may ultimately reduce the high degree of residential segregation that characterizes most U.S. neighborhoods, cities, and regions today.

Research

In this paper I have stressed action programs and paid little attention to the research needed. Further research might immeasurably improve my crude benefit estimates, but I am more concerned with other research needs, since I believe the magnitudes of my estimates are in "the right ballpark." Research on the impacts of different forms of housing allowance on housing supply and housing suppliers, as well as on recipients of allowances, is vitally needed and must be carried out.

I am also concerned with research leading to appropriate planning actions for each metropolitan area, where public housing planning and management activities will play a major role in each area in discovering the best methods for achieving the benefits of residential desegregation at least economic cost and with a minimum of physical and psychological discomfort. Much of this research will be of a community involvement variety, directed toward helping different neighborhoods find better methods for self-improvement and/or create environments that lead to the migration patterns each desires — within the context of the overall community and region and its own and federal resources.

Another type of metropolitan research should be analytic, aided where possible by simulation or other urban modeling method. Preferably, the model should be capable of representing small areas (or neighborhoods and subcommunities), their present characteristics, and the changes brought about by public and private actions, programs, and projects. The model should be capable of relating housing (including changes in demand and supply functional relationships), manpower and education programs, transportation programs, and areal environmental programs to areal in- and out-migration, labor force, employment, and personal income. The reactions of different social, economic, and ethnic groups to one another, and to public and private actions should also be included.

The Forrester modeling apparatus,[46] while suitable for conditionally forecasting the long-range values of demographic, social, and economic variables for an entire region and its major areal components, relies primarily on untested and uncalibrated (perhaps uncalibratable) "attraction parameters" for its submetropolitan allocations. Its treatment of the short-run dynamics of location does not promote confidence in its longer-run forecasts.[47] My own inclination, relying on the later uses of the Lowry formulation and my own reinterpretation,[48] would turn instead to a formulation such as the Community-Action-Program Model,[49] designed for early use (1966–67) in research and evaluation efforts by the Office of Economic Opportunity. This model, put aside to be "calibrated" with combined local and 1970 Census small-area data, deserves a test both of its analytic powers and the capability it would yield local planners in assessing alternative housing, manpower, access, and employment programs. The model system can be briefly described in this way:

This model system [shown in Figure 1] is primarily intended to reflect the implications — for populations of identified economic and social characteristics within small areas of a community — of alternative sets of public programs aimed at increasing employment and/or income. The system traces, through time, the response of such household characteristics as size and income to employment opportunity and to the effects of public programs. Newly formed and migrating households are allocated among small areas within a region according to the size, cost, and location of available public and private housing. Selected attributes of the community and of each small area are then computed algebraically from the characteristics of these and the previously established households.

Data representing the existing population, housing demand and supply, and labor market are supplied to the system, as are forecasts (or estimates) of future changes in employment by major industry types for each time interval and quantitative descriptions of the projects sought to be reanalyzed. The model is then run through a number of cycles representing

[46] J. W. Forrester, *Urban Dynamics* (MIT Press, 1969).

[47] Leo P. Kadanoff, "From Simulation Model to Public Policy," *American Scientist*, January-February 1972, pp. 74–78. Brown University personnel are attempting to make Forrester's formulation more "realistic" and useful (Kadanoff, p. 78).

[48] Ira S. Lowry, *Model of Metropolis*, Rand Corporation Memorandum RM-4035-RC, 1964; also "A Short Course in Model Design," *Journal of the American Institute of Planners*, May 1965.

[49] G. Kruschwitz, A. Colker, and D. Lamb, "A Community-Action-Program Impact Model," *Socio-Economic Planning Sciences*, vol. 3 (1969), pp. 37–63.

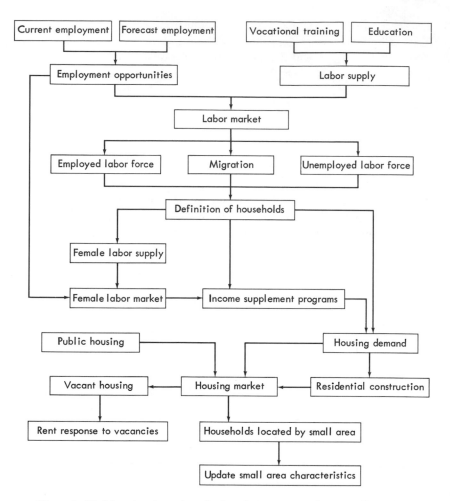

Figure 1. Model system to analyze dual market structure of metropolitan areas.

future time periods of interest to the user. In the process of each cycle, new population and community characteristics are prepared for input to following iterations, and selected attributes are displayed. These attributes are analyzed during or after each run of the model to examine the impact of the project mix being tested. If the user wishes to change the project mix on the basis of his analysis, he may restart the model at the initial time period with a new project mix, or he may add, delete, or modify projects between successive iterations.[50]

[50]Ibid., p. 44.

This modeling system can best be utilized with calibrations against small-area data from 1950, 1960, and 1970, and with certain community attitudinal data.

I hold no particular brief for either subjective (i.e., attitudinal) or objective analytical approaches. In reality, a combination is best, particularly where the research is action oriented and is to be used to evaluate the short-range and longer-range impacts of public and private actions.

I do not wish to end this paper on a research-oriented note, nor do I believe it is necessary to perform significantly more research into the substantial disbenefits and social costs of residential segregation. Rather, I favor immediate demonstration and experimentation programs, leading to full-scale efforts in which creative local action is tied to broad federal incentive programs to achieve a modern land use policy. I am keenly aware of the psychological discomfort that too rapid residential desegregation can bring, but I see no alternative that promises the same national gains — measured both qualitatively and quantitatively — as substantial residential desegregation.

I only hope that *local creativity* is sufficient and that the American sense of fairness can match what appear to be excellent federal initiatives — housing allowances, revenue sharing, and manpower development programs — to avoid another century of social and economic deprivation for a growing mass of our people. In this next century, even more than the last, we can ill afford the luxury of residential segregation.

TAX REFORM
TO RELEASE LAND

MASON GAFFNEY

Taxes on land and buildings are important influences on land use, and are within the control of government. Real estate taxes are a major source of revenue to local governments (LGs) in the United States, as well as being a major cost of owning property. Currently under legal attack in the United States is the local real estate tax as the backbone of public school finance. The premise is that children should not be deprived of reasonable education because their school district lacks an adequate tax base. Regardless of any reforms in this system of local taxing for local services, it seems probable that real estate taxes will persist at some level of government — they are too important a source of revenue to be abandoned. They might or might not be reduced.

Real estate taxes do more than raise revenue; they influence land use, often strongly. Their influence arises not merely from their level, but from the relative tax on land versus that on buildings, from the relative tax on unimproved land versus that on improved land, from the frequency and reasons for reassessment of property, and from other aspects of the imposition of such taxes. Some of the land use effects may be unintended by the legislators and administrators responsible for the taxes, but many of the effects seem clearly to be desired and sought. Real estate taxes cannot absolutely compel some land uses nor absolutely forbid others, as can zoning or building codes; but they provide powerful economic incentives, which are

MASON GAFFNEY is a research associate at Resources for the Future and was formerly professor of economics at the University of Wisconsin, Milwaukee. He has also taught at the universities of Missouri and Oregon and at North Carolina State College and is the author of numerous monographs and articles on urban expansion, containment of urban sprawl, property taxation and land use, economic theory, conservation, and resource economics. Born in 1923, Mr. Gaffney received his B.A. from Reed College and his Ph.D. from the University of California, Berkeley.

operative constantly over long periods of time and in the long run may be as effective as absolute prohibitions or mandates.

Local real estate taxes affect the landholder directly, and also indirectly by affecting the way local governments (LGs) use other land use controls. Most local zoning today has become fiscal zoning, calculated to fortify the local per capita tax base. That is not news, but it is only the most familiar example of the role of the real estate tax in the pattern of local particularism.

The purpose of this paper is to describe the many ways in which real estate taxes influence urban and suburban land use. Some of these effects are rather obvious and expected; but others, on analysis, turn out to be different than a quick and intuitive judgment would predict. In general and in total, real estate taxes as administered in the United States tend to favor the land speculator over the builder, the larger owner over the smaller, and the suburbs over central cities. De facto, real estate taxes as ordinarily administered are an instrument of economic discrimination. They might, if properly restructured, become instruments for socially more constructive land use.

MOTIVES OF LOCAL GOVERNMENTS

The art of central government is one of motivating local governments to act in the wider public interest – to serve the nation by serving themselves. Local governments (LGs) have objectives and operate under constraints and incentives just like persons and firms. Economists have analyzed persons and firms since Adam Smith at least and examined how public policy can work with the market to harness private motives to public ends. But they have neglected the analogous question about LGs, and so have political scientists.

Local governments borrow the sovereignty and police power of the state, and are assumed in law to represent a public interest. But what public? Each represents a small and particular public. There are even cases – in California, of course – of special service districts that are armed with sovereignty and its trappings, immunities, privileges, and exemptions representing as few as one landowner.

Since local governments borrow the sovereignty of the state, the states have the power and duty to structure local incentives to constrain LGs to serve all by serving themselves. And so the states do, in many ways, but they have fallen behind the problem. Today the tension between parochial LG interests and broader public interests approaches the flash point. It is past time to be defining the tensions and aiming to resolve them. This is the point of this forum and this paper.

The local viewpoint differs from the national in that the local turf is more completely open to the movement of labor and capital. The LG is defined as an area of land. Men and wealth come and go, and the level of their returns is set by national market forces, much as the waters of the sea find a common level by interflowing. So the benefits of local spending lodge mainly in higher local land values, because land alone is stationary for long. By the same token, the cost of taxes lodges in lower land values. Land is the equity interest in the municipal corporation. Land income is the bottom line of its income statement. Many municipal motives may best be understood, therefore, as efforts to maximize land income and values.

There is a harmony here between local and national interest. The private owner maximizes net income from a given land area by carving it up and improving and using it so as to maximize its net service flow. The private owner's greed, harnessed by the market, makes him allocate his land for housing and complementary life-support facilities in a surprisingly socially oriented way. One sometimes hears "highest and best use" belittled as though it were a public nuisance, but basically it means the use serving the most human needs. That basic rule must be qualified to account for external effects, but the qualifications are not the rule.

The same rule holds for the LG, which is a group of landowners in league to preside over the collective capital that they use jointly. The LG is a halfway house between the individual landowner and the state. Landowner control is modified by democracy, which gives the whole system some of its characteristic tensions and compromises. But landowners, as the permanent party of every LG, take a strong and steady interest in local government out of proportion to their numbers. It is reasonably accurate for many purposes to think of the LG as a collective landowner, maximizing land income. In so doing it serves the national good.

While there is that basic harmony of local and national good, LGs feel at least four pecuniary incentives that make their goals clash with the larger metropolitan and national welfare. LGs want to avoid dilution of tax base. They want to minimize tax export. They want to fence off local public goods from aliens. And they want to avoid pure competition among their members. No doubt there are more, but these are prominent, and a sufficient basis for the problems of local exclusivism that vex us today. The factor of ethnic bias is treated in other papers in this book.

Avoiding Dilution of Tax Base

The states delegate to LGs certain service duties and certain tax powers to finance them. Many duties, such as drainage, vary as functions of area rather than of people; but others, notably education, vary with population. The property tax is redistributive. So old settlers in each LG are sedulous to see that immigrants contribute as much in taxes as they require in added spending. Indeed, they go further. They try to limit new entry to those who will enrich the tax base by the maximum possible amount. Added to this is often a crabbed and misanthropic outlook on strangers, and a lack of urgency to develop annexed vacant land, which has led to extremes of exclusivism.

Whoever said Americans idolize motherhood never looked into suburban zoning. Whoever said the property tax is regressive is not listening when the rich grumble about taxing property to finance services to persons. For the state to require LGs to "tax the rich man's property to educate the poor man's child" is to invite them to fence out poor families. The tension is partly resolved by the fact that good schools are, like other local services, capitalized into higher real estate values. The bromide that property benefits only from services to property and not from services to people is false. But it is true that school benefits are in proportion to children and not to taxable real estate. The municipal manager finds it his duty to keep out children without a large complement of taxable real estate, and wears a black armband on Mothers Day.[1]

This attitude is not limited to suburbs. President of the U.S. Conference of Mayors, Milwaukee's Mayor Henry Maier, advocates removing "whole square miles of people" from central cities.[2] Big city mayors have been doing that for several years, with federally subsidized programs for highways, urban renewal, land clearance, slum clearance, code enforcement, airport expansion, open space purchase, attraction of industry, campus expansion, harbor expansion, street widening, and so on. It is not just the lure of the suburbs that has lowered the density of central cities so far below what it was 30 years ago.

This exclusionary attitude is not an urban monopoly by any means. Cities have at least some tradition of welcoming immigrants — that is how they became cities. Some rural and sylvan areas never have wanted growth, which is often one reason they remained rural or sylvan. Northern Maine is a celebrated case, owned by a handful of timber companies who have opposed the incorporation of any towns that might tax them to finance schools and attract immigrants. In the settlement of the West the very formation of counties was fought by large ranchers whom the counties might tax. The Homestead Act, planting smaller farmers everywhere, overcame the resistance in most counties, and the need for farm labor softened the exclusionary

---

[1] Indeed, our current Malthusian agitation may derive its plausibility and social status by committing the fallacy of composition on the problems of school finance in suburbs where many social leaders live and form their views of the world, seeing it as a spaceship suburb threatened by school taxes. It is an unfair extension: children do not dilute world wealth in the same way they dilute suburban tax bases.

[2] Presidential Address, U.S. Conference of Mayors, New Orleans, *Washington Post*, June 18, 1972, p. C12.

attitude. Today, as the average native student demands longer and costlier schooling, and as migrant labor competes, every rural county feels a new impulse to exclude the poorer. Migrant labor does the job without requiring schools and without voting.

Minimizing Tax Export

LGs like to help their constituents avoid paying taxes to higher levels of government. This takes several forms.

Within counties using the property tax, smaller LGs try to underassess real estate. Boards of equalization fight this competitive underassessment with overt success but sometimes fail to redress covert underassessment. Low-use zoning is underhanded underassessment, because it depresses resale values during the period before the zoning is breached or lifted. The LG in effect sets its county assessment low by its own motion. This ploy is invidiously reserved for LGs whose citizens can collectively afford to forgo resale value during a prolonged holding period before the zoning is changed.

A complement of low-use zoning is tax assessment based on present use rather than market value. Local assessors often find this acceptable to boards of equalization that would reject more overt forms of competitive underassessment.

Any local tendency to encourage commerce is discouraged in states that levy heavy sales taxes and, unlike Illinois and California, do not return a share to the LG where collected. With no return, any local sacrifice of environment to build up commerce would only pour more taxes into the state treasury.

Property assessment also plays a central role in avoidance of state and federal income taxes. Income property is tax depreciable. Law and Internal Revenue Service (IRS) practice allow repeated depreciation by successive owners, ridiculous as that may be. The law recognizes that land does not depreciate, so each successive owner can depreciate only the building, not the land. When he buys he must allocate the cost between depreciable building and nondepreciable land. Enter the local tax assessor. It is IRS practice to accept the local assessor's allocation of value between land and buildings. Local assessors, by undervaluing land relative to buildings, thus help their constituents depreciate land and so avoid a large share of the income tax due on real estate, and help convert it from a tax payer to a tax shelter. This is the modern version of competitive underassessment, one that costs the federal treasury billions annually and goes virtually unchecked. This practice creates a strong local bias to underassess land, which in turn tends, through its direct effect on landowner incentives, to keep land from serving the needs of the median consumer.

The income tax hits ordinary income much harder than capital gains — more than twice as hard, when one knows the angles on capital gains — and the name of the tax-avoidance game is converting income into capital gain. One's LG helps. Rather than use public money to help established industry and commerce earn ordinary income, the LG extends its capital infrastructure into new land to create capital gains, selling tax-exempt municipal bonds to raise the capital. The "unearned increment" on the land is the untaxed increment as well.

The LG also devotes extra effort to securing state and federal spending and public works that will raise local land values. To this end it reserves sites, holding them ready for a new branch of the state university, a military base, a highway interchange, a defense plant, or whatever. To this end it also seeks to attract citizens with influence at court, which adds to its bias for the wealthy.

Blending into the minimizing of tax export is the maximizing of outside aid. An entire culture of local politics has grown up around the art of pleading poverty. Cities are always "strapped," in "crisis," requiring "relief," and so on, in spite of the rise of their real estate tax base. This is silly, but a game people play in dead earnest as they compete for federal dollars. Underassessment is a central part of the game, sequestering latent fiscal assets. So is regressive assessment, assuring that local taxes hurt and arouse sympathy and an image of desperation.

Fencing Off Local Public Amenities from Aliens

LGs provide many public services, such as schools, parks, police and fire protection, libraries, and others. These municipal amenities yield a flow of services to their users — a form of income to these persons that is tax free. Local taxes used to finance the production of these local amenities are deductible from the individual's taxable income, unlike cash payments for items of individual consumption. The availability and quality of these local services raise local land values, as anyone who seeks to buy a house in a neighborhood with good schools quickly learns; and the increases in land values are largely tax free, due to the capital gains provisions of income tax law. At a time when a penny saved is two pennies earned before taxes and tax-free income is almost the only kind worth having, these are weighty values.

The problem here is restricting the use of these local amenities to local residents. The goal is a tenure or right of use that is common but not too common — common within the small group of local residents, but private against outsiders. This source of pressure is often very strong. All residents of the local area have much to gain from exclusive use of local amenities, but only the large landowner has something to sell if aliens invade the local area by purchase of property. The tenant and small owner have little or no salable tenure in local amenities — only a shadow equity in the old swimming hole based on use and custom, familiarity, and their small numbers. They can suffer real losses from the invasion and crowding of their old haunts.

To maintain the unstable balance between common amenities and limited access, suburbanites have developed the cult of open space, a philosophy that transmutes the exclusionary particularism of the golf course into the nobility of Naturalism. The apotheosis of open space is to suburban particularism what "national defense" is to the federal budget. The anomaly of open space behind cyclone fences is only a contradiction to those who don't get the subliminal part of the message. Every movement requires a philosophy and Naturalism has been recruited to serve the local treasury.

Avoiding Pure Competition

The historical Mercantilistic city was a monopoly, using municipal policy to exploit its trade territory by restricting competition. Today the motive is less sharply defined due to greater mobility, but it is by no means dead. Owners of old buildings are sensitive to competition from new ones, which pull away tenants. They know that renewal at higher density adds to supply and helps lower rents, while renewal at lower density is removal, which delivers tenants into the hands of landlords. They mask this with talk of "good planning," "human scale of density and size," psychoses of crowded laboratory rats, birth control, saving historical shrines, aesthetic absolutes, and other diversions and digressions. So far they have gotten away with it.

LOCAL MERCANTILIST POLICIES

Local governments have other, more basic incentives on which the four discussed above are superimposed. They want to serve their constituents well at low cost (subject to Parkinsonian tendencies among bureaucrats, of course). They seek efficiency, internal equity among voters (even including tenants), renewal, ordinary (i.e., productive) income, growth of the local market, and succession of land to higher uses (i.e., uses serving more human needs). There is a continual tension between the goals, to understand which is to understand much of municipal behavior.

LG response to these combined incentives is municipal "Mercantilism" or "particularism," interchangeable terms emphasizing the pursuit of parochial self-interest at the expense of outsiders. LGs pursue Mercantilism by bending all their powers to the goal. These include establishing boundaries, taxing, zoning, allocating capital budgets, planning public works, policing buildings, pricing municipal services, influencing utility rates, negotiating for new industries, and a few others.

Balkanization

The basis of local particularism is segregating the tax base by creating and defending tax enclaves. Industrial tax enclaves are one type, but they get more than their share of the spotlight. Resources are a larger member of the family. "Trees don't go to school," says the timber owner, "why should I pay taxes?" Mineral owners don't say anything, they just lie low with nearly total success. Farm landowners, whose real estate weighs in at over $200 billion, have sold themselves as a collective welfare case. (Their national average property tax rate is about 1 percent of market value.) Factory owners on the other hand are blamed for school children, as though hiring were siring.

It is a double standard to ponder, as national unemployment rises to crisis levels while the birthrate drops toward zero population growth. Creating jobs is not really antisocial, it just seems that way to the local school board. Those who deploy their capital to employ men are doing a favor to the nation, and are not adding a bit to national school costs. So the establishment of industrial enclaves, which exclude residences, should not be singled out for avoiding school taxes, any more than farmland, timber, minerals, and utilities. Employers should pay taxes because they own property, not because they hire fathers.

Enclaves established to provide tax havens do not resist "growth" of everything, but only of population. They love to annex land and attract taxable capital. From the parochial viewpoint of modern municipal Mercantilism, the best industry is the most capital-intensive industry that hires the fewest fathers per dollar of tax base. Such industries are hypersensitive to property taxes, and so tend to attract each other and cluster in low-tax enclaves. This is splendid for them, but hard on everyone else.

Some suburban residential enclaves, often mixed with rural ones, have effectively excluded racial and ethnic minorities and low-income people of every race. Such enclaves have recently been the center of legal and political efforts to desegregate races and classes and to tap segregated tax bases by invasion. The enclaves may well deserve the invasion, but let us not forget the larger tax bases not touchable in this way: forests, farms, minerals, vacation resorts, factories, utilities, stores, and warehouses. A move to statewide property taxation for schools will do more to equalize school resources than anti-zoning cases. And let us not forget that invading a segregated tax base will almost surely result in relocation of people and businesses in areas they might well not have chosen but for the lure of the richer tax base they could share there. Again, statewide school finance has the advantage of equalizing fiscal resources without requiring or inducing people or businesses to move in quest of more favorable tax treatment. Some of the longest leaps in the annals of suburban sprawl have resulted from developers' pioneering in peripheral rural counties to enjoy their low tax rates.

Administrative Modification of the Property Tax

Assessors have much latitude, de facto. Most assessors are, for better or worse, chameleons of municipal policy, and use their latitude to help effect predominant local goals as seen by the local powers.

Regressive assessment has been found in many LGs, although never in pure form. It is mixed with other biases. Some, like the bias against newer buildings, tend to countervail regressivity. But most biases probably reinforce it — for example, the bias for land, the lag in revaluing declining areas downwards and new areas upwards, the bias against subdivision, the bias against the unorganized and possibly against blacks, the "wholesale rate" given to large speculative acreage and larger lots, and basing assessment on present use rather than value.

Some recent studies showing or suggesting regressive assessment are by Oldman and Aaron in Boston; Theodore Smith in Hartford; the Urban League in Atlanta; and Gaffney in Milwaukee.[3]

It may be hard to prove regressive or racist motives. They may not even prevail, although I personally believe they are an influence. The point of consistency is fiscal particularism, the desire to protect and enrich the local tax base.

"Hearth-tax" assessment is a strong tendency. A site is assessed in part by value, but adjusted for number of families there. The result, and I surmise the idea behind it, is to remake the property tax into something more like school tuition.

Sites without buildings are assessed most lightly of all. No hearth, no tax. We shall see that taxing buildings reduces population while taxing land increases it. The LG fighting immigration will naturally hit buildings harder.

[3] Oliver Oldman and Henry Aaron, "Assessment-Sales Ratios Under the Boston Property Tax," *National Tax Journal*, vol. 18, no. 1 (March 1965), pp. 36–49; Theodore Smith, *Real Property Taxation in the Urban Center* (Hartford: J. C. Lincoln Institute, January 1972); "Report of the Atlanta Urban League on the Fulton County Property Tax," mimeographed (The Atlanta Urban League, September 1971); Mason Gaffney, "What is Property Tax Reform?," *American Journal of Economics and Sociology*, vol. 31, no. 2 (April 1972), p. 149; and "The Property Tax is a Progressive Tax," S. J. Bowers, ed., *1971 Proceedings of 64th Annual Conference of National Tax Association* (Columbus: National Tax Association, 1972), p. 415.

Land assessment based on present use is part of the pattern. It is not true that taxing ripening land ad valorem forces premature use, but it is true that raising land assessments at the time of subdivision or other conversion to higher use is a powerful force postponing such conversion. It creates a locked-in effect, like the capital gains tax that waits on sale. The assessor's propensity to assess land use rather than value is reinforced and abetted by low-use zoning, discussed below.

There is tension here, and ambivalence. LG taxpayers would like the undeveloped acreage to share the load. But they hold back, in an uneasy truce: we don't tax you; you don't crowd our schools.

The property tax is also modified by exemptions provided by state law. LGs are not omnipotent over this, but they have a choice of what exemptions to fight. The Milwaukee tax commissioner, for example, fights to disexempt dormitories, hospital annexes, and nursing homes — capital that serves people's needs. On the other hand he does not fight to tax cemeteries that preempt as much land as industry and hold most of it in reserve for future burials while life-support systems are taxed instead. Nor does he fight to tax the vast grounds surrounding many institutions, or to assess golf courses at market value. Cities blame the states and plead impotence, yet much of the exempt land is owned by agencies of the city itself: industrial land banks, harbor commissions, redevelopment authorities, and many agencies with advance sites. Thus cities evince a preference for the kinds of tax exemption that reduce the supply of buildings (other than private schools, which help hold down school taxes).

Forcing Property Consumption by Direct Control

One way to enrich the property tax base is to require every resident to use no less than a standard complement of land and capital, and exclude those who will not. This is forced consumption.

It is a pretty expensive indirect way to collect taxes, something like Charles Lamb's description of a mythical Chinese practice of burning down a house to roast a pig. It could raise a family's yearly debt service or other yearly capital costs by $10.00 in order to increase tax returns by $1.00. The lower the tax rate, the greater the forced consumption of real estate required per dollar of tax revenue. And low tax rates do not weaken the motive, which is to avoid *increasing* rates, from whatever level.

LGs force land consumption by using zoning, subdivision control, building codes, and condemnation power.

Zoning. Low-density zoning is the focus of today's perception of this set of devices, and is discussed by others in this forum. It is simply forced land consumption. Indirectly it also forces the individual to consume more capital, because large homes go with large lots. It very directly forces LGs to sink more capital in all public works, the costs of which vary as functions of area, not population.

It is ironic that low-density zoning is viewed by some as a defense against urban expansion. It forces urbanites to consume more land, and cities to spread out, even if working ideally. The way it normally works, it thwarts demand for better land and sends developers probing outward seeking weak spots in the zoning umbrella. High-density land use thus erupts capriciously here and there, and threatens everywhere, rather than clustering where it belongs. The protection of nature and open space against man, purportedly a reason for low-density zoning, is not achieved. Man is frustrated in his quest for land, and more of nature is displaced than if he were satisfied. Zoning to protect nature is a boomerang policy. Touted as a solution, it has become a large part of the problem.

It is ironic that zoning is used as a defense against higher school enrollments and hence against higher taxes, for low density inflates most other public costs. Jumpy, uneven, unpredictable sprawl inflates them even more. The added costs are net social costs to the nation; the school savings are just transfers, local gains achieved by imposing the cost on others, or depriving children altogether. The national result is a tragic waste of resources to no purpose.

Agricultural zoning is the most extreme kind of exclusionary zoning, followed by large-lot zoning in horsey exurbs. But zoning is universal. Zoning extends clear to the center of the city, where it takes the form of floor-area ratios, height limits, and setbacks. At every stage it interdicts market choices for more intensive use. Usually this is a direct bias against the poor. Luxury high-rise apartments and some office buildings cater to the affluent, but the indirect effect of suppressing them also hits the poor, as the rich are forced to bid for more land.

As you might expect, LGs overzone for uses regarded as fiscal surplus generators, and underzone for deficit-makers. There is often a lack of careful counting of supply and demand, and a tendency to reserve most of the land for a small share of the market, regionwide. The fiscal motive is mixed with a variety of subjective value judgments and weakly based, strongly held opinions about high-rise apartment living, ethnic outgroups, and aesthetics. Some results of exclusionary zoning are capricious and hard to explain rationally, as with any human endeavor: what is regarded as a local liability often reflects more prejudice than analysis. But even with perfect knowledge, there would be a zoning bias.

Too much land is zoned for commerce and industry in most cities. Some rich suburbs zone them out as nuisances, but that is the exception: few can afford the luxury. The classic "good reason" for zoning is to protect ivy-covered cottages from gas stations and rendering plants, but in most LGs the zoning gives these nuisance uses a wide choice of sites among dwellings. The ivy-covered cottages are the nuisance: they produce the fiscal pollutant, school kids. Many have to invade industrially and commercially zoned land, because so little is zoned residential.

The main limit on commercial zoning is imposed by influential merchants to stifle competition. Zoning boards entertain as quite legitimate, legal, and respectable the plea that commercial zoning be denied a newcomer because it would hurt someone else's business. The common law rule against monopolies is easily forgotten. This is in keeping with the historical municipal Mercantilism of monopolistic city-states.

Zoning often determines property tax assessments. From the land speculator's viewpoint, the ideal is farm zoning and a low assessed value during the ripening period, with the option to secure high-density zoning at the time of his choosing. Many have succeeded in achieving this. The rest of the community appreciates the speculator's not diluting the local tax base by developing, but would also appreciate his enriching it by paying taxes. There are other pros and cons in each case, too, and great variety in the compromises struck. But there is a common theme: zoning is used to hold down property tax assessments on ripening land. Zoning helped to change the property tax from a tax on present and potential land value to a tax on land use, activity, and human occupancy. It reinforces and legitimizes the assessment discrimination that occurs even without zoning. The assessment discrimination, in turn, helps keep land in low-density use or cold storage, withheld in either case from the poor.

Subdivision control. LGs have power to refuse subdivisions, and can make them meet standards. It is an obvious occasion for upgrading, and goldplating street improvements has become the rule. An aerial photograph shows vast areas in subdivision paving, planned to repel through traffic, used entirely for local access. The result: expensive lots, as intended.

Some LGs impose what are in effect special taxes on new building tracts by requiring donations of land for school sites. These add to the price of new houses, limiting supply and excluding poorer buyers.

A pernicious byproduct of imposing extra costs on subdividing is an exaggerated propensity to build without subdividing, where possible. This means stringing buildings out along trunk roads financed by city, state, or the United States. Interior land is sterile, or worse, divided into bowling alley lots. Settlement is linear, guaranteeing a minimum of linkage, and a maximum of interference and congestion. The resultant low density makes public transport uneconomic, leading to total dependence on private autos — another exclusionary device.

Building codes. The worthy purposes of codes, like other devices, are easily subverted to exclusionary ends, and probably have been. "Every building a Cadillac" is hard on Datsun budgets. Occupancy limits further require that the Cadillac have empty seats.

Grandfather clauses let standards be focused on new buildings, the cutting edge of supply, without threatening old ones. This, too, acts against renewal.

It is grotesque to watch HUD struggling with its Operation Breakthrough, as though cheap housing waited on engineering advances. The theory of Cultural Lag has been a commonplace for decades, yet technocratic minds keep seeking physical solutions to institutional problems. American industry has offered us a good cheap dwelling unit called a trailer for as long as the life of the theory of Cultural Lag. The reason it does not solve our housing shortage is not to be found on the assembly line, but in the Assembly Chamber. LGs will not let them in, largely because they dilute the tax base.

Condemnation. Many cities condemn old buildings for safety and health reasons. This does, where applied, bring euthanasia to structures forced into the geriatric stage by policy. But the emphasis is on clearance, riddance, and removal, not on rebuilding. Like federal urban renewal, condemnation lends itself to policies of exclusion.

LG authorities would condemn old buildings more vigorously if welfare were all locally financed. Large federal sharing in welfare makes old slums much less a local liability than otherwise. The main local liability remains the school child.

Condemnation operates in reverse when a forsaken gargoyle, cornice, aesthetic or "historical" antiquity is threatened by market forces. People who look the other way when poor families are driven from their condemned homes may often be found rallying to save a shrine that symbolizes what they define as history or tradition. If it stands in the way of a housing project, so much the better.

Taste conformity. Some LGs have architectural review or fine arts commissions and the like, with certain powers to save antiquities, prohibit nonconforming styles, and so on. Ostensibly they are concerned with aesthetics, and no doubt they are, but taste standards are subjective and often absolutist. As Veblen taught, an objective factor in taste is waste, preferably dignified by age and obsolescence, tempered by modesty in display. But modesty in display entails setbacks, leading to immodest land requirements, the ultimate symbol of financial respectability, reserve power under leash, and priority of status. Class bias may masquerade as anger at the greed of developers, and fear of children as love of beauty. The end result is another fence against the poor.

Regressive Regulatory Bias

Utility rate regulation nearly everywhere ignores the fact that distribution cost gets lower as density rises and gets higher with distance from the load center. Yet at today's low densities, distribution (or collection) has become far and away the major cost in almost all utilities, so total costs are dominated by density of settlement. The cost varies as a function of area primarily, and only incidentally with volume per meter. Rates do not reflect these differential costs. Discounts, indeed, go to the large individual buyer, irrespective of density. Many large individual buyers are at low density and far out, and should pay higher rates.

Thus "rich territory" subsidizes the lean, and small lots subsidize the large. Utility rates are a regressive tax. Owners of large lots and of undivided vacant land are spared part of the costs of services available to them and hence are under less pressure to subdivide their land.

If the surpluses wrung from small users of land in this fashion went to local school boards, LGs might welcome the poor. But the surpluses are pooled, instead, over utility networks covering many LGs. The local school district is hit with the cost of the children living at high density, while the benefit of low per capita utility costs is diffused over a wide system. As a result many LGs use their power over certain mass systems, mainly sewer and water, to control immigration. They can block subdivision with "sewer power" by refusing sewers, pleading undercapacity – and then fail to increase capacity.

Meanwhile, building continues at the low densities appropriate to private individual water wells and septic tanks. Capital costs are high, and screen out the poor. Large-tract platting preempts land and precludes subdivision. In terms of sewer and water service this pattern of land settlement makes no sense at all. It is a device of local fiscal particularism, calculated to fortify the per capita tax base. And it is growing. Those who put much hope in cracking snob zoning as the route to reform, take note. LGs have several lines of defense.

Allocation of Municipal Funds

The tendency of cities to tilt capital and operating budgets toward their upper classes is widely observed. In recent years, Milwaukee cleared a large urban renewal project area, evicting scores of families stacked up in the ghetto – but scheduled all its capital budget for city utilities into expansion onto raw land, zoned for large lots. The specifics are available but the point is not Milwaukee. If it were just one city we could laugh at the human circus. But this is a national epidemic, and where are these "whole square miles" of poor people to find a resting place short of the whole square miles of tax-exempt land reserved for cemeteries?

Industrial Promotion, Federal Programs, and Other Policies

In seeking industry, there is a hierarchy of desirables. It is based largely on capital intensity. Capital means taxes; labor means school children. Cities seeking industry use all their selling wiles to favor capital over labor.

Cities have primary control over sales of cleared land under federally sub-sidized urban renewal programs. Sales and conditions are dominated by fiscal bookkeeping, in keeping with other policies.

There are dozens of ways that city policy affects land use – too many to catalog here. Step by step, a city's motives determine the result. Today, the motive is to repel poor people, and many programs develop that thrust.

Without itemizing every policy, note the implication of the fact that there are many. If local government is to function meaningfully it must have powers and areas of discretion. Anti-Mercantilist policies of central govern-ment should aim at restructuring incentives, therefore, rather than at impos-ing federal control on every specific power, as by categorical grants. The virtues of local autonomy are those of independence, human scale of organi-zation, contact with local needs, and quick responses. These are to be pre-served and cherished. To overcome LG Mercantilism by direct controls is to destroy local autonomy, a price too high to pay, especially since we don't have to. The alternative is to make it fiscally advantageous for LGs to attract people so that they will compete for families instead of for capital and land. This brings us to the subject of taxes.

THE PROPERTY TAX, LAND USE, AND MUNICIPAL MERCANTILISM

The property tax is at the heart of fiscal Mercantilism in today's American cities. It is a control over land use – the most powerful and pervasive of all, and the most flexible. It has been used as an exclusionary device, but it can be, and to some extent has been used as a promotional device, depending on how the assessor allocates real estate value between land and buildings. The property tax can be a lever for the reform of LG Mercantilism.

Property taxes affect several aspects of land use: intensity, frequency of demolition and renewal, size of parcel, choice of location of improvements, and the time when land is ripe for higher use. In the aggregate, property taxes affect the supply of buildings and floor space in each LG jurisdiction. The property tax not only raises money, it controls land use, redistributes wealth, and dominates LG Mercantilism. It wants a close analytical look. Analysis may entail some pain. But, as your dentist says, it only hurts a little, and it should improve your bite.

The property tax is at least three taxes: one on land, one on buildings, and one on personal property (in practice, business inventories). Each has its distinctive effects. I treat the first two separately, and omit the last, which is the smallest, in the interest of brevity.

The effect of property taxes depends among other things on how high the real rate is. A rough national mean today might be about 1½–2 percent with a wide dispersion about the mean. At these levels the tax rate is still not very high next to interest rates at 8 percent or so, and annual inflation at 4 percent or so. But the effect of the tax rate may outweigh the effect of interest at an equal rate if the interest is only forgone interest on equity, because the tax is a cash outgo. There are many LGs, too, where real rates are above 3 percent, or are threatening to be. There are a few up around 7 percent with Newark and Boston. Here the property tax is a major control.

Intensity of Use

Taxes on buildings. The property tax on buildings is a percentage of their value and is therefore something like an increase in the mortgage interest rate. Interest is the largest cost by far in building, as it is with all very durable goods; over the life of a building, interest on investment is greater than the principal, the latter representing payments to construct the building. The property tax added onto this cost and recurring annually for 50–100 years is the second largest cost, unless rates are uncommonly low.

The effect of raising building costs is to reduce building. And when one does build, everything about a building that is marginal is made submarginal. Every individual site, considered in isolation, is less intensively improved. Chopped off are marginal increments to quality, beauty, safety, pollution control, convenience, fireproofing, quakeproofing, insulation, durability, height, and all aspects of intensity (excepting lot coverage, discussed separately). In essence, one applies less capital per unit of land. It is a matter of diminishing returns of capital applied to land.

It is a sad fact of life that egoism precedes altruism, and much of what is marginal to an owner is that which is there to impress, please, and avoid offending and endangering his neighbors. What is marginal to the owner is of more than marginal value to the health of neighborhoods, so the loss of marginal increments to one owner's capital is a collective loss of consequence. In some jurisdictions it has been found that building owners neglect exterior appearance specifically and selectively because they believe it influences assessors. The celebrated case of the Seagrams Building assessment in Manhattan, although extreme, lends credence to this notion. The Seagrams Building assessment was raised 50 percent because of its good looks.[4]

Taxing buildings makes capital dearer, motivates people to substitute land for capital, and encourages horizontal spread. Vertical rise meets increasing capital costs, whereas horizontal spread enjoys decreasing capital costs, up to a point, and saves on capital by consuming more land.

This produces the anomaly that taxing buildings, although it lowers intensity, acts to increase lot coverage. By putting a premium on horizontal spread, it encourages the building to invade the yard. This might be overcome by enlarging the lot, but here one runs directly into his neighbor trying to do the same thing. A corollary is artificially forced demand for land, and higher land prices. In time this also leads to urban expansion and larger lots.

High rise is sometimes painted as a desperate expedient of poverty, but it is more accurately seen as a luxury that lets us enjoy the benefits of closer living without walling off all open space. The luxury is available when capital is cheap. Taxing buildings makes capital artificially dear and prices this luxury out of the market.

Where lot coverage is limited by zoning and buildings are taxed, horizontal spread cannot substitute for height. The net result is limited height and a reduction in the carrying capacity of the land of the LG. The tax is another form of forced land consumption — less direct than zoning, and with other side effects.

Taxes on land value. These would be neutral in their effect on land use under the simplifying but unreal assumption that there is a perfect market for capital. The tax cost does not add to the interest cost of holding land, but displaces it. Forgone interest on equity falls as the tax lowers the price of land. Simple algebra shows that the decline of interest cost exactly equals the increase of tax levy — that is the classic theory of tax capitalization (see Appendix, section I).

But in fact, interest rates vary among people. They are regressive — the poor pay more. Land taxes, assuming true assessment, are not regressive. Substituting taxes for interest therefore undoes the effect of regressive interest rates. It hits the rich owner harder than the poor. This is the theory of *differential* capitalization of land taxes. It gives the land tax a progressive quality (see Appendix).

Differential capitalization increases the bidding power of the poor for land, causing them to encroach on lands held by the rich. This occurs through

[4]*Life*, August 16, 1963, p. 4.

subdivision of large holdings, accelerated release of ripening land to higher uses, consolidation of very small holdings, and sales of land from the rich to the poor.

The effect of land taxes on intensity of land use is therefore not a simple plus or minus. The effect is equalizing as among classes. Land taxes let the poor, who live crowded on poor land, live less crowded and move to better land. They lower density for the poor by raising it for the rich, who own most of the land.

That is not widely understood. It is often advanced that land taxes "force land into use," and result in higher density. This simplicity is catchy and will not easily give way. But it is misleading. Land taxes crowd the rich, but open up more land for the poor. Only from the standpoint of the wealthy are land taxes simply intensifying. The land tax is rather redistributive.

In terms of finding land to house and serve the mass market and the poor, this kind of redistribution is a virtue. But at the local level, it runs counter to Mercantilist needs by increasing population, attracting immigrants of only average wealth, and whetting competition. This is why the exclusive taxation of site values has not been more widely supported by LGs. The state and national incentive structures are not gauged to make its results unambiguously attractive to them.

Land taxes focused on central land also tend to lower intensity of land use in fringe areas by meeting demand on central land and so weakening outthrusting demand. Those who choose to go exurban thus achieve lower density, too.

Timing of Demolition and Renewal

Short-run effects. When a building is old, the effect of building taxes is probably to lengthen its life, and certainly to defer the renewal of its site.

It is not the taxes on the old building itself that lengthen its tenure. On the contrary, they may cause premature demolition and replacement by a parking lot or a nothing if the owner can count on the assessor then lowering the valuation, a point on which local practice varies.

What does defer renewal is the threat of taxes on the successor building. Building on a parcel of real estate is the occasion for a large increase in the tax bill. This throws a weight into the scales of decision between old and new. The year that would be optimal for renewal in the absence of taxes now looks premature to the owner, because of the tax difference.

So long as taxes depend on the use to which land is put, they intercede in the competition of the market in favor of the lower taxed use and alter decisions at the margin. Here it is a matter of one particular application of that general principle: the margin of decision between old and new. Building taxes are heavier on the new and weight the decision against it. They may defer renewal for any number of years and decades, depending on particulars. Because of neighborhood effects, which are mutually reinforcing, what defers renewal of the individual site for 25 years may defer renewal of neighborhoods and cities for 50 years or in some cases forever. The city may die. Some cities are dying in this way. Perfectly good land is abandoned, rendered unrenewable by the cumulative neighborhood effects of counterproductive tax policy.

Land taxes are more neutral than building taxes in the renewal decision, and in perfect capital markets they might be completely so. In practice they accelerate renewal because they drain cash from holdouts waiting for high bids from builders. According to the portion of tax theory that looks at marginal incentives and ignores the wealth and liquidity effects of taxes, land taxes are simply neutral, and in an important sense that is true. But taxes affect behavior in more than marginal ways. They affect it through changing relative wealth and holdout power and credit ratings. The effect of a cash drain on a holdout far outweighs the effect of an equal value of forgone interest on equity because the cash drain lowers his wealth and liquidity. The cash drain of land taxes also conveys information to many owners who are only vaguely aware that they are holding a resource of high salvage value to society. Land taxes build a fire under sleeping owners. Anyone who talks with owners of ripening land soon learns that many who are not in debt perceive their holding costs in terms of taxes more than forgone interest, though the latter be five to ten times as high; and in legislature assembled they put their faith in preferential low assessment of ripening land when they want to forestall its urbanization. If money talks, the tax dollar outtalks the interest dollar, at least the dollar of forgone interest on equity, which speaks in a whisper.

Long-run effects. Taxes also affect the planned life of buildings. Because they act like higher interest rates, they discourage durability, which may be perceived as substituting capital for labor. From this, it is easy to infer that building taxes act to shorten planned life. Easy, but wrong, for the taxes also force substituting land for capital. In the discussion of intensity of use, that meant spreading out in space. Here it means spreading out in time, letting structures stand a long time before demolition.

So we seem to have two contrary forces at work. Building taxes cause us to build less durable structures, but then to defer demolition. These two forces are consistent in that each helps save on capital. They are at odds in that the first appears to shorten life, the second to lengthen it.

The matter is resolved by distinguishing service life from carcass life of buildings. Taxing buildings makes us shorten service life, but lengthen carcass life, thus creating a geriatric afterlife of buildings during which they occupy space without doing much good. Houses are built for faster recovery of capital but slower recovery of site, so that the shells of old structures, the ghosts of departed values, stand to haunt us after they have been drained of most of their serviceability.

This reinforces the short-run effect. Old buildings stay with us a long time, thanks to taxes on buildings, and they stay with us yielding less service.

There are those who oppose demolitions on the ground that they destroy housing for the poor. Federal Urban Renewal Programs and other removal programs have been frightful in this respect, and wanton demolition for "slum clearance" is surely to be condemned. The proposal made by John and Ursula Hicks to exempt new buildings while taxing old[5] is to be faulted for forcing premature demolition. But taxing buildings as generally practiced in the United States today is not defensible on the grounds that it defers demolition because it does so only by weakening the profit motive to rebuild and increase supply. Indeed, taxing old buildings, taken by itself, often causes premature demolition, long before land is ripe for renewal. In tandem with the tax threat against new buildings, it lengthens the dead period between buildings when land is held out of service.

As to land taxes, they are again more neutral, subject to the qualification that the market for capital be perfect. But taxes affect behavior in at least two ways. There is the effect on marginal incentives, discussed above; then there is the wealth effect. Land taxes are neutral in respect to marginal incentives, but they have a definite wealth effect, especially in contrast to the taxation of buildings. Taxing buildings drains wealth from, and creates liquidity crises, for builders; taxing land serves the same discipline to nonbuilders and to the holders of obsolete and inadequate improvements. By this mechanism land taxes affect the market sharply.

Size of Parcel

We have seen that taxing buildings causes the substitution of land for capital. The immediate impact is increased lot coverage. The secondary impact is bigger lots. If there is just so much land in a city, lots cannot get bigger, and the result is simply higher land values. But if a city can spread out, it does, under this influence.

Similarly, taxing buildings discourages subdivision where that means more capital per acre. It discourages converting old estates to middle-class housing, for example, because the tax bill would rise.

[5] J. and U. Hicks, *Report on Finance and Taxation in Jamaica* (Kingston: Government Printer, 1955), chapter 10.

Apartments might seem to be an exception because they involve assembly, but the exception is only specious. The ownership of apartments is unified, as a rule, but the *use* is subdivided. So subdivision, broadly construed, includes the building of apartments. A tax on buildings is quite consistent in its bias against this kind of land use.

Land taxes are not neutral in their effect on the size of parcels, for a reason already cited. Interest paid or forgone is the main cost of holding land. Interest rates are regressive, and as a result, the use of land is regressive. This means that those who enjoy low interest rates spread out over land that at the margin yields them less service than it would yield their credit-pinched rivals. Land taxes displace the interest cost of holding land by a tax cost. They fall harder on those who enjoy lower interest rates and larger land holdings. They tend therefore — assuming true assessment — to equalize land holdings.

Choice of Location

The effect of taxing buildings is not merely incremental in the manner treated so far. It changes the relative bidding power of different uses, and changes the structure of cities.

In a perfect market, uses needing high accessibility cluster around a center of maximum access. Access is mutual, so the presence of those seeking access is a net benefit to others seeking access, and clustering is self-reinforcing, up to a point. Likewise, uses needing specific mutual access, or access to the same people or things, cluster in specialized neighborhoods and districts. Aggregate transportation needs are minimized, for any level of linkage. There is a logic to market decisions — the "highest and best" use in the market sense also has a good claim to approximating highest and best use in a more ultimate sense of social good.[6] So it is a social cost of moment to deny the market allocation of land without some good reason like a playground, mini-park, or street.

Two rival uses compete on equal terms for land, and represent equally high and good use, when they have the same imputed site value, S.

$$(1) \qquad\qquad S = PVR - C$$

where PVR is the present value of revenues (net, discounted), and C is cost of construction. It is the *difference* between PVR and C that makes site value,

[6] For further discussion and sources, see Mason Gaffney, "Land Rent, Taxation, and Public Policy," *Papers of the Regional Science Association*, vol. 23 (1970), pp. 141–153; and "The Sources, Nature and Functions of Urban Land Rent," *American Journal of Economics and Sociology*, July 1972, pp. 241–57.

not the absolute size of either. Thus a gas station can sometimes compete with an apartment; though present value of revenues is less, so is construction cost. But the effect of building taxes varies with C, the tax base. As between two uses equally high and good, i.e., with an equal *difference* of PVR and C, the building tax intercedes in favor of the one of lower construction cost (C). Although its revenue is less, the gas station outbids the apartment because the apartment would have paid more building taxes.

This is a matter of leverage. A given percentage increase in cost cuts deeper into the residual land value afforded by the more intensive use, because its cost is higher relative to the land value. Let us give that some precision and generality.

We begin by converting the stream of future building taxes to a lump sum, their present value (PV). "Present value" of the stream means if you borrowed PV and paid it off on the installment plan over the life of the building, your annual payment would be the amount of your building tax. The PV of an annual payment of $1 over sixty years is a lump sum of around $13 (discounting future dollars at 7 percent per year compounded). So a property tax rate of 1 percent of building cost is equivalent to a present value of 13 percent of building cost.

This comes out of what a builder can bid for land. He reduces his bid by 13 percent of the cost of the planned building (C). The higher is C, the more the disadvantage.

Let us couch this in terms of the percentage drop in what competing uses can bid for a site. The absolute drop, for each 1 percent of tax rate, is:

$$(2) \qquad\qquad -\Delta S = 0.13C.$$

That drop as a percentage of site value is:

$$(3) \qquad\qquad -\Delta S/S = 0.13C/S.$$

C/S for a high-rise structure might run 8/1. Since $8 \times 0.13 = 104$ percent, the tax reduces the bid by more than 100 percent and so wipes out the site value.

For a $70,000 gas station on a $140,000 hot corner, C/S is ½. Since ½ $\times$ 0.13 = 6½ percent, the oil company can bid only 6½ percent less than if there were no taxes. The effect of building taxes is to give the less intensive use a comparative advantage over the more intensive.

That does not mean the total abolition of high-rise buildings everywhere. This is not the way the world works. It means gas stations get more land, and better land. (They also spread out.) Apartments get less land, and worse. (They also are built shorter.) Gas stations move into the center; apartments move outwards. This helps account for the anomaly of intensive uses popping up on poor land and mixed in with much lower uses, while low uses preempt much of the central land. In general there is a poorer matching of buildings and uses with sites.

The above is a picture of urban disintegration. Our ways of imposing taxes play a role in making cities sprawl. Sprawl, in turn, with attendant suburban enclavization, weakening of metropolitan community ties and facilities, and automobile dependency, spawns many of the problems of class conflict that concern us now.

More directly, the bias against uses with a high building-cost/site-value ratio (C/S) is a bias against the poor, who live crowded at much higher density than the rich and on land of lower unit value as a rule.

I noted earlier that the tax on buildings affected incentives somewhat as would a rise of interest rates. Here we reach the limits of that parallel. The building tax is more specifically targeted against intensive use than is the interest rate. In the extreme, on an unpaved parking lot yielding income with no building, the building tax does not lower its value a bit, while a higher interest rate would lower the value. More generally, in (1), building taxes are proportional to C, while higher interest rates have an effect which is proportional to PVR. Thus the artificial scarcity of capital caused by the building tax is more disruptive to the integrity of urban linkages than is a natural scarcity of capital reflected in high interest rates. Indeed, high interest rates would also make roads and allied infrastructure costlier, raising horizontal transportation costs and raising the premium on central location.

Ripening of Land for Higher Use

Criteria of ripeness. Under dynamic conditions, land is often in transit from one use to another and usually higher use. In anticipation of a move, it develops an "expectation value," or speculative value, that is higher than income from the current best use will support. When should the owner take the quantum jump and initiate the higher use? When is the land ripe for the change?

The choice of ripeness date (D) is difficult because a durable building, indivisible in construction, must be placed on the land to shift its use. As demand for the site grows with each succeeding year, the hypothetical optimal improvement that one would put up if he were going to build in that year changes. Each succeeding year's optimal building yields more net present value to the land.

To avoid premature, preclusive underimprovement or other irreversible error one postpones building – but not forever. R. T. Ely identified himself with the doctrine of "ripening costs" in which he argued the case for deferral, but he failed to supply a criterion for ripeness. *D*-date (ripeness) arrives when the value imputed to the site by each succeeding year's hypothetical optimal building stops rising faster than the interest rate.[7] (This is the same as selecting the date that maximizes present value of the land as of any fixed calendar year.) By not building in Year 1 you forgo — and thus in effect invest — the present value of site (S_1) realizable by building in Year 1 to gain S_2 in Year 2, or $S_3, S_4, \ldots, S_n$. If any

$$(4) \qquad\qquad S_n > S_1(1 + i)^{n-1}$$

then the value of holding the uncommitted site grows faster than money in the bank and is a good investment.

In addition, there is current site income (a_1) from the tag end of the prior use, or from some interim use. Adding these in, a site is not ripe so long as

$$(5) \qquad\qquad (a_1 + \Delta S)/S_1 > i \,.$$

Note that ΔS is not just the yearly rise of land value in the market, but is $S_2 - S_1$ as defined in the previous paragraph. *S* is "use value." It is below market value until the optimal year of building, at which time use value has risen to equal market value. Market value is use value at *D*-date (ripeness) discounted, so market value grows at the investor's rate of interest. Use value (S) grows faster than that until ripeness, by definition of ripeness.

Taxing buildings affects ripeness. We have seen that taxing buildings reduces site values derived from buildings and applies leverage against intensive building. It follows that taxing buildings affects the growth rate of site values, assuming that the optimal building-cost/site-value ratio (C/S) changes with ripening. Thus taxing buildings affects the date of ripeness.

I shall show the following. As land ripens, the effect of taxes on the ripeness date depends on whether further waiting would lead to a higher or lower C/S ratio. Normally it leads to a lower ratio; *C* rises, but *S* rises by a higher rate. The effect of taxes is then to retard ripeness. They make one more disposed to sacrifice an earlier for a later use.

This is the kind of elusive relationship that algebra was invented to nail down. To simplify, assume no current income from a prior or interim use. To simplify the notation, the present value of the stream of future net revenues,

[7]Mason Gaffney, "Replacement of Individual by Mass System," *Proceedings of American Real Estate and Urban Economics Association*, vol. 4 (1969), pp. 21–68. This piece also treats the effect on ripeness of later generations of use, a point omitted here.

PVR in equation (1), is denoted simply as *R*. The growth rate of use value (*S*) is:

(6)
$$\frac{\Delta S}{S} = \frac{\Delta R - \Delta C}{R - C}.$$

Let *T* be the present value of future building taxes, expressed as a percentage of *C*. (We previously illustrated *T* as 13 percent for a 1 percent tax rate; about 15–40 percent is normal, depending on the tax rate and the discount rate.) After taxes, assumed to lodge in lower site values:

(7)
$$\frac{\Delta S}{S} = \frac{\Delta R - \Delta C(1 + T)}{R - C(1 + T)}.$$

Taxes proportional to ΔC reduce ΔS, because ΔC comes out of ΔS. But taxes also reduce *S*, the denominator of the rate. Which factor prevails? The rules of algebra provide an answer.

The effect of taxes is to raise the growth rate of *S* if:

(8)
$$\frac{\Delta R - \Delta C(1 + T)}{R - C(1 + T)} > \frac{\Delta R - \Delta C}{R - C}.$$

By cancellation (or inspection), (8) implies

(9)
$$\frac{\Delta C}{C} < \frac{\Delta R}{R}.$$

By inspection, (9) is true if *C/R* is falling. I shall call *C/R* the cost/benefit ratio. From (1), *R* is $(C + S)$, the sum of building and land value, so:

(10)
$$\frac{C}{R} = \frac{C}{C + S}.$$

Thus *C/R* is simply the share of building cost in real estate value. Falling *C/R* implies falling *C/S* as well.

Intuitively we think that land ripens into higher intensity, but intuition is a blind guide here because it compares incommensurables: building *value* per unit of land *area*. Economic intensity compares commensurables: building value and land *value*. Our *C/S* and *C/R* are proper indices to economic intensity.

For several reasons, I believe ripening usually entails a drop in C/R. C rises, but R rises at a higher rate, so C/R falls. These reasons are developed in section II of the Appendix. So the usual effect of taxing buildings is to retard ripeness by raising the percentage growth rate of the use value of the site. I conclude that the paramount effect of building taxes on ripeness is to defer it.

The demonstration above must be tempered to allow for the evasive action of the taxpayer faced with the threat of a tax on buildings. This modification is in section III of the Appendix.

Occasionally, ripening would lead to a higher C/R. Then the effect of building taxes is to advance ripeness by making the later use relatively less attractive. The point of consistency is that intensity loses either way. Taxing buildings makes landholders more patient to wait for lower uses, but less patient to wait for higher uses. But section II of the Appendix shows that excessive patience is the rule.

Neighborhood effects add to the retarding influence of building taxation. Part of ripening is not waiting so much for greater demand but for greater certainty. Certainty means waiting for neighbors to commit themselves. But Alphonse waiting for Gaston simply perpetuates uncertainty when Gaston is waiting for Alphonse. Much of the rationale for ripening is a hyperindividualistic one that does not bear examination from a social viewpoint and can only be painted a social good by committing the fallacy of composition. "We have no plans," said a San Francisco land speculator, "we're waiting for other people's plans." In such a context, whoever leads off ripens his neighbor's land and shortens the sterile downtime of land between major improvements. Building taxes that retard the improvement of one site thus retard the ripeness of neighboring complementary sites by generating uncertainty. Uncertainty of this kind in a highly complementary urban neighborhood is an external nuisance every bit as noxious as odors, fumes, noises, and shadows.

I remarked earlier that the property tax on buildings affects investor behavior somewhat as would a rise of the interest rate. In respect to ripening that is not true. A higher interest rate would also require the use value of sites (S) to grow faster to remain unripe; but a higher building tax rate has no such effect. Indeed, the macro nationwide effect of having buildings taxed in all jurisdictions is to lower the level of interest rates that investors require land to earn.

Turning to land taxes, they would be largely neutral if credit markets were costless. It is widely believed that they speed up ripening, but the belief has been wrongly rationalized. It rests mostly on assuming that land taxes are piled on top of interest costs of holding land. But land taxes are capitalized into lower values, and thereby supplant interest costs rather than supplement them, as already noted. The reason that land taxes hasten ripening is that ripening land is mostly held by strong hands whose comparative advantage lies in holding assets where the main cost is paying interest on loans and forgoing interest on equity. Hastening the ripening of such land is simply an aspect of the transfer from rich to poor that land taxation effects via differential capitalization (see Appendix, section I).

Frequently the date of ripeness is outside the owner's direct control and depends on when public works are extended. Today, in many suburban areas, sewers are controlling. Here, land taxes cannot speed ripening until sewers are built. But they can then speed private building to match public building and effect great savings on public capital of all kinds.

Land taxes also have important distributive effects. Future sewers have a present value to landowners. Values rise above farm levels — not once and for all, but incrementally along a line wiggling around a basic compound interest growth curve. This annual accrual of value is a current income, in the true economic sense, just as depreciation is a current cost. Land taxes levied ad valorem on the base of this selling value are a way of tapping this accruing income for the public. Appreciation is proportional to value; the tax is proportional to value; therefore the tax is proportional to the appreciation.

Arguments against taxing appreciating land do not therefore hold water on the grounds on which they are usually presented — i.e., that ripening land yields no income. They do, however, make sense to the local interests whose welfare is the bottom line of the municipal enterprise. Land taxes redistribute income from landowners to other voters and immigrants. From the parochial Mercantilist view this is bad. From the national view, where the welfare of migrants and labor are a greater concern, it might be valued more positively.

It is traditional to blame premature building and sprawl on ad valorem assessment of ripening land. Premature extension of public works is more guilty, coupled with postmature conversion of ripe land close-in, made unripe or submarginal by taxes on building.

Aside from wealth effects, land taxes are neutral in their effect on date of conversion, so long as they are not contingent on the date selected. Noncontingency is the same principle that makes land taxes neutral towards other land use choices. Suppose someone were panicked by rising land taxes into premature urbanization of farmland, as is sometimes feared. What would he gain? Either he would overimprove and lose money the first few years; or he would gauge his building to the slim early market, and in a few years be locked into an underimprovement while his land assessment and taxes kept on rising.

If he behaves rationally he will not convert land sooner because of tax carrying costs. The time permanently to convert land use, with or without taxes, is when the rapid rise of value begins to taper off. Then the land is ripe. This happens when the city has grown out to abut the land in question. Land taxes should tend to help conversion be less disorderly than now by equalizing carrying costs among owners of different credit ratings. Land assessments should also be given a quantum jump when public works are supplied, triggering action, prompting owners to fill in compactly and developers to sell quickly, lest the public investment in the works be sterile.

Land taxes would encourage premature conversion if the assessor maladministered them, i.e., if he raised them until the owner improved the land, then locked the assessment at that level. Under that system, the owner could buy himself a low assessment by early underdevelopment. Some assessors do maladminister like that. The solution is the building-residual method of assessment: assess the land at what it would bring if vacant; then assign the building the residual value.

Aggregate Local Effect of Property Taxes on Supply of Buildings

Building taxes. The overall effect of taxing buildings is to reduce the service flow from a municipality of given area. We have seen this in several aspects.

Intensity falls, in terms of quality, durability, and height especially. There is some compensatory tendency toward increasing lot coverage, the strength of it depending on whether people have somewhere else to go. If they do, lots get larger as buildings ramble.

Site renewal slows down greatly. This slowdown, coupled with less durable buildings, creates slums and out-of-service land. Each old building robs neighboring sites of their renewability, and the extreme result is nonrenewable, abandoned neighborhoods.

Building taxes magnify the motive to withhold land for ripening. The virtue of avoiding premature commitment is distorted into the vice of postmature commitment. Within a neighborhood the delay can be indefinite, as each separate owner, waiting for certainty, imposes uncertainty on others. In the still larger scene of the entire metropolis, postmature building in truly ripe areas disperses demand outwards. Development takes place in outer areas that are made to look ripe from a local viewpoint, even after taxes, but are grossly premature in the regional plan. This is the more likely when central city tax rates become substantially higher than suburban.

Taxing buildings tends to favor larger parcels and discourage subdivision and apartments.

Last, taxing buildings weakens the relative bidding power of more intensive uses in competing for land, and changes the structure of cities. Gas stations and parking lots push high buildings out of the center. Out-of-service lands break up complementary clusters, and cause urban sprawl.

The combined effect is to reduce the service from any given amount of land and to diffuse demand over a wider area than is necessary, economical, or socially desirable. This result is a kind of forced consumption of land, plus forced consumption of capital, as sprawl inflates the infrastructure costs of urbanization. This heavy capital cost dashes the hope that moving out to cheap land in the old frontier tradition may open up land for housing the mass market.

Land taxes. The overall effect of taxing land is toward equalizing the intensity of use between rich and poor by displacing regressive interest costs with the tax. That means intensifying the use of land, because most land is held by the rich; but it means more land per family for most families, because the median family is far below the mean in income and even lower in wealth.

Taxing land is redistributive, the more so when the proceeds go to finance schools and welfare. So long as localities were infected with a wish to grow, and an egalitarian philosophy, land taxes found strong support. In today's mood of local Mercantilism, which questions growth and leans to elitism while still seeking local efficiency and community, tension and ambivalence surround the local taxation of land.

EFFICIENCY, EQUITY, AND POLICY

Policies of forced consumption of land and capital achieve their ends at high cost in social efficiency. They reduce density below what sovereign consumers evidently desire, running up heavy public costs in the process. They retard renewal and create slums. They frustrate the mass market desire for cheap land and cheap housing.

They make cities disintegrate in several ways. Building taxes weaken the relative power of intensive uses to compete for the most accessible land. Underemphasis on land taxes, as by underassessment and zoning dodges, causes the most rentable land to go to the strongest hands with superior financial power, rather than to the most productive use. A weak seller far out often looks better to a builder than a strong holdout close in. Zoning as we practice it is self-defeating, because a builder's biggest profit comes from breaking the zoning rather than following the rules and paying a high price for land already zoned to his needs. Long extension of the ripening period creates too many niches for shoddy interim uses that disfigure the American city.

The policies force consumption of more land and capital than consumers want. And they inhibit adequate development of mass systems like transit and sewerage that depend on high density.

The set of policies also militates against social equity and sense of community. They are consistently biased against the poor and school-age children and their parents, contributing to class division and the generation gap. They are biased against people, contributing to the unemployment problem that federal policy alone has now proven powerless to abate. If Tawney was right that a society is rich when material goods are cheap and human beings dear, then these policies work to impoverish society. They treat people as a pollutant.

Remedial policy can be at once radical and conservative. It needs to be radical in the sense of being pervasive and transcendent. That is, we need policies that will change local incentives and nudge local decisions in the humanist direction, as opposed to a series of running battles forcing local officials to go against what they perceive to be their interest.

Policy can be conservative in the sense that small changes can tip the balance between exclusionary and philanthropic policies. Cities have powerful incentives to attract people, as well as to resist them. The two large forces are about evenly balanced. It was not long ago, after all, that the growth booster was an American stereotype. Heaven protect us from his most barbaric manifestations, but he does display a set of motives for welcoming immigrants. What is needed now is to tip the scales of local incentive in favor of receiving human immigrants, as opposed to exclusive emphasis on capturing capital, public works, and territory.

Policy can also be conservative in retaining local control over local matters. There is great administrative efficiency in having each local government handle as much as possible, motivated towards efficiency by having its own bottom line to maximize. It is not important that the profit or equity be large. It is important that profit vary with, reward, and motivate local efficiency.

It would not work to withdraw local zoning power. Zoning and other exclusionary devices are means to ration access to local public schools, and in lesser measure to parks, streets, and other common properties. To take away the LG's exclusionary powers would cause them to starve the teachers and sell the parks for commerce. They would not pay for good schools if these simply attracted more large, poor families to share the schools and dilute the tax base. Fighting the good fight against snob zoning will boomerang on the warriors if it results in lowering school support. The object after all is not just access to land for housing, but also to good schools. The object is not just to equalize school access, but to improve schools.

The most important feasible radical-conservative policy change to achieve these goals today is to shift "foundation" school financing to the state level, and the property tax along with it. A year ago that was far out. Suddenly it is imminent and probable.

School children entering a community complete with a generous voucher for tuition, social dividend, or other device for allocating state funds by school population would be a local fiscal asset. LGs would compete to attract them. It would become financially respectable to be a human being.

Much else would then fall into place as a result of voluntary local action. And the property tax itself, as a state institution, could be remodified: all the exclusionary features that characterize local assessment practice could be changed. The site value tax with exemption of buildings would make more sense than it does now from the local viewpoint. And rates could be much higher than now, with less fear of repelling fiscal surplus generators. Property could carry more of the tax burden, lightening the load on regressive sales and payroll taxes.

A concurrent change should be a higher emphasis on user charges gauged to social cost. Exclusionary policies now are an indirect device to ration use of local commons. They are very inefficient devices with more side effects than effects, and readily perverted to antisocial goals as we have seen. If we don't like autos we should tax autos, not houses.

User charges today are perverse. We tax water supply and exempt private wells, tax sewer use and exempt septic tanks, tax mass transit and exempt autos and streets, and so on. Within mass systems, rate regulation makes rich territory (which houses poor people) subsidize lean territory and rich people. All this needs to be worked over, on marginal cost principles. The effect on land use would be a conservative, economical, accountant-directed humanitarian revolution.

Changes in federal tax policy are also needed. Congress needs to take the fun out of land speculation by hitting capital gains in a dozen ways, thus encouraging cities to use their capital budgets to serve their median citizens rather than the strong hands who hold speculative land and inveigle councilmen. Washington might also share the social dividend of school finance, raising the revenue by kinds of tax reform that encourage better land use.

Cities could expand with sharp edges, coordinating zoning and tax assessment with extension of municipal services, developing close-in land compactly for median citizens, letting the wealthy average-raisers outside pay their own way.

Congress needs to stop the competitive underassessment of land by local assessors, described above, which makes a mockery of the federal income tax by letting people avoid taxes by depreciating land not just once, which amounts to complete exemption of land income, but several times, which amounts to a large subsidy for holding title to land. There is no substitute for federal review of assessments – a federal board of equalization, in effect. Otherwise, local assessors will continue overvaluing buildings relative to land to inflate the depreciable share of real estate owned by their local constituents.

These economic policy suggestions do not displace the legal steps discussed by others here, but supplement them in our mutual quest for the lost sense of American community and purpose. These are exciting times, and there will be much excitement in implementing and detailing the policy shifts sketched above. Nobody said it was going to be easy.

APPENDIX

I. Differential Capitalization of Taxes on Land Value

Let a = annual net income of land before land tax (but after other taxes)
  i = rate of interest
  t = rate of yearly property tax on land value
  V = market value of land = assessed value of land.
With $t = 0$

(1) $$V = \frac{a}{i}.$$

This is simple "capitalization" of income into value.
  With $t > 0$

$$V = \frac{a - tV}{i},$$

$$V(i + t) = a,$$

(2) $$V = \frac{a}{i + t}.$$

Equation (2) is the classic algebra of tax capitalization: the tax is capitalized into a lower value.

Now assume that credit rationing divides the capital market into two groups, Poor and Rich, who pay (or forgo) two different interest rates, p and r.

(3) $$p > r.$$

Equation (2) now tells us what each group can bid for land, using p or r in place of i. This is *diffential* capitalization. Rich outbids Poor for land yielding each the same net income (a), and even for land yielding Poor more income, up to:

(4) $$\frac{a_p}{a_r} \geq \frac{p + t}{r + t}.$$

But taxes (t) lower the bids of Rich more than bids of Poor. Bids of the Poor are cut in half when $t = p$, but bids of the Rich are cut in half at the lower $t = r$. More generally, equation (4) says that raising t dilutes the effect of p being higher than r, tending to equalize bidding power of Rich and Poor.

I have simplified by omitting that the lower bidder must figure on taxes on a value established by the higher bidder, but the simplification merely understates without changing the conclusion.

To restate in terms of yearly carrying costs, c,

(5) $$c = V(i + t).$$

The poor pay more to carry a given piece of land, because the cost is mostly interest. Again I understate by simplifying. The poor not only pay higher rates, they borrow on shorter terms, so their carrying costs include a heavier amortization factor as well. The self-financed landowner has no debt to amortize, and no cash drain but taxes.

But as t is made larger, V falls, so Vi falls, and the impartial tax cost displaces the regressive interest cost.

The effect of the tax is greater when land is appreciating. Let V rise yearly by g, a percentage. Deduct this from c (we could instead have added it to income). Now

(6) $$c = V(i - g + t).$$

(6) shows that g leverages or fortifies the effect of p being greater than r, in contrast to t which dilutes the effect.

Thus appreciating land gravitates to "strong hands," i.e., those who borrow at the prime rate, or don't have to borrow at all. And by the same token the equalizing effect of land taxes is most pronounced when applied to appreciating land. A numerical example based on (6), when $p = 0.08$ and $r = 0.05$, follows.

$$\text{Ratio of Carrying Costs } \frac{c_p}{c_r} = \frac{0.08 - g + t}{0.05 - g + t}$$

$t \backslash g$	0	0.02	0.04
0	8/5	6/3	4/1
0.02	10/7	8/5	6/3
0.04	12/9	10/7	8/5
0.06	14/11	12/9	10/7
0.08	16/13	14/11	12/9
0.10	18/15	16/13	14/11

II. Why Land Generally Ripens into a Lower Intensity

Let C = capital cost of building

R = present value of future net revenues or cash flow from building

S = use value of site = $R - C$

$$\frac{C}{R} = \frac{C}{C + S} = \text{cost/benefit ratio } (C/R) .$$

1. There is a hierarchy of land uses, qualitatively different. While each one is of variable intensity, they are discrete, with a quantum jump from one step to the next, as from grazing to row crops, row crops to orchards, acreage to lots, singles to walk-ups, walk-ups to high-rise, and so on.

Demand is generally rising, and land succeeds from one generation of use to another. Each use has an inner margin where it is the lower use, less intensive than its inner rival; and an outer margin where demand is weaker, or land is less suited, and it is the higher use, more intensive than its outer rival.

"Marginal" land connotes low intensity, but the connotation is misleading. It is based on a physical or per acre concept, while economics is concerned with values. The essence of economic marginality is that $C/R \rightarrow 1$, the cost/benefit ratio approaches unity. In these terms, marginal land is the *most* intensively used. As demand rises and costs fall, land yields a surplus. As the rings in the hierarchy of land uses expand, and a site shifts from the outer to the inner margin of its ring, it becomes less marginal and more rentable, and C/R falls.

2. Land ripens because of falling building costs as well as increasing demand. Obsolescence is a continuing expectation, an ineluctable factor in all decisions (independent of inflation and overstated fatalism about union wage rates, not at issue here). Of course, falling C means lower C/R.

Another general reason to expect falling *C* is economy of scale. As demand grows, a larger building is appropriate. There are great economies of scale in building.

Land can also ripen into a new generation of use at lower density. A quarter or more of many central business districts has ripened into parking lots, for example, and many a house has been knocked down to expand a gas station apron.

Another kind of falling cost generally to be expected is lower borrowing rates of interest. This results from better creditworthiness of land as the proposed use becomes less marginal, innovative, or experimental in an area. As the land ripens into a better credit rating, *R* rises because it is the discounted value of future revenues, and a lower discount rate is relevant.

This last factor is partly circular, but that is the nature of credit ratings. It depends on the cumulative process of forming conventional opinion among lenders, few of whom supply much venture capital.

3. Empirical studies generally show that *C/R* is lower on better lands. It is very low in Champaign County, Illinois, or Benton County, Indiana, the best grain land. It is very low in Kuwait, the best oil land. It is quite low in Manhattan, the best urban land; generally lower on retail land than residential; lower in central cities than fringes; lower in rich suburbs than poor ones. It is lower for Site I timber lands on the western slope of the Coast Range in Oregon than for Site VI lands in the high Cascades. To some extent that may reflect underutilization of better land due to cartel behavior, the soporific effect of surplus income on owners, and other institutional factors, but it probably is more basic than that — basic as that is!

4. Time generally brings public works, paid by others, to lower costs. This is one factor in increasing demand, already postulated, but it is also a factor in lower costs. Thus extension of city sewer and water precludes septic tank and well.

Figure 1 is a schematic representation of these relationships.

III. Effects of Building Tax on Intensity and Ripeness Combined

In equations (7) and (8) in the text, I proceeded for simplicity as though *C* and *R* in each year would be the same despite the threat of building taxes. Actually, the landowner would turn to less-intensive alternatives so *C/R* would fall. This would almost certainly entail an absolute decline in both, as well.

Thus, consider all cases where

(1) $$C(1 + T)/R > 1.$$

That means

(2) $R - C(1 + T) < 0.$

i.e., the use value is negative, taxes have made the particular use of land submarginal. But they have not made the land itself submarginal. The owner can find a lower use whose

(3) $C(1 + T)/R < 1.$

Now posit a base intensity-path, without taxes, following the course charted in Appendix II, with C/R falling; apply building taxes, and let the

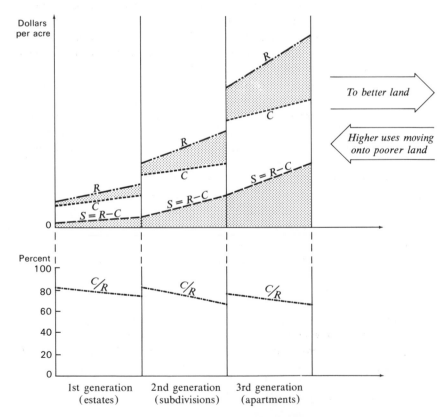

Figure 1. Costs, revenues, use values of sites, and intensities (or cost-benefit ratios), comparing succeeding discrete generations of uses as land ripens into higher uses.

taxpayer change his path, to avoid taxes optimally. He will lower C/R where it is highest, i.e., at the beginning of the path. Thus C/R will be lower at the start and will drop less along the path. This, in turn, reduces the high after-tax growth rate of S, and reduces the retarding effect on ripening.

The net effect of all this is a combination of two evasive wiggles. In general, he builds less, later. The emphasis depends on particulars. He may build much less and a little later; or a little less much later; or any combination.

LEGAL ASSAULTS ON MUNICIPAL LAND USE REGULATION

IRA MICHAEL HEYMAN

For good or ill, the institution of land use regulation is far from being a dead letter. I firmly believe that we are, or will be, relying more heavily on regulation as time progresses, especially to protect environmental goals. But a major trend away from the municipal monopoly on land use regulatory powers has emerged, and there are strong tendencies toward the reorganization of governments at the state and local levels and the assignment of land use regulatory powers to higher echelons. This trend should have important impacts on future land development processes.

A BRIEF HISTORY

Zoning and subdivision regulation on any real scale came into being in the United States during the first quarter of the twentieth century. The objectives were relatively benign, and the assumptions were simplistic. The most important objectives were threefold: to segregate inconsistent uses; to prevent con-

---

IRA MICHAEL HEYMAN is professor of law and city planning at the University of California, Berkeley. He previously practiced law in New York and served as law clerk to Chief Justice Earl Warren. He is the author of numerous articles on land-related environmental problems and has acted as consultant to the Tahoe Regional Planning Agency, the San Francisco Bay Conservation and Development Commission, and a number of government agencies concerned with limiting development for environmental ends. Mr. Heyman was born in 1930 and has an A.B. degree from Dartmouth College and an LL.B. degree from Yale University.

Author's note. This paper was prepared as a speech intended to provoke discussion among the participants of the RFF conference recorded in this volume. Thus, many of the ideas are not fully worked out, and the author cautions the reader that the purpose of the exercise is to paint a relatively broad picture and discern probable major trend lines. The investigation is far from definitive.

gestion; and to provide for the economical provision of public services. To accomplish these, within the then-conceived limitations of governmental structure and constitutional prohibitions, zones would be established at the municipal level within which certain uses (with attendant bulk and yard requirements) would be permitted as "of right," that is, without need for individualized administrative treatment and merely by proof of compliance with the stated law. Zones would be cumulative from single-family homes to relatively unrestricted use. They would also be few in number and large in size. A minimum of legislative and administrative flexibility was envisioned. Amendments, especially boundary changes, would occur when conditions changed, but only on an extraordinary vote in the case of protest. An individualized administrative variance might be issued, but only for unique hardship cases.[1]

There were at least five crucial assumptions upon which the original system was built. First, a simplistic segregation of uses would result in a quality urban environment. Second, it would be possible, in drawing the zoning map, to formulate an intelligent all-at-once decision to which the market would conform. Third, the governors of the system would rarely change the rules. Fourth, nonconforming uses would go away. Fifth, municipal power would accomplish the goals. Most of these have proved to be wrong.

Undoubtedly, land use control at the municipal level has had some beneficent effects, especially as it has become more sophisticated. It has reduced some situations that give rise to land use conflicts and has thus aided certainty of expectations and marketability of property — especially residential property. It has permitted somewhat better planning for the provision of public services. It has been increasingly useful for various environmental ends. It has permitted a local neighborhood majority to act in concert in situations where one or two landowners could destroy neighborhood values. It has helped to maintain the special character of selected areas, such as ones of historic importance. It has provided a vehicle for shifting some public costs to development, especially through subdivision exactions.

But land use control at the municipal level has largely failed to accomplish many of the original and emerging goals. It has not been able to withstand pressures created by an active market. The extraordinary congestion in downtown Manhattan and San Francisco is proof of this. It has not been able to withstand intermunicipal competition for tax revenues and business activity.

---

[1] In "Innovative Regulation and Comprehensive Planning," *The New Zoning* (N. Marcus and M. Groves, eds., Praeger, 1971), I spell out the reasons for my belief that we will rely more heavily on regulation as time goes on, and review and analyze early zoning objectives at much greater length.

The felt shortages of strategically placed open spaces in metropolitan areas attest to this. A host of other examples could be mentioned.

Perhaps one of the principal effects of land use control at the municipal level has been to buttress exclusionary tendencies. This objective was undoubtedly unintended, at least consciously, by the fathers of land use control. But it was not wholly unanticipated. It is instructive to recall the words of the district judge in the famous *Euclid* case who, as we know, was reversed in the United States Supreme Court:

> The plain truth is that the true object of the ordinance in question is to place all the property in an undeveloped area of 16 square miles in a strait jacket. The purpose to be accomplished is really to regulate the mode of living of persons who may hereafter inhabit it. In the last analysis, the result to be accomplished is to classify the population and segregate them according to their income or situation in life.[2]

It seems safe to say that a great many people prefer to live in the midst of cultural homogeneity. The typology of homogeneity is difficult to state. In its simplistic forms: many whites want to live apart from blacks, or at least low-income blacks; many blacks want to live apart from whites; many middle- and upper-income people want to live apart from lower-income people; ethnic enclaves have a tendency to persist, for both inclusionary and exclusionary reasons.

Presuming that the generalization is roughly true, how do groups of relatively homogeneous people seek to assure relative cultural isolation? The very wealthy can often buy exclusivity in large estates protected by restrictive covenants. Those who reject mainstream values can depart for rural communes. But the middle class, especially the white middle class, does not have these options. It seeks to rely on governmental, quasi-governmental, and private institutions.

The most accessible governmental institutions are local ones. And the ones most amenable to such use are the rich profusion of suburban general-purpose municipal governments that abound, and can still be created, in our metropolitan regions. And, as previously stated, it is to these governments that we have heretofore entrusted general jurisdiction over land use controls.

We should not be surprised, therefore, that land use controls, together with a number of other manipulations of legal institutions at the local level (such as the refusal to create a public housing authority) have played an important part in barring low-income persons, especially members of minority groups, from access to many suburban areas.

[2] 297 F.307.318 (N.D. Ohio 1924), rev'd. 272 U.S. 365 (1926).

Municipal land regulation has been far from a total success in accomplishing many of its more benign objectives, but as Robert Weaver reports,[3] and as the National Commission on Urban Problems (Douglas Commission) suggested earlier,[4] it has been fairly successful as an exclusionary tool.

ATTACKS ON MUNICIPAL LAND USE REGULATION

Six of the major sources of assault on municipal land use regulation are explored in this paper: the environmentalists; the lawyers; the market; the manifold proponents of open housing (especially the civil rights movement); state governments; and the federal government.

The Environmentalists

The Council on Environmental Quality recently published *The Quiet Revolution in Land Use Control*, by Fred Bosselman and David Callies, in which the authors review nine innovative land use regulatory systems, most of which have been fashioned and adopted to protect physical environmental values. The striking feature of all of them is that they interfere, often substantially, with the municipal land use control monopoly.

The systems are premised on the realization that a municipality cannot provide rational treatment for ecological systems that transcend local boundaries. Moreover, many of the systems reflect the fact that a local jurisdiction, because of perceived self-interest, will take actions that are harmful to the combined interests of a larger constituency. California provides two striking examples.

The San Francisco Bay Conservation and Development Commission now has almost exclusive jurisdiction over development in San Francisco Bay.[5] This amounts largely to regulating the filling and dredging of the Bay and adjoining tidelands. Prior to the creation of this regional agency, nine counties and a host of cities, whose geographical boundaries extended into the Bay, were the sole determiners of whether shallow portions of the Bay would be filled. Such filling was proceeding at a rapid rate for various types of

[3] Robert Weaver, "Housing and Associated Problems of Minorities," in this book.

[4] *Building the American City* (House Doc. No. 91–34, December 12, 1968), pp. 211–17.

[5] Fred Bosselman and David Callies, *The Quiet Revolution in Land Use Control* (Council on Environmental Quality, December 15, 1971), p. 108 (hereinafter cited as *The Quiet Revolution*). See also Jack Schoop and John Hirten, "San Francisco Bay Plan: Combining Policy with Police Power," *Journal of the American Institute of Planners*, vol. 37 (January 1971), p. 2.

development. No local government saw reason to interfere — action by a single unit would simply deprive that jurisdiction of revenue and business-producing activities with no assurance that its competitors would act similarly. Moreover, no locality perceived that its sanctioned fill would create large problems. This situation resulted in the transfer of a rather important quantum of land control power to the San Francisco Bay agency — an upper echelon of government, which could at least consider regional benefits and costs in its regulatory decisions.[6]

The Tahoe Regional Planning Agency is an even more significant innovation because it has almost full power to supersede the land use regulations of local governments (some six in the Tahoe Region).[7] It has already adopted a plan and ordinances that significantly control zoning, subdivision standards, grading, and shoreline development. Additional ordinances are under preparation. Again, the reason for the shifting of power upward was the realization that local governments, practically speaking, were unable individually to withstand the extraordinary development pressures that were bound to result in a significant decay of the total regional environment.

California is far from unique. Bosselman and Callies analyze the Massachusetts Wetlands Protection Program, the Maine Site Location Law, the Wisconsin Shoreland Protection Program, the Twin Cities Metropolitan Council, the Vermont Environmental Control Law, the Hawaii State Land Use Commission, and other systems. A brief review of some aspects of these systems will illustrate the point.

An important ingredient of the Massachusetts legislation is state agency control of coastal wetlands.[8] The Massachusetts Department of Natural Resources is authorized to issue protective orders defining the boundaries of the coastal wetland areas and prohibiting any development except under carefully controlled circumstances. As the study reports, "the orders are filed in the title records and become binding restrictions on the use of land. To date about one-third of the state's coastal wetlands have been covered by protective orders and another one-third are in various stages of public hearings."[9] While the legislation permits stricter regulation by local entities, it interestingly makes no provision whatsoever for local government participation in the state's regulatory program. The state agency is directed to hold its own public hearings and to work directly with private landowners in the

[6] See Note, "Saving San Francisco Bay: A Case Study in Environmental Legislation," *Stanford Law Review*, vol. 23 (1971), p. 349.

[7] P.L. 91–148 (91 Cong., Dec. 18, 1969). See *Report of the Lake Tahoe Joint Study Committee* (March 1967).

[8] *The Quiet Revolution*, p. 205.

[9] Ibid., p. 209.

issuance of protective orders and to administer its own permit system. As might be expected, local officials, if they are interested, are consulted by the department, and the few town boards that desired direct involvement were accommodated. Generally speaking, however, primary (and nearly complete) land use control over vast areas of coastal wetlands has passed from local to state control.

Vermont's Environmental Control Law[10] is much more pervasive. This 1970 act created a State Environmental Board of nine members and seven regional commissions of three members each. Any residential subdivision consisting of ten or more lots of less than 10 acres, any housing, commercial or industrial development of substantial size, and any development above the elevation of 2,500 feet requires a permit from the State Environmental Board. Applications for permits are reviewed by a state interagency committee, which sends recommendations to the regional commission. The commission holds a public hearing at which comments may be offered by local planning commissions. The regional commission then decides whether or not to issue the permit. In order to grant a permit, ten conditions must be met. Some of these relate to environmental characteristics — water pollution, waste disposal, water availability, soil erosion, scenic and aesthetic values. Some relate to other matters — burden on government services, highway congestion, conformance with local and state plans. Appeals from commission decisions can be made to the State Environmental Board by the applicant, state agencies, and local governments. The Vermont Environmental Control Law also calls for the State Board to adopt a state capability and development plan and a state land use plan.

The Vermont system, which is a model for state and regional assumption of land use control, was stimulated by a boom in second homes and ski resorts and a backdrop of very little local exercise of land regulatory powers. Vermont had a perfectly adequate set of enabling acts, however, and the local decisions to forgo use of them was a choice for market dictation of the development process. But when it became clear that environmental values were seriously jeopardized, the state intruded in a manner that substantially undercut the probabilities of future local control.

The other examples in the Bosselman-Callies monograph tell much the same stories. And the examples they give are only the seminal undertakings. Similar agencies are now being created or proposed in nearly all the states, even those with mature local governments and a historic bias toward home rule. It is only a matter of time, for instance, before California creates a state

[10]Ibid., p. 54.

coastal commission and multipurpose environmental agencies with jurisdiction over open-space preservation, among other matters, in her great metropolitan areas such as the San Francisco Bay area, Los Angeles County, and San Diego County.[11]

The lesson of this trend is clear. Municipal governments will be increasingly shorn of significant land use control powers in order to protect environmental values.

The Lawyers

Another assault on municipal land use regulation is coming from the legal fraternity through one of its most prestigious (and conservative) institutions – the American Law Institute (ALI). The Institute, which has sponsored various restatements of the law and model and uniform statutes that have had considerable impact, has been struggling with a Model Land Development Code for nearly four years.[12] There is good reason to believe that the effort will produce a product that is acceptable to the Institute membership and that will be adopted in the near future. Whether or not this occurs, the draft sections already circulated are affecting lawyers' attitudes and are providing bases for new legislation in a number of states. Three major sets of provisions in the circulated drafts of the Code are of importance to the subject of this paper.

First, the draft Code's planning section, which replaces the old Standard Planning Enabling Act, calls for what might be called an impact statement relating to social concerns.[13] The Code provides for long-range planning and short-run programming, with emphasis on the latter. In both instances, the Code suggests (although perhaps it should require) text analyzing the probable social and economic consequences of provisions of a proposed plan or program, including the impact on population distribution by characteristics (such as race and income) and an evaluation of the consequences of alternative plans and programs. While this direction is addressed to local governments, the identification of these outcomes could have powerful influences upon extramunicipal politics.

The second set of provisions of particular relevance appears in the section on land use regulation and represents an attempt to "legalize" land use con-

---

[11] Bills have been introduced and vigorously debated concerning both matters.

[12] American Law Institute, *A Model Land Development Code*, Tentative Draft No. 1 (4–24–68); Tentative Draft No. 2 (4–24–70); and Tentative Draft No. 3 (4–22–71). Citations below are to Tentative Drafts No. 2 and No. 3 (hereinafter cited as *ALI Draft 2* and *ALI Draft 3*).

[13] *ALI Draft 2*, § § 3–102(5); 3–103(2); 3–104(2); 3–105(2)(e).

trols which, as practiced, consist largely of ad hoc or piecemeal decision making despite the facade of prestated standards and certainty.[14]

These provisions therefore impose explicit and detailed procedures for making rules and for granting permits. The latter require records as well as hearings and written findings. Again, these sections are directed at local governments, but the disclosure of the actual reasons for local decisions is intended to facilitate extralocal review.

Finally, and of most importance, the Code provides the detailed machinery for state planning, state regulation, and state administrative review of local land use decisions.[15] It is unnecessary to review these provisions in detail here, for many of the features have already been discussed in connection with the Massachusetts and Vermont statutes. But three aspects deserve mention.

First, the Code provides for a State Land Planning Agency with power to designate geographical areas of critical concern to the state and to subject local regulation in such areas to state review and approval.[16]

Second, the Code identifies four types of development of special "state or regional benefit" and requires local governments to approve such developments, even if they are inconsistent with local land use regulations, if the "probable net benefit . . . exceeds the probable net detriment" as determined under ten explicit factors stated in the Code.[17] The State Planning Agency may be a party to the proceeding, and the local decision is appealable to a State Land Adjudicatory Board. One of the four categories is "development by any person receiving state or federal aid designed to facilitate a type of development specified by the State Planning Agency by rule." The notes to the section make it clear that this category includes subsidized housing, such as public housing and sections 235 and 236 housing. This provision follows to some extent the Massachusetts Zoning Appeals Law,[18] which authorizes developers of low-income housing to apply to the local government for a "comprehensive permit" in lieu of all other permits. If the permit is denied, the developer can appeal to a state board – the Housing Appeals Committee – which has the power to vacate the denial and direct the issuance of a permit if the denial was not "reasonable and consistent with local needs." Under another portion of the statute, local regulations are consistent with local needs if they are "reasonable in view of the regional need for low and

[14]Ibid., § § 2–303 to 2–305.
[15]*ALI Draft 3*, Articles 7 and 8.
[16]Ibid., § § 7–201 to 7–208.
[17]Ibid., § § 7–301 and 7–502.
[18]40B Mass. Gen. Laws Ann. § § 20 to 23 (Supp. 1971).

moderate income housing." This, and a succeeding sentence, are a bit of legislative legerdemain that results in the setting of quotas. The local government is then protected if it refuses permits once the quota has been reached.

Finally, under the Model Code, the State Planning Agency is empowered to define large-scale development that is likely to present issues of state or regional significance, and to subject such development to special review processes somewhat similar to the processes applicable to development of special state or regional benefit.[19]

The American Law Institute Code does not go nearly as far as the Vermont statute, for instance, in superseding local land use controls. Nor does it go so far in selected areas of regulation as do the two California regional agencies previously discussed or the Massachusetts wetlands legislation. Nevertheless, it sets up the general machinery for significant state intrusion upon local land use control by setting forth specific criteria against which to judge whether particular local land use decisions make regional and statewide sense and by subjecting such decisions to state administrative review where the presumptions of regularity and validity that normally attend judicial review are largely unavailable to the local government. Finally, the Model Code, unlike the environmental statutes, permits the state agency to supersede local vetoes; in other words, to license certain development over the objections of local governments.

The Market

A third assault on municipal land use regulation will predictably come from the new participants in the land development market. Richard Babcock has pointed out that in the past fifteen years the "housing industry has undergone evulsive change" with "corporations, national in scope, immense in capital, and diversified in market ambitions, announcing . . . entry into the housing field by acquisition or by internal expansion . . . . These sophisticated aggregates are chagrined to discover that village codes are a major barrier to marketing their dwelling-related products,"[20] many of which, for various reasons, consist of all or component parts of low-income housing.

The participants as Prototype Site Developers under "Operation Breakthrough," for instance, include such national firms as Aluminum Corporation of America, General Electric, and Republic Steel.[21] These firms, and others

[19] *ALI Draft 3*, § § 7–401 to 7–405.

[20] Richard Babcock, "The Courts Enter the Land Development Market," *City*, vol. 5 (January–February 1971), p. 59.

[21] Carter Burgess and Sidney Friedberg, "NHP: A New Opportunity for Housing," *George Washington Law Review*, vol. 39 (1971), pp. 870, 888–89.

such as Westinghouse's Urban Systems Development Corporation and Aerojet-General Corporation are investing considerable money in a variety of innovative housing techniques both with and without the sponsorship of the Department of Housing and Urban Development (HUD).[22] By February 1970, the National Corporation for Housing Partnerships had raised over $12 million from an impressive array of corporate sponsors including Armco Steel, Kennecott Copper, Reynolds Aluminum, and Boise-Cascade.[23] Standard and Poor's in 1971 reported that "A development of major significance in recent years has been the growing penetration of the total housing market by the large, well-financed, and often publically owned tract and community builders."[24]

Babcock concludes that "the impact of this change in the housing industry on the allocation of governmental power can be profound."[25] This conclusion seems warranted. First, these new participants can effectively seek state and federal legislative and administrative intervention to override municipal bars to their products. A good example is the recent spate of legislation creating state boards to license prefabricated housing, thus overriding inconsistent local code provisions.[26]

Second, well-capitalized industrial entities are in a position to invoke judicial review of local exclusionary regulations and to test their validity. They can finance the delay, especially if big projects are involved. This will create opportunities for repetitive judicial reflections on the rationality of local regulations that are inconsistent with regional needs.[27]

The Use of the Courts by Proponents of Open Housing

A fourth attack on municipal land use regulation has come from litigation by proponents of open housing. Dan Fessler's paper in this volume addresses the legal questions raised in the vast number of lawsuits brought mainly by lawyers deeply involved in the civil rights movement. Some noteworthy battles have been won. If federal or state courts could be convinced to adopt legal theories that could be easily relied upon to strike down municipal land

---

[22] *Business Week* (March 17, 1970), pp. 32–36.

[23] *Business Week* (Feb. 14, 1970), p. 83.

[24] *The Outlook: Building for the Future* (Standard and Poor's Corporation, 1971).

[25] Babcock, "The Courts Enter the Land Development Market," p. 59.

[26] See *Automation in Housing* (September 1971), pp. 42–43, reporting the adoption of such acts in nineteen states, and consideration of such acts in nearly every other state. See also Note, "An Analysis of the Probable Impact of the California Factory-Built Housing Law," *Stanford Law Review*, vol. 23 (1971), p. 978.

[27] See e.g., *In re* Kit-Mar Builders, 439 Pa. 466, 268 A.2d 765 (1970); *In re* Girsh, 437 Pa. 237, 263 A.2d 395 (1970).

use regulations that operate to exclude low-income persons from residency, the utility and impact of municipal land regulation would be seriously undercut. It seems somewhat doubtful at this point in time, however, that doctrines with such sweeping impact will be embraced by the judiciary.

Fessler discusses three potential bases for federal court negation of local regulations such as large lot zoning, exclusion of multiple dwellings, and prohibition of mobile homes: equal protection, supremacy, and substantive due process.

A successful *equal protection* attack might proceed from a judicial determination (1) that the purpose of a particular regulation was to exclude members of racial minorities; (2) that a regulation producing such an effect, regardless of purpose, was invalid; or, more broadly, (3) that a regulation having the effect of discriminating on the basis of wealth was invalid. Judicial acceptance of the third proposition would seriously weaken the validity of much zoning, especially in the suburbs. And the cases would not be difficult to litigate because the factual basis could be proved statistically. But, for the reasons Fessler indicates, it is highly doubtful that the federal courts (or state courts) will embrace this view. Similarly, it is doubtful that the courts will adopt the second position, although there is some arguable precedent for it.[28] More likely, the federal courts will only interdict local regulation on the basis of equal protection when it is shown that the locality adopted or perpetuated a regulation for the purpose of excluding (or ghettoizing) a racial minority.[29] Such a judicial position would require individualized proofs of a difficult order in each case and would seriously blunt the efficacy of the judiciary as a tool for achieving open housing.

The *supremacy* doctrine — that state and local laws that are inconsistent with federal law based on express powers (in this case, the Thirteenth Amendment) are invalid — offers an attractive opportunity, as Fessler establishes, to the federal executive and legislature to sweep away a variety of local regulations that exclude disadvantaged minorities. But the judiciary alone will not do this, it will require the action of the political arms of government.[30]

[28] *Dailey* v. *City of Lawton*, 425 F.2d 1037 (10th Cir. 1970); *Kennedy Park Homes* v. *City of Lackawanna*, 436 F.2d 108 (2d Cir. 1971). But see *James* v. *Valtierra*, 91 S. Ct. 1331 (1971), where "motive" or "purpose" was not found, and despite "effect" of racial exclusion the local regulation was upheld.

[29] *Dailey* v. *City of Lawton; Kennedy Park Homes* v. *City of Lackawanna; Crow* v. *Brown*, 332 F. Supp. 382 (N.D. Ga. 1971).

[30] In *Shannon* v. *HUD*, 436 F.2d 809 (3d Cir. 1970), the court read the history of housing and civil rights legislation to create a national policy requiring HUD to take into account racial concentration in dispersing federal housing subsidies. It is quite doubtful, however, that a federal court on supremacy grounds would invalidate local laws that exclude without a direct and bold Congressional statement to that end. The probabilities for such legislation do not seem high.

Finally, Fessler investigates the doctrine of substantive *due process*. This doctrine essentially asks the judges to substitute their value judgments for those of the legislature on matters not treated of directly in constitutions (i.e., matters other then speech, religion, search and seizure, and criminal procedure). The judges are importuned to rule that a particular regulation is invalid, usually as applied, because it does not accomplish a particularly important purpose and/or it unreasonably interferes with other values. Thus, for instance, a litigant attacking a zoning ordinance that completely excludes mobile homes from a town might argue *seriatim* that the exclusion serves no useful purpose, that the exclusion is inconsistent with other town regulations (permitting, for instance, semipermanent occupation of motel units), that the exclusion is inconsistent with the regional need for locations for lower-income residents, and that the regulation thus arbitrarily interferes with the rights of the owner to use his property.[31]

Fessler concludes, properly in my view, that it is unlikely that federal courts will make free use of the *substantive due process* approach in reviewing local regulation.[32] On the other hand, as Fessler argues, it is much more likely that state judges will be willing to find local regulations with exclusionary impacts "unreasonable," especially if the state constitution, or state legislation, contains language leading generally in that direction. Some recent cases might indicate a trend line.[33]

What the foregoing indicates is that judicial attack on municipal land use regulation will most likely continue to exert pressure toward either regionalization of the low-income access problem or at least selected judicial vetoes of particular municipal policy decisions that operate to deny access to low-income residents. The frequency of such suits will increase as the new participants in the market find such grounds effective. But judicial attack will not produce rapid across-the-board change, because the courts appear unwilling to premise decisions on sweeping doctrinal grounds.

Before leaving this topic, reference should be made to the recent decision of the California Supreme Court in *Serrano* v. *Priest*.[34] *Serrano* held unconsti-

---

[31] See e.g., Judge Hall's classic dissent in *Vickers* v. *Gloucester Township*, 181 A.2d 129, 148 (N.J. 1962).

[32] But see *Southern Alameda Spanish Speaking Organization* v. *City of Onion City*, 424 F.2d 291 (9th Cir. 1970) and the District Court's subsequent determination, No. 41490 Memo. of Decision by Sweigert, J., filed 7-31-70.

[33] E.g., *In re* Girsh, 437 Pa. 237, 263 A.2d 395 (1970); *In re* Kit-Mar Builders, 439 Pa. 466, 268 A.2d 765 (1970); *Board of County Commissioners* v. *Casper*, 200 Va. 653, 107 S.E.2d 390 (1959).

[34] 5 Cal.3d 584, 96 Cal. Rptr. 601, 487 P.2d 1241 (1971).

tutional the California scheme for financing public education, determining it to be a denial of equal protection of the laws, under the federal and California constitutions, to discriminate on the basis of wealth in the provision of public education. The culprit was reliance on the property tax, at least for a good portion of the local education bill. The solution will probably be to greatly increase the financing of public secondary and primary education from the state level. Such a solution would have interesting implications on exclusionary land regulation, even if restricted solely to education. At least in California about one-half of the local property tax goes to local school districts. Shifting this revenue drain to the state level would deprive the municipality of its principal public *raison d'être* for exclusion, the shortage of local funds. If *Serrano* is extended to other municipal services, the argument for exclusionary zoning becomes even weaker. Adoption of the *Serrano* doctrine *might* make some suburban cities less unfriendly to the dispersion of some of the disadvantaged to their jurisdictions; it would certainly make it harder to justify refusal to accommodate newcomers. It *might* make laws like the Massachusetts quota system unnecessary. It *might* make negotiations carried out by regional entities more fruitful. But the extension of the *Serrano* doctrine to other states or to other municipal services is highly uncertain.[35]

State Governments

The environmental movement is largely responsible for the creation of a number of state (and regional) agencies that are playing an increasingly important role in land regulation. These agencies have usually been given negative powers and can do no more than veto land uses and development licensed by local governments. But we are beginning to witness the evolution of state agencies that function positively. The state planning agency proposed in the ALI Model Land Development Code, for instance, is given power to override local development vetoes in selected cases. And developments in New York provide a good example of state efforts with the potential for positive action.[36]

Nelson Rockefeller, when first elected governor of New York in 1958, moved rapidly to strengthen the Office of the Governor as a policy planning

[35] But see Kenneth Karst, *"Serrano v. Priest*: A State Court's Responsibilities and Opportunities in the Development of Federal Constitutional Law," *California Law Review*, vol. 60 (1972), p. 720.

[36] The following description of developments in New York is based largely on Vincent J. Moore, "Politics, Planning, and Power in New York State: The Path from Theory to Reality," *Journal of the American Institute of Planners*, vol. 37 (March 1971), pp. 66 ff.

center. This move was followed by a number of steps that have made state planning and implementation more effective in two regards. First, the activities of state functional agencies are better coordinated. Second, a variety of state public benefit corporations have facilitated financing, programming, and construction of capital facilities, including low- and moderate-income housing.

In the course of Rockefeller's first three terms (1958–70), New York created the Office of Planning Coordination, a series of multicounty regional planning boards, a planning-programming-budgeting (PPB) system, a number of "super departments," and a series of public benefit corporations, as mentioned above. The regional planning boards have become neither regional general-purpose governments nor state instruments operating regionally with some local representation, as originally hoped. The rest of the apparatus, however, has clearly strengthened the state hand and, concomitantly, drained some powers away from local government. Continuation of this trend seems probable.

The public benefit corporation is a central feature in the New York approach. One example is the State University Construction Fund. The other, of particular interest to this paper, is the New York State Urban Development Corporation (UDC), the board of which is appointed by the governor. UDC has the authority and capacity to undertake four types of projects: residential projects consisting of low- and moderate-income housing, industrial projects, civic projects, and land improvement projects. It is empowered to acquire land by purchase or condemnation, to override local zoning and building codes, and to build, sell, manage, or lease any of its projects.

As reported by Moore,[37] UDC facilitates private investment in subsidized housing and needed industrial development by doing the necessary planning, site acquisition, and political negotiation to obtain required zoning and code changes before the private developer is brought into the process. UDC is reimbursed out of the mortgage proceeds and "receives a fee for its developer services and risks."

As of October 1, 1970, two years after its establishment, UDC had seventeen projects under way, including 7,500 housing units, and had committed another 43,000 units in twenty-six different localities. While its policy has been to go into a city only when invited by local officials (although this has meant a mayor's invitation even over the objection of city council members), this might change, at least in degree, when UDC becomes financially independent.

[37]Ibid.

New York has a record of pioneering with innovative techniques, many of which are later adopted in other states. A successful program of the sort described will undoubtedly be copied by other urban states. Thus we see another source of erosion of the municipal monopoly on land use regulation.[38]

Federal Stimulants

From the great variety of federal programs ranging from planning grants to river basin commissions, I have selected only a few prominent undertakings, or prospects, that bear particularly on the continued vitality of municipal land use regulation.

There are two especially noteworthy programs that have been adopted and one program that, if adopted, will further erode the municipal monopoly over land use controls: metropolitan clearinghouse review; HUD policy regarding the distribution of subsidy funds for housing;[39] and pending measures involving national land use policy.

The Office of Management and Budget Circular A-95, which implements Title IV of the Intergovernmental Cooperation Act of 1968, provides for review of applications for assistance under more than 100 federal grant and loan programs by state, regional, and metropolitan clearinghouses.[40] The reviews, which are advisory only, seek to identify the relationship of the proposed project to area comprehensive plans. The review requirements, originally established for metropolitan areas by a 1966 statute,[41] have stimulated the creation of numerous councils of government and the preparation of regional and metropolitan plans.

A-95 review, as practiced, will obviously not regionalize land use regulation. But it does provide an evolutionary base for negotiation between a regional agency and local governments regarding municipal exclusion of development of regional consequence. The experience of the Dayton, Ohio, area exemplifies this possible trend. There, the Miami Valley Regional Planning Commission devised a plan "to disperse in four years 14,000 units of feder-

---

[38]Various other laws shifting licensing power to state levels have been passed, especially concerning installations which localities resist but which are deemed necessary for the general welfare. Siting of power-generation plants is a good example.

[39]If revenue sharing, with payments directly to local governments, comes to pass, it will exert a contrary pressure.

[40]William Brussat, "Realizing the Potentials of A-95," *Planning 1971* (American Society of Planning Officials, 1971), p. 57; Vincent Smith, "The Intergovernmental Cooperation Act of 1968: Opportunity for State Government," *Planning 1971*, p. 61.

[41]Section 204, Demonstration Cities and Metropolitan Development Act of 1966.

ally subsidized housing throughout the Dayton, Ohio, metropolitan area on a 'fair share' basis, computed on the basis of both community needs and capacities – in other words, a plan to build low- and moderate-income housing, including public housing, in white suburbs.[42] The plan was unanimously adopted in 1970 by the local elected officials who constitute the commission, and its chances of success appear substantial. A-95 type review is one of the levers for commission implementation, but, more important, it appears to have been the prime stimulant for the creation of the regional commission that provided the crucial framework for building metropolitan consensus.

In *Shannon* v. *HUD*[43] the Third Circuit Court of Appeals held that federal statutes have created a national housing policy, which mandates that HUD act affirmatively to eradicate residential segregation, both de jure and de facto, in federally assisted housing.[44] HUD has issued project criteria for public housing funds and housing subsidies that favor projects located away from areas of minority concentration.[45] In addition, HUD is seeking to give priority funding on water, sewer, urban renewal, and model cities grants to communities that adopt areawide planning goals and provide housing accessibility on a nondiscriminatory basis.[46] Secretary Romney reported in December 1971 that, of 117 low-income housing projects started during the latter half of 1970 in six metropolitan areas (Baltimore, Washington, San Diego, San Antonio, Pittsburgh, and Jacksonville), 77 were in suburban areas and 40 within central city areas. Whether or not these figures are significant, it seems apparent that HUD is making a serious effort to disperse low-income housing. The political future of such efforts is problematic.[47] But recent legislative activity gives reason to expect more, rather than less, federal action in the future.[48]

A variety of legislation has been introduced in the past few years with the objective of requiring the states to engage in land use planning and regulation.

---

[42] Lois Craig, "The Dayton Area's 'Fair Share' Housing Plan Enters the Implementation Phase," *City*, vol. 6 (January–February 1972), p. 50.

[43] 436 F.2d 809 (3rd Cir. 1970); noted *New York University Law Review*, vol. 46 (1971), p. 561.

[44] See also *Gautreaux* v. *Chicago Housing Authority*, 296 F. Supp. 907 (N.D. Ill. 1969).

[45] *Congressional Quarterly*, vol. 30 (January 8, 1972), pp. 50–55.

[46] Ibid., p. 64.

[47] The Ashley proposal, H.R. 9688, 92 Cong. 2 sess., for instance, for metropolitan housing councils patterned on the Dayton experience (*Congressional Quarterly*, vol. 30, January 8, 1972, pp. 50–55), was recently defeated in the House.

[48] See survey of legislative activity in *Congressional Quarterly*, vol. 30 (January 8, 1972), pp. 50–55.

In their latest embodiments,[49] states would be induced to create state land-planning processes and land use programs to control the siting of key growth-inducing facilities, the construction of large-scale developments, and the protection of areas of critical environmental concern.[50] Such legislation can be seen as a part of an emergence of a nascent "national urban growth policy" discussed in 1971 by Norman Beckman.[51] Serious interventions of these sorts will by necessity undercut municipal self-determination.

SPECULATIONS ON THE FUTURE

What are the probable land development consequences of today's broad trend toward regionalization? At the outset two points should be noted. First, the various sources of pressure towards change have different goals and strengths. The environmental movement, for instance, is not centrally concerned with the dispersion of low-income persons throughout a metropolitan area as is the civil rights movement. Second, it is considered less of an invasion of local prerogatives to create a regional or state agency that can veto a development licensed by a local government than to empower such an agency to license a development that a local government has traditionally had authority to veto.[52] Therefore, objectives that can be accomplished through a system that reviews local determinations, and weeds out unacceptable development, stand a better chance for implementation than objectives that require imposing a regionally important development on unwilling localities.

The seemingly most powerful stimulant toward regionalization of land use regulation is the environmental movement. Four chief reasons support this assertion. First, the conditions it opposes are concretely perceived as ones requiring extralocal control: air and water pollution, loss of open space, disappearance of undeveloped shoreline, and freeway traffic. Second, these conditions are part of everyday life and not ones that are visited primarily on

[49] S. 632, S. 992, 92 Cong. 2 sess. See Land Use Policy and Planning Assistance Act of 1972, Report of the Senate Committee on Interior and Insular Affairs, Report No. 92–869 (June 19, 1972).

[50] For a broad treatment of these matters, see Herman Ruth, "Elements of a National Policy for Land Use," *Planning 1971*. See also Melvin Levin, "The Big Regions," *Journal of the American Institute of Planners*, vol. 34 (1968), p. 66.

[51] "Development of National Urban Growth Policy: Legislative Review 1970," *Journal of the American Institute of Planners*, vol. 37 (1971), p. 146; "Toward Development of a National Urban Growth Policy: Legislative Review 1971," *Journal of the American Institute of Planners*, vol. 38 (1972), p. 231.

[52] This statement excludes, of course, matters that traditionally have been administered at the state level, such as highway location and construction.

deprived classes or racial groups. Third, a large constituency of politically able and influential persons are interested in these problems. Finally, for many people the costs of environmental quality do not enter into the calculus of decision making because the trade-offs involved are remote or the added costs as distributed do not seem consequential. There are few persons, for instance, who consider the probable increase in electricity rates occasioned by regulations prohibiting the use of low-grade fuel oil with a high sulfur content. Similarly, there has been very little public concern with the cost consequences of the automobile emission standards promulgated under the Clean Air Act of 1970.

If the recent past evidences what is likely to occur in the near future, we can predict the creation of numerous regional and state agencies empowered to veto locally licensed development.[53] The veto power will take the form of both zoning-type regulations (such as the Hawaii state conservation zone where urban development is prohibited in advance) and performance standards (such as the regulations of the Tahoe Regional Planning Commission requiring elaborate mechanical systems to preclude siltation otherwise produced by land development). Such regulations will almost invariably render development more expensive by internalizing costs that previously were externalized. Thus, in the Tahoe example, for instance, the developer and his buyers will have to pay the cost of cleaning up storm runoff rather than having discharged wastes cause pollution that is harmful to other users of the lake. And the probabilities are substantial that the regulations will be considerably more onerous than at present, especially as the regulating agencies will, at the outset at least, be devoted to the single goal of environmental protection and will not be charged with responsibility for solving associated social problems, such as housing and employment.

If these predictions are correct, the environmental movement will produce agencies that will slow down development and make it more expensive, thus increasing the exclusionary effects of present local land use regulations. (Low- and moderate-income housing projects, for instance, will have to satisfy two reviews, not the single local one as at present.) Local government resistance to regional edicts involving these subjects will not be intense because the local constituents, at least in the suburbs, will generally agree with the regional goals. Agreement, in fact, will be easy because the regional regulations will operate primarily to the disadvantage of nonresidents who might like to move in; existing homes and businesses will be largely unaffected. The acceptability of tough regional environmental regulations will be even more pronounced

---

[53] Nearly every environmental agency studied by Callies and Bosselman exercises this type of authority.

where courts embrace the *Serrano* v. *Priest* doctrine. For if the states assume a larger share of fiscal responsibility for schools and other local services, suburban governments will find it less necessary to attract industry (and provide housing for workers) to solve their fiscal problems.

Four of the other pressures for change will act at variance with the environmental stimulant in form and, to an extent, in goals. Open housing proponents are seeking to emasculate local veto powers. Market pressures operate similarly. State efforts of the sort exemplified in New York and provided for in the ALI Model Land Development Code authorize state licensing of regionally important development over local objection. Federal policy is conflicting, but HUD dispersion policies and metropolitan clearinghouses for federal subsidies seek to overcome the potency of local opposition to development of regional importance.

The proponents of open housing, while seemingly well-organized, do not appear to be nearly as powerful politically as the environmental movement. Their constituency is considerably smaller. The goals are central to a relatively small group; in fact, dispersion is viewed ambivalently by many minority persons and resisted in the suburbs.

Despite the foregoing, it is possible that the proponents of open housing will occasionally be able to wrest concessions from suburban representatives, perhaps as the price for supporting the creation of an environmental agency at the regional level. This might be demonstrated by some theorizing about the San Francisco Bay Region.

The minority population in central cities of the Bay region continues to grow. Political organization within this population has become much firmer. More minority members occupy offices of considerable influence. Many minority members are quite suspicious of proposals to create regional agencies of any kind. These are seen as part of a strategy to strip local governments of power just at the point when minority voters are likely to take over control of some of these governments. (Oakland and Richmond are good examples.) These fears, whether real or imagined, jibe nicely with the fears of some suburbanites who equate regional government with central city rule. The attitudes of the minority population also could lead to cooperative relationships with groups whose economic interests are most endangered by effective environmental controls. Given a situation where minority political leaders control an important swing vote, it is not inconceivable that the price for creating a regional entity with powers to protect environmental values will be the assignment to such an agency of power and responsibility involving social concerns as well. If the San Francisco Bay Conservation and Development Commission were being proposed today, the quid pro quo might well be access by minorities to housing near new industrial employment opportunities in the suburbs. This would make particularly good sense because a strict prohibition on filling in the Bay has made it increasingly difficult to locate new industry in the central cities where minority concentrations are highest.[54]

While coalition political efforts of the sort described will be successful only occasionally, combinations of housing producers and state and federal officials might prove to have greater vitality.

Open housing proponents will undoubtedly continue to bring court actions that will exert pressure in selected instances. Judicial intervention alone will not seriously undercut municipal land regulatory power on a national scale unless, as is doubtful, federal courts adopt a position that equal protection renders invalid regulations that have the *effect* of excluding persons on the basis of wealth or race. In the absence of such a holding, litigation will be successful where discriminatory purpose can be shown and, more broadly, in those states where courts are willing to judge the reasonableness of particular regulation by taking into account its regional implications. In most instances, this will require case-by-case litigation with each determination based on the particular mixture of facts that are proved. Such litigation creates opportunities for upsetting a particular regulation hitherto invulnerable to attack, but case-by-case assaults in expensive lawsuits will not alone produce sweeping change. The availability of judicial remedies, however, might be a useful political lever in a number of negotiations.

The strength of open housing proponents should be augmented by the resources of the new participants in the housing market. If the present trend continues, and it might well be furthered by federal programs like "Operation Breakthrough," large politically influential corporations will have a financial stake in breaking down parochial barriers to low- and moderate-income housing. Such corporations should perceive the advantages of state and regional agencies that can license development barred by local regulation, and should be willing to spend money and exert influence in support of the creation of such agencies. Moreover, to the extent that litigation can play a useful role, such corporations predictably will be willing and able to pursue judicial remedies. Their cases will be strengthened because they will be "representing" not only their shareholders but also the consumers of their products.

State governments might well follow the lead of New York in creating instrumentalities with authority to supersede local decisions for selected types of development. They will be importuned to do so by housing producers, open housing proponents, and central city politicians. Moreover, espe-

---

[54] The mayors of large cities, for obvious reasons, have also been active in supporting legislation to permit metropolitan dispersion of low-income residents.

cially in the large urban states, the plight of the disadvantaged is increasingly viewed as a state problem. One must not discount, however, the large suburban representation in state legislatures and the vitality of suburban resistance to the erosion of "home rule" powers.

The federal government might play an important role. The most realistic possibility is through metropolitan planning and review agencies of the sort stimulated by the A-95 process. William Wheaton in 1967 called for a metropolitan allocation agency with power to negotiate with local governments concerning population placement by racial and economic classes, the location of metropolitan facilities, and the location of revenue and employment-generating sources.[55] The agency's stick would be control over state and federal grant-in-aid. Such an instrumentality is only one step away from the emerging A-95 agencies and could be an effective means for implementing a variety of federal policies, including the HUD principles guiding the location of federally subsidized housing. Other means are also available.[56]

The other pressure for change is coming from the lawyers as reflected in the ALI Model Land Development Code. An intriguing aspect is the attempt to legalize planning decisions — by establishing and enforcing procedures that require disclosure of the reasons underlying decisions to permit or bar a proposed development, and by requiring estimates of the social and environmental effects of such decisions. Such a system of required disclosure would affect local planning determinations in two important ways. Local officials would have to face up to the moral and regional consequences of their actions. And local decisions would be vulnerable when subject to effective extralocal judicial or administrative review. Both effects tend to impose de facto limitations on parochial decision making.

CONCLUSION

We are witnessing a substantial transfer of land use control from the local to regional and state levels. Professionals have long called for this move, and lawyers, as well as planners, are now beginning to act institutionally to achieve it. More important, however, there are new participants in the process, and the group exerting the greatest contemporary pressure is the environmental movement. As power moves upward in response to the pressure, newly created state and regional agencies are likely to exercise their negative powers to prevent development that would have adverse impacts.

[55] William Wheaton, "Metro-Allocation Planning," *Journal of the American Institute of Planners*, vol. 33 (1967), p. 103.
[56] See notes 48 and 49, supra.

The stringent exercise of these powers will probably restrict the actions of landowners far more than zoning does now. If rulings are based on environmental considerations alone and social goals are ignored, development will become more expensive, heightening exclusionary impacts.

The new agencies will provide a governmental framework that could be used to achieve social outcomes. Whether they will be so used will depend on the vitality of the new participants in the housing market and the proponents of open housing. The ability of the housing groups to produce state and federal interventions that override local development vetoes will determine the substantive outcome of the movement of land regulation power upward.

CASTING THE COURTS IN
A LAND USE REFORM EFFORT:
A Starring Role or a Supporting Part?

DANIEL WM. FESSLER

In opening this discussion of zoning laws and their effect upon a poor man's search for housing, it may be appropriate to observe that poverty law, like Ulysses in his epic journey, has been everywhere but "home." Yet the rising level of disruption in living patterns occasioned by urban renewal, coupled with a growing consensus that as an immediate living environment and source of employment opportunity the central city constitutes an island of misery, indicates that the poverty law movement may soon be "homeward" bound. If this prediction represents an accurate prophecy, it may be followed by a second: that such a homeward journey will encounter a substantial barrier in the multiheaded Hydra that guards the more affluent suburban and exurban areas of our society — zoning ordinance schemes.

In this paper I examine the sophisticated, widely deployed client service organizations that are increasingly at the command of low-income citizen suitors and assess the chances for their success or failure in attacking exclusionary land use controls. I begin by charting the dimension of the legal arsenal currently at the disposal of the educationally and economically disadvantaged, an arsenal placed in a dynamic perspective by the legal services movement. After describing these clients' service organizations, I review re-

---

DANIEL WM. FESSLER is professor of law at King Hall, the Law School of the University of California, Davis, and was formerly a special assistant attorney general. He recently argued as counsel *amicus curiae* in the landmark decision in *Hawkins* v. *Town of Shaw*, 461 F.2d 1171 (5th Cir. 1972), regarding the minimum entitlement demands of the poor on the institutions and services of municipal government. With Charles M. Haar, Mr. Fessler is the author of "Beyond the Wrong Side of the Tracks: Municipal Services in the Interstices of Procedure," *Harvard Civil Rights–Civil Liberties Law Review*, vol. 6 (1971). Mr. Fessler was born in 1941 and holds undergraduate, law, and graduate law degrees from Georgetown and Harvard universities.

cent poverty law developments in order to indicate the potential force that
the poor may marshal through this medium. Moving from this survey of
battle lines to legal strategy, I examine both the Due Process and Equal
Protection clauses of the United States Constitution against the background
of recent case law for indications of an aggressive or passive judicial posture.
The Supremacy Clause and opportunities for employing it to override local
land use preferences in the name of a national housing reform policy are also
considered. After assessing the theories upon which local land use control
may be attacked, I consider the question of whether the state or the federal
judiciary is the most propitious forum and the issue of local versus central
control. Whatever the efficient legal theory, any judge contemplating an activist or interventionist role will be confounded by the fact-finding and planning limitations of the judicial forum. How can such a judicial officer perceive
"the big picture"? How can the court take into account the relevant points
and parties in interest? The discussion emphasizes the limitations that may
inhere in taking a judicial rather than a legislative approach to satisfying the
legitimate social and economic aspirations of those disabled and disadvantaged by the battery of exclusionary zoning devices. For it is these devices
that hold the greater proportion of undeveloped and partially developed
urban and suburban land beyond the economic reach of all but the most
affluent members of our society.

THE LEGAL SERVICES MOVEMENT

An Array of Force

Within the memory of one generation, the concept of the poor going to
court in order to redress real or imagined social and economic injustices
would have been at best an academic exercise. In an era in which the marketplace controlled the division and availability of legal talent, the poor were
simply without means to procure a judicial review of any executive or legislative decision. This reality has not entirely disappeared, but a change is occurring. Today, on a variety of substantive fronts, scattered along a multiplicity
of geographic locations, state and local courts are being enticed into efforts to
redress the balance, if not to reconstitute the social contract framed by those
in possession of economic wealth and political advantage. In a composite
sense, these efforts are a firm indication that the combination of determined
and passive force that sustains the status quo is threatened with assault by an
ancient but heretofore little-used weapon — litigation in the hands of the
disadvantaged. As an alternative to what has proved a futile quest for reform
through the agencies of legislative and executive branches of the government,

this appeal is to a nonmajoritarian and, in that sense, antidemocratic tribunal. The attractiveness of such a course is easily identified. It offers both speed and relative precision to groups that, to this hour, have been either noncombatants or ineffective forces in the logrolling and jockeying for position that yield the distribution of advantage and opportunity within a society.

The concept of taking "city hall" to the local courthouse has never gained broad popular usage in American legal practice. A diversity of factors account for this sparse record. Until quite recently, local governments were insulated from judicial scrutiny by a concept of sovereign immunity. Equally disabling was the rather stringent judicial attitude toward the qualification of an individual citizen to call into question the exercise or processes of executive or legislative decision making. The lawyers' label for this jurisdictional difficulty is "standing." Both sovereign immunity and standing are doctrinal manifestations of a fundamental attitudinal limitation on the willingness of the judiciary to enter the political thicket. Removed beyond the range of effective attack by this double insulation was the value judgment regarding optimum land use capsulized by local building and use ordinances.

Perhaps more decisive in limiting pressure upon both the personnel and the institutions of local government was the absence of any interested segment of the bar. The very individuals or groups who found themselves without economic or political power were the least likely to obtain the "for hire" services of the private bar. Lacking favorable procedural and substantive precedent and faced with the magnitude of the potential defendant, the citizen-plaintiff was dissuaded from seeking a day in court.

Yet in the opening years of the 1970s, with what may strike some as alarming speed, the theoretical barriers to judicial redress seem to have slipped, if not fallen, while the ranks of advocates have become populated by an aggressive and ambitious group evidencing little inhibition about involving either state or federal courts.

Legal services for those without the ability to pay the going rate are not new in this country. Indeed, the earliest manifestations of a legal aid society in America can be traced back nearly a century. Having been initiated to provide legal assistance to immigrants, these efforts were from their inception an urban phenomenon. By the end of the nineteenth century, legal aid societies had been initiated in a number of large cities. In keeping with the attitudes toward public assistance at that time, the community legal aid societies rendered legal advice and representation to the urban poor as a charitable service. While some legal aid offices were manned by a salaried staff, the typical operation functioned with part-time volunteers who attempted to steer prospective clients toward members of the bar who shared a service-oriented concept of a lawyer's professional responsibility. Though assuredly not without accomplishment in individual cases, the typical society was miserably underfinanced, invariably drowned in the wake of a massive case-load, and the source of grossly noncompetitive salaries. Hardly a willing con-tender against the forces of city hall, such an operation was incapable of a sustained law reform effort.

A dramatic shift in the heretofore sporadic governmental involvement was achieved with the advent of the Office of Economic Opportunity (OEO). Both the pressing need for legal services and the fact that nearly all state and metropolitan governments had eschewed any opportunity to assist the local legal aid societies prompted OEO to set up the Legal Services Program in 1965 as one of its major Community Action Programs.

The infusion of federal support (80 percent of a local project's budget is assumed by OEO) was a vital aspect of the post-1965 legal services move-ment. But of greater long-run import may be the "neighborhood identity" and macro law reform objective that the OEO legal services concept has stamped upon this fiscally invigorated movement. As outlined in the project requirements, projects are to engage in a broad program aimed at reforming both civil laws and administrative practices that adversely affect the poor. In more specific terms, the grantee project is charged with the development of a law reform effort that will contribute to the economic development of the community served. To this end, and in order to preserve the integrity of the neighborhood community, the OEO-funded legal services project is enabled to provide advice and representation to organized citizen groups. The model thus developed — a community-based project for promoting community services — is of particular utility in articulating the grievances of the dis-advantaged as well as their aspirations for a future social and economic re-alignment. The legal service grantees are expanding the legal aid scheme of providing legal representation for individual clients on individual matters and escalating the reform objective by commencing lawsuits in the name of the disadvantaged as a class.

While accurate statistics on the legal services movement are not readily available, it is generally agreed that as of 1970 there were some 260 individual legal service grantees. These ranged in size from the California Rural Legal Assistance (CRLA) functioning on a statewide basis to smaller grantees oper-ating neighborhood law offices within a designated municipality or municipal subdivision. In combination, the 260 grantees staff more than 850 law offices and employ approximately 2,200 full-time lawyers. The ranks of these law-yers are frequently augmented by the part-time efforts of law students seek-ing "clinical experience," as well as those of paraprofessionals recruited from the community. In contrast to the estimated expenditure of $5.4 million by all legal aid operations in 1965, the budget for federally funded legal services in fiscal 1969 was $58 million – a level that has been maintained in subsequent fiscal years.

Worthy of particular mention is the OEO-sponsored legal services backup center specializing in housing and economic development. This center, named after former Chief Justice Earl Warren, is located on the Berkeley campus of the University of California. While the greater burden of financing and advancing the legal services movement has fallen upon the Office of Economic Opportunity, the Departments of Housing and Urban Development, of Health, Education, and Welfare, and of Transportation have conducted experiments in funding specialized legal service models. The efforts of HUD have taken the form of two specialized legal services offices in Model City Target Areas.

The accomplishments of the legal services movement to date suggest little ground for comfort or complacency on the part of those benefiting from the current content of local ordinances. The détente between federal and state governments in the area of public assistance has been shattered, perhaps beyond the ability to maintain the existing system, by a series of legal services-sponsored suits that culminated in favorable decisions before the United States Supreme Court. In the area of education, the earliest efforts were aimed at repressing the last vestiges of racial discrimination, but of late there has been an increasing emphasis on the question of school finance. Much remains to be done in this area. Indeed, the vexing issue of school busing is adding dimension to the campaign. By a decision obtained from the Supreme Court of California in the summer of 1971 the historically sanctioned and nationally practiced scheme of tying public school finance to the tax revenues of a given locality was struck down as violative of the Equal Protection Clause of the United States Constitution. In other areas, the efforts of the law reform advocates have borne preliminary success. Somewhat analogous to land use disputes are the municipal service equalization suits that have been waged in a number of communities both large and small. Half-completed campaigns have been successful in the areas of consumer protection, landlord tenant relations, employee's wage garnishments, and the availability of health services.

The competition for land use can be expected to produce confrontations between those who seek a low-income housing opportunity and the established community that is fighting to retain the fiscal and aesthetic integrity of a local status quo. Before I proceed to this specific topic, some general observations on the role of litigation may be in order. First, litigation, or the threat of litigation, is a weapon with which the politically and economically disadvantaged may seek to influence the institutions and officials of local government regarding a host of value judgment decisions, including future land use allocations. Second, the dynamics of the litigation process almost ensure that external value systems and criteria will enter into the process of deciding the issues of "general welfare," equality, and minimum entitlement. Thus, not only is litigation potentially "disruptive" of a local status quo or "power structure" but is inherently at war with a solution that reflects the alignment and realignment of pressures and interests at the purely local level. Even a local judge must decide a legal point with reference to the external criteria reflected in prior case law, and his decision is subject to appellate review by a tribunal of out of towners. These observations suggest that litigation under either constitutional (state or federal) or statutory theories offers an alternative way to bring to a crisis stage the demand for some relief for those who hold the "short end of the stick" on the "wrong side of the tracks." Third, notwithstanding the value of the legal services movement to this previously neglected group, many students of the judicial branch doubt that this apparently most available of governance institutions has the capacity to resolve land use controversies in a manner calculated to produce optimal advantage to the society.

An Emerging Crisis

Two factors seem destined to bring the poor and their advocates into collision with the land use restrictions representing the value judgments of the politically and economically advantaged. The first is the undeniable fact that land is scarce, and in this urban society underdeveloped land is even scarcer. The second is a phenomenon of our decade, the interest of the poor in mobility. The physical decay and general environmental deterioration of the central city has already produced an exodus of the economically affluent. The disappearance of this discernible class of "doers" also reflects their loss of faith that surroundings compatible with cultural advancement and economic prosperity can be restored. It is this absence of venture capital and commitment on the part of the affluent that casts the darkest shadow over both the present and future of our once great urban centers. The interest of the disadvantaged in joining this exodus doubtless follows in part from a perception of these broad and disquieting trends, but for the most part it can be traced to the flight of jobs, for employment opportunity constituted part of the baggage carried off by the affluent. If an individual hindered by low-income status were to decide that his unemployment could be solved only by moving to the suburban and exurban areas, and if – in the words of a currently popular refrain – he were to put "100 down and buy a car," he is likely to find a less than hospitable reception awaiting him in San Jose, to name but one suburban community! The prospective low-income resident is likely to find that a locally adopted comprehensive zoning plan operates to place the greater proportion of land that would otherwise be potentially available as housing beyond his economic reach.

The zoning schema thus encountered is likely to consist of any or all of six basic exclusionary devices: (1) minimum building size requirements usually taking the form of floor space restrictions; (2) exclusion of multiple dwellings; (3) restrictions on the number of bedrooms; (4) lot size requirements; (5) a frontage, or lot width, requirement; and (6) a prohibition on mobile homes. While the de jure thrust of these devices is to exclude the specific deviance or attain the objectives articulated, their de facto impact is economic discrimination against the low-income citizen. A recent report by Paul and Linda Davidoff, who were members of the Urban Policy Project of the Twentieth Century Fund, suggests that these exclusionary land use controls place the greater percentage of undeveloped urban land beyond the reach of all but the most affluent.[1] Their conclusion is that the discriminatory impact sweeps far beyond the immediate interests of the economically disadvantaged to prejudice the economic futures of all but the most advantaged 10 percent of the American urban population. Having surveyed the availability of vacant land in New York, New Jersey, and southwestern Connecticut, the Davidoffs suggest that "public law is being used to preserve perhaps 80 percent of the vacant residential land in metropolitan areas for perhaps 25 percent of the population and, if in fact most of this housing is available to families with incomes above $20,000, then less than 10 percent of all families can compete for it."[2] In this context, the label "snob zoning" is not an abusive accusation.

Given this climate, it may not be an exaggerated vision of the immediate future to anticipate that challenges to local exclusionary land use controls will come from three groups: low-income clients acting through their poverty law advocates, those interested in developing low- and moderate-income housing for profit, and people in the lower and middle income brackets who seek a place in the suburbs. It now remains to offer what is represented only as informed speculation on where these efforts will lead.

THE THEORETICAL APPROACHES TO REFORM AND RELIEF

There are four analytically discernible theories that might be pursued in an effort to defeat the application of "snob zoning" barriers or overturn their existence. Two of them involve federal constitutional claims, the third rests upon an application of state constitutional claims, and the fourth seeks to use

[1] "Opening the Suburbs Toward Inclusionary Land Use Controls," *Syracuse Law Review*, vol. 22 (1971), p. 509.
[2] Ibid., pp. 524–25.

the concept of federal supremacy to parlay the value judgments of a national housing policy into a vehicle capable of overriding the local ordinance restriction. Within the context of a federal constitutional argument, academic discussion has suggested, and the earliest cases have attempted, an application of the Equal Protection and Due Process clauses of the Fourteenth Amendment. In the discussion that follows I analyze briefly the essence of each theory, assess the probability of success given the current status of the law, and, finally, devote a few words to the issue of standing.

The Constitutional Approach

Federal constitutional claims, whether pursued within the conceptual limitations of an Equal Protection claim, or predicated on a Due Process assertion, seek to entice the judiciary to substitute its own value judgments for those of the legislative and executive branches of the government. The hesitancy on the part of courts to enter the political thicket long ago caused judges to divide the activity of government into two broad spheres. The first concerns the question of "what" it is that the government proposes to do or not do; the second, the issue of "how" that objective is pursued. Placed in the framework of traditional legal terminology, the division is thus between substantive and procedural questions.

A political history of the United States Supreme Court reveals (with one error of major exception, discussed in the next paragraph) a recognition that the "what" question, which involves the issue of wealth allocation within the society, is most peculiarly suited to the processes of legislative determination and executive administration. On the issue of "how" the government proposes to treat a citizen, the courts have asserted a greater willingness to scrutinize the procedures employed to the end that citizens might be treated in a manner that comports with "fundamental notions of fair play." Although the problem-solving capacity of the judicial branch is at optimum efficiency in determining the "how" issues of procedural fair play, the evidence is clear that courts are capable of asserting a power of substantive review. Most recently, such review has been undertaken within the context of the Equal Protection Clause. Nearly fifty years ago, however, an assault on discriminatory zoning schemes was attempted by advocates armed with the concept of Due Process. In deference to this early effort, I initially consider the utility of persevering with this historically established posture.

Substantive Due Process

For a brief period of time at the turn of the century the United States Supreme Court was active in substituting its vision of the republic's future for that embodied in the ordinances of the state and national legislatures. The results were, by any standard, disastrous. Utilizing the asserted power of judicial review conferred by the Due Process Clauses of the Fifth and Fourteenth Amendments, the Court struck down such social legislation as the graduated income tax, child labor laws, and the minimum wage for women. In each instance, the Court was able to rationalize the substitution of its social and economic policy judgment for that of the legislature on the ground that the legislature's activity denied private citizens the right to dispose of their property or labor. The hue and cry that greeted this judicial legislation left a mark upon the Court, and for many years the judiciary was highly hesitant. It was the unfortunate fate of those mounting the earliest challenges to zoning ordinances that their cases should mature before the United States Supreme Court during the late 1920s when the activist inclinations of the Court were still in a state of deep freeze.

The challenge to the early attempts at comprehensive land use planning did not find the initial zoning schemes totally lacking in obvious merit. Long before the advent of the twentieth century the involvement of the judiciary in the resolution of land use disputes had a prominent place in the common law system. Such involvement flowed from the attempt of one or a number of citizens to enlist the "law" and thus to solidify and "objectivize" their desire or vision and to enforce the resultant land use pattern upon a recalcitrant neighbor. The theory employed was that of "nuisance." A case for a private nuisance was made out when one in possession of a prior and socially approved use claimed an injury from the land use scheme pursued by a neighbor whose activity was second in time. The common law maxim which sought to accommodate the activities and visions of neighbors was *sic utere tuo ut alienum non laedas* ("use your own property in such a manner as not to injure that of another"). So long as society was in concord with an essentially static land use pattern, the concept of nuisance permitted resolution of the occasional dispute, generally at the expense of the novel or deviant use. The impact of industrialization, with its consequent pressure upon urban populations, destroyed whatever commonality there may have been in a socioeconomic vision of land use. In the face of such confusion, the nuisance vehicle functioned without apparent direction or not at all. This was the condition that prompted the earliest experiments with legislative solution. The resultant theory of a comprehensive land use plan achieving a legal imperative through legislation was hailed as an accommodation of traditional values and dynamic experimentation. "A place for everything and everything in its place." Alfred Bettman, the attorney who lodged an *amicus curiae* brief supporting the constitutionality of a comprehensive zoning plan adopted by Euclid, a small suburban community in Ohio, stated:

The term public nuisance has ceased to have any definite meaning as a measure of legislative power . . . a lawyer would often hardly hazard a guess as to whether his client's proposed industry will or will not be declared a nuisance. . . . The zone plan, by comprehensively districting the whole territory of the city and giving ample space and appropriate territory for each type of use is decidedly more just, intelligent, and reasonable than the system, if system it can be called, of spotty ordinances and uncertain litigations about the definition of a nuisance.[3]

The year was 1926. Bettman's case, *Village of Euclid* v. *Ambler Realty Co.*, 272 U.S. 365, was the first to bring the concept of comprehensive zoning before the high court.

Perhaps it was the force of Bettman's argument that touched a longing for a rational or predictable order. Perhaps it was the temper of the times. Doubtless it was a combination of the two that inspired a majority of the high court to assume a highly noninterventionist posture when subjecting the value judgments implicit in the Euclid ordinances to judicial review. While asserting that such legislative enactments must find their ultimate justification in some aspect of the police power, the majority was clear that the ordinance should not be set aside unless it could be shown to be "clearly arbitrary and unreasonable, having no substantial relation to public health, safety, morals or general welfare."[4] Buttressing the noninterventionist posture of this reviewing standard was the companion presumption of validity and the concept of judicial deference to legislative expertise. In the relatively few cases that have been considered since the decision in *Village of Euclid*, the Court has adhered to what has amounted to giving carte blanche to local municipalities to effect land use planning and control through zoning ordinances. The only articulated restraints were that such ordinances could neither be arbitrary nor unreasonable. Such restraints were devoid of meaningful inhibition given the recognition of legislative primacy in the articulation of policies deemed to promote the public health, safety, morals, or general welfare. In the nearly fifty years that have elapsed since the *Village of Euclid* decision, zoning for

[3] Bettman's brief is quoted in Richard F. Babcock, *The Zoning Game – Municipal Practices and Policies* (University of Wisconsin Press, 1966), pp. 4ff.

[4] Such was the beginning, and yet even at this stage a prophetic warning had been sounded by the lower court which had struck down the Euclid ordinances upon the conclusion that: "The purpose to be accomplished is really to regulate the mode of living of persons who may hereafter inhabit it. In the last analysis, the result to be accomplished is to classify the population and segregate them according to their income or situation in life" (*Ambler Realty Co.* v. *Village of Euclid*, 297 Fed. 307, 316 [N.D. Ohio 1924]).

When one compares the results reported by the Davidoffs with the argument advanced by Bettman, it is evident that there is no longer a "place for everything" or everyone.

aesthetics, for control of population density, and, in some instances, for protecting existing property values has been upheld time and time again. As recently as 1954, the United States Supreme Court in *Berman* v. *Parker*, 348 U.S. 26, 33, declared "it is within the power of the legislature to determine that the community should be beautiful as well as healthy, spacious as well as clean, well balanced as well as peacefully controlled." Although recent decisions in Pennsylvania and New Jersey reveal a more aggressive stance, nonintervention still characterizes most judicial response. Indeed, the recent emphasis upon environmental questions has been noted by one court as exacerbating the difficulty faced by a judicial tribunal that would seek to substitute its judgment for that of the legislature. Reference is to the decision of the United States Court of Appeals for the Ninth Circuit in *Southern Alameda Spanish-Speaking Organization* v. *Union City*, 424 F.2d 291, 294 (1970).

For the low-income would-be resident of a given municipality the question of standing poses an almost insurmountable barrier to the prosecution of a Due Process claim. The literal language of the Fifth and Fourteenth Amendments, that no person shall "be deprived of life, liberty, or property, without the Due Process of law," suggests that the standard of judicial review can only take into account the relative advantage and disadvantage imposed upon those living or owning property within the municipality. There is thus no occasion to regard the interest of the nonresident who may be excluded or tangentially prejudiced. This lack of standing has resulted in the role of party plaintiff being taken by the developer who would construct moderate- or low-income housing in areas where such use would be contrary to existing zoning ordinances. The history of large-scale land developers within the past thirty years has left an unpleasant aftertaste that lingers within the memory and experience of many municipalities, and obviously affects the unarticulated attitude of a good many judges. Until such time as the standing problem can be overcome and the grievance of the low-income potential resident assessed directly, the tainted history of disinterested exploitation that marks the past of many large-scale developers prejudices the outcome of nearly every Due Process case.

In one important context, the standing difficulty has been surmounted. The recently inaugurated federally assisted housing development programs have spawned qualified project sponsors consisting of representatives of low-income citizens. In the *Southern Alameda Spanish-Speaking Organization* (SASSO) case, the Ninth Circuit Court of Appeals had no difficulty in recognizing the direct standing of SASSO in its challenge to the nullification by voter referendum of an approved zoning change that opened a certain tract of land in Union City, California, to low-income multifamily dwellings. At the time it commenced the litigation, SASSO had acquired an option to purchase a tract of land lying within the rezoned area for the purpose of constructing a 280-unit medium-density housing project. Although the decision in *Southern Alameda Spanish-Speaking Organization* thus represents a tactical victory on the standing issue, the ultimate conclusion of the court, when it balanced the police power prerogatives of the local governance structure (there speaking directly through a voter referendum) against the Due Process guarantees, resulted in a denial of relief. Passing on plaintiff's Due Process claims, the court concluded "nor can it be said that the resulting legislation on its face was so unrelated to acceptable public interest standards as to constitute an arbitrary or unreasonable exercise of the police power. Many environmental and social values are involved in a determination of how land would best be used in the public interest. The choice of the voters of Union City is not lacking in support in this regard" (424 F.2d, at 294).

In sum, it can be said that there are three impediments to achieving reform through Due Process claims. First, there is the noninterventionist standard of review adopted by the courts, a policy little changed since its first enunciation by the United States Supreme Court in *Village of Euclid.* Second is the question of standing, which involves the basic unwillingness of courts to accept that nonresidents of a community possess a requisite life, liberty, or property interest cognizable in weighing a balance against the police power objectives represented by local legislative efforts. The final difficulty is, in reality, a manifestation of the second. Since the poor lack direct standing, they are frequently forced to see their beneficial interests squandered in lawsuits brought by developers whose selfish and exploitive economic interests pervade the litigation. A far more stringent or interventionist standard of judicial review is at least potentially attainable under an Equal Protection theory, a topic to which I now turn.

Equal Protection

A potentially viable Equal Protection claim can be established if one can demonstrate a substantial disparity in either the quality or quantity of governmental treatment accorded to identifiable classes of citizens within the same community. Experience in other aspects of poverty litigation has demonstrated that the life span of such a complaint is directly related to the stringency employed by the reviewing court in evaluating the fact of discrimination against the preferred government excuse. If the plaintiffs can qualify for the challenge to restrictive land use ordinances and for an application of the "strict review" standard, the chance of ultimate success is excellent. One avenue is founded on the criteria utilized for the classification; the other rests upon the gravity of the individual or "personal" interest adversely affected. A pattern of discrimination that *either* is predicated upon a "suspect basis of classification" *or* encroaches upon a "fundamental personal interest" of the disfavored citizen is "invidious"; and a violation of the Equal Protection Clause is established unless the defendant can justify his conduct through the vindication of a "compelling governmental interest." A failure to qualify for the strict review standard will nearly always prove fatal to this type of litigation.

Failing to attain the "New Equal Protection," recourse is to the traditional standard under which a reviewing court will defer to a governmental practice if it can be rationally related to any legitimate governmental purpose (even a speculative or imagined one). The governmental defenses of aesthetic or environmental quality, the preservation of community identity, the stabilization of a population so that governmental services might be rationally planned and allocated, and the conservation of the governmental fisc are all legitimate governmental purposes. Yet as recently as two years ago the United States Supreme Court in the welfare residency case specifically held that neither the facilitation of governmental planning nor the conservation of the public purse was a "compelling governmental" interest sufficient to save from Equal Protection condemnation a residency requirement deemed to transgress the petitioner's "fundamental personal interest" in an asserted right to interstate travel.[5] Since both the conservation of chronically insufficient public funds and the requirements of a population stabilized for community identity and planning purposes will be major themes in nearly every answer to a zoning ordinance challenge, it should not require great experience to realize that the issue of selecting the standard of review is a conclusive, not a preliminary, stage of Equal Protection litigation.

The posture of a challenge to restrictive land use controls predicated upon an Equal Protection theory is not encouraging, given the already established criteria for attaining the strict review standard.

By far the most direct route to the attainment of a strict review or interventionist standard of Equal Protection analysis would be to achieve an identification of the low-income citizens' quest for urban land upon which to construct or rent a home as the pursuit of a "fundamental personal interest." Such a proposition is not without indirect support in the dictum of very early Supreme Court cases following the Civil War. In the first *Civil Rights Cases*, the majority of the Court spoke in terms of "those fundamental rights which are the essence of civil freedom, namely, the same right . . . to inherit, purchase, lease, sell and convey property. . . ."[6] This language is greatly weak-

---

[5] *Shapiro* v. *Thompson*, 394 U.S. 618 (1969).

[6] 109 U.S. 3, 22 (1883). And see, *Jones* v. *Mayer*, 392 U.S. 409, 438–43 (1968).

ened by being in the context of a racial discrimination case. More to the point, it seems doubtful that the United States Supreme Court, which only two years ago expressly refused to find a fundamental personal interest in public assistance benefits (which it had previously recognized as constituting the "very means to subsist, food, *shelter* [emphasis added] and the other necessities of life"),[7] would be willing to sweep the quest for a housing location into this rather ad hoc category.[8]

In *Dandridge* v. *Williams*, 397 U.S. 471, 484-85 (1970), the majority expressly equated the constitutional status of "social welfare" legislation and substantive regulation with that of "state regulation of business or industry." As such, Maryland's maximum grant regulations for welfare recipients were to be reviewed according to the old or passive standards, under which "[a] statutory discrimination [would] . . . not be set aside if any state of facts reasonably may be conceived to justify it." As is pointed out in the dissent of Mr. Justice Marshall, the state's only justification in *Dandridge* for its classification was the conservation of its limited resources. However, the majority of the Court approved another rationale which the state had wisely added upon appeal: "It is enough that a solid foundation for the regulation can be found in the State's legitimate interest in encouraging employment and in avoiding discrimination between families of the working poor" (id. at 482).

The counseling point for those engaged in challenging zoning ordinances is clear. It should be anticipated that the efforts of a governmental unit may well be rewarded if it urges goals other than the conservation of the public fisc as justification for its classification scheme. For example, it might state that special geographical or topographical problems are the reason for zoning certain areas to exclude intensive development, special traffic patterns, or community identity questions, or it might cite long-range planning considerations. For, as the United States Supreme Court has stated, "The problems of government are practical ones and may justify, if they do not require, rough accomodations — illogical, it may be, and unscientific" (*Metropolis Theater Company* v. *City of Chicago*, 228 U.S. 61, 69-70 [1913]). In light of this

---

[7] *Shapiro* v. *Thompson*, 394 U.S. 618, 627 (1969).

[8] Fundamental personal interests have been identified by the Court to include the following: the right to procreate, *Skinner* v. *Oklahoma*, 331 U.S. 535, 541 (1942); the right to vote, *Kramer* v. *Union Free School District No. 15*, 395 U.S. 621, 627 (1969), and *Reynolds* v. *Simms*, 377 U.S. 533, 561-62 (1964), *Carrington* v. *Rash*, 380 U.S. 89, 96 (1965), *Harper* v. *Virginia Board of Elections*, 383 U.S. 663, 670 (1966); the right to political association, *Williams* v. *Rhodes*, 393 U.S. 23 (1968); the right of interstate travel, *Shapiro* v. *Thompson*, 394 U.S. 618 (1969); and, the right to receive public primary and secondary education, *Serrano* v. *Priest*, 487 P.2d 1241, 1259 (S. Ct. Calif. 1971), and *Hobson* v. *Hansen*, 269 Fed. Supp. 401 (D.D.C. 1967, aff'd sub nom. *Smuck* v. *Hansen*, 408 F.2d 175, 183 (D.C. Cir. 1968).

direct and unfavorable precedent, the "suspect classification" route would appear more promising.[9]

If the disparity in land use opportunities dictated de facto or de jure by the mandate of zoning ordinances happens to coincide with the racial composition of the favored and disfavored neighborhoods, a garden variety strict review equal protection suit is theoretically before the court. Indeed, from the vantage point of theory, it may be suggested that only in the presence of clearly demonstrable racial discrimination should law reform advocates be counselled to use a federal constitutional theory and a federal forum to resolve a land use restriction dispute. Yet reform litigation, if it is to be successful, must survive the passage from "theory" to a workable judicial hypothesis; the transition from the pages of legal periodicals to those of law

[9]In concluding this brief discussion of the "fundamental personal interest" route to the strict review standard of Equal Protection analysis a caveat must be sounded. I have previously noted that a citizen's right to engage in *interstate* travel was accorded judicial recognition as being "fundamental" in *Shapiro* v. *Thompson*, 394 U.S. 618 (1969). See also, *United States* v. *Guest*, 383 U.S. 745, 758 (1966). It is difficult to conceive of how this holding would be of utility in an attack upon local zoning requirements adopted by a given municipality. The impact of local ordinances upon a right of interstate travel would be slight for they would not burden access to the balance of the territory within a given state. Yet their impact upon intrastate movement is direct, and within the local context, substantial. Thus if the Court were ever to hold a right to *intrastate* movement included within the defined fundamental personal interest the stage would be set for meaningful attack upon "snob zoning" ordinances. Not only would they be tested under the strict or interventionist standard of judicial review, but, with the right to travel (here meaning a right to migrate) as the asserted interest, the standing problems of the non-resident would be erased. Though clouded with what is perhaps an intentional lack of clarity, the Court may have already moved in the direction of such a holding.

Dunn v. *Blumstein*, 92 S.Ct. 995, 1001 (1972), involved an Equal Protection challenge to the durational residence requirements that surround the franchise in Tennessee. At stake were a one-year residency requirement within the state and a three-month requirement within the county in which the voter desired to register. The one-year residency within the state was challenged as a burden upon the right of interstate travel. Its demise under the strict review standard mandated by *Shapiro* v. *Thompson* came as no surprise. However, apparently included within the Court's holding was the three-month requirement of residency within the county. This last qualification of the franchise could obviously bar bona fide residents of Tennessee who had made a mere *intra-state* move from one county to another. The opinion of the majority, speaking through Mr. Justice Marshall, makes no distinction between the *inter* and *intra* state application of these clearly separable durational requirements. Both would appear swept within the statement "the durational residence requirement [note the singular] directly impinges on the exercise of a second fundamental personal right, the right to travel" (92 S.Ct. at 1001). Significantly missing from this assertion is the term "interstate." Neither the concurring opinion of Mr. Justice Blackmun nor the dissent of Chief Justice Burger casts light upon what appears to be a deliberate vagueness in the majority's position. There is a further limitation in the entire discussion of the interest in travel as an alternative to the primary holding which turns upon the fact that the right to vote is, itself, a fundamental personal interest sufficient to ensure application of the strict review standard even if no right to travel were involved.

reports. Before discussing the current or projected attempts to effect this passage, a general observation seems appropriate. The prosecution of equal protection assaults upon restrictive zoning ordinances as variants of a racial discrimination pattern limits the effective scope of this litigation to only those communities wherein segregated housing and land use patterns can be isolated and clearly disparate opportunities for exploitation and enjoyment demonstrated. The problem occasioned by such restrictive land use practices is, however, far more universal than the incidence of either de facto or de jure racial discrimination. Equal protection, if it cannot be advanced beyond this point, is incapable of completing a "homeward journey" on behalf of the economically disadvantaged.

Perceiving the limited utility of a racial discrimination premise, proponents of equal protection strategies have suggested that future litigation place primary reliance upon classifications drawn along lines of economic wealth as an alternative "suspect" criterion. Such a strategy offers a substantial advantage in that economic discrimination will permeate the record of nearly every case that documents the origin and impact of restrictive land use controls. This advantage of potential universality, however, must be discounted by a frank realization that "wealth" has not incurred the same degree of infamy as "race" as an inherently suspect basis of classification. True, the United States Supreme Court less than four years ago declared that "a careful examination is especially warranted where lines are drawn on the basis of wealth *or* race . . . two factors which would *independently* render a classification highly suspect and thereby demand a more exacting judicial scrutiny" (*McDonald* v. *Board of Election Comm'rs of Chicago*, 394 U.S. 802, 807 [1969]) (emphasis added).

With deference to former Chief Justice Warren's opinion, it is submitted that in the words of a former Chief Executive: "That dog won't hunt." The dictum in *McDonald* cannot overcome the fact that in no case has the Court ever found in the fact of economic discrimination, standing alone, an invidious classification. The concept that a citizen's race should be an absolute constitutional irrelevancy not only harmonizes with the Court's recognition of the main purpose of the Fourteenth Amendment but also seems imminently sound. To contend for the same degree of condemnation each time the government takes into account a citizen's economic position is to assume a posture which cannot be sustained on either hard judicial precedent or popular sociopolitcal assumptions.

This is not to suggest that access to those fundamental interests which depend upon the state for their protection and provision ought ever to be conditioned on the respective ability of a citizen to pay for a "fair trial," or the "exercise of the voting franchise." Such seems to have been the conclusion of the Supreme Court of California which, after a lengthy discussion of the status of "wealth as a suspect classification," declared that: "Until the present time wealth classifications have been invalidated only in conjunction with a limited number of fundamental interests – rights of defendants in criminal cases . . . and voting rights" (*Serrano* v. *Priest*, 487 P.2d 1241, 1255 [1971]). Clearly, there are some economic considerations that enjoy official government sanction, such as approved airline, bus, and train tariff regulations, which qualify the exercise of the "fundamental personal right of interstate travel." This will be so until the principle of capitalistic provision is eliminated from a society which shows little tendency in favor of that development.

Analysis of the rationale that has motivated the Supreme Court to hold "wealth" a suspect criterion vis-à-vis the machinery of criminal justice and the franchise would strongly suggest a perception that inherent in these two areas are functional means to achievement or preservation of constitutionally protected rights of "life, liberty, and property." An attempt to qualify the low-income citizen's quest for a residence location would, at first blush, seem to satisfy the literal language of the test. But until the United States Supreme Court can be convinced to reexamine and overturn its assertion in the *Dandridge* case, the housing interest will not be accorded inclusion in the litany of fundamental personal interests. In the absence of a tie-in to demonstrable racial discrimination and the availability of the strict review standard, the widespread utility of a federal theory of equal protection in the area of restrictive land use reform is in doubt.

It is the source of some satisfaction that this discussion of the equal protection theory can still end on a tentatively hopeful note. If one reviews the cases regarding the standard of equal protection scrutiny, one is left with the disquieting thought that the standard selection represents the conclusive phase of litigation. For the record indicates that if the Court selects the strict review standard predicated upon either the finding of a suspect classification or the identification of a fundamental personal interest, the state cannot win. Only in the Japanese internment case during the Second World War was the state able to prevail. The petitioning citizens were indisputably correct in noting that they were being classified for treatment by the government strictly on the basis of their national origin or race. The government's reply was candid and direct. The Court accepted wartime exigencies as amounting to a compelling governmental interest and vindicated the constitutionality of the government's activity as against the equal protection claim. On the other hand, should the Court decide that access to the strict review standard cannot be sustained, the authorities are at one in commending to the Court a deference to the legislative or executive judgment if that judgment can be connected to any legitimate governmental purpose even if the Court is obliged to speculate or imagine the existence of such purpose.[10] Scholarly critics have noted the questionable utility of a procedure in which all of the ultimate value judgments regarding the merits of the case were necessarily compressed into the pretrial maneuvering of the parties regarding the inceptive issue of standard selection.

In November 1971, the Supreme Court was faced with a challenge by Mrs. Sally M. Reed. The gravamen of Mrs. Reed's complaint was that the substantive law of Idaho discriminated against women citizens in a statutory provision which declared that as between persons equally qualified to administer estates males must be preferred to females. In seeking judicial intervention, Mrs. Reed took the position that "sex" was a "suspect" criteria as offensively invidious as race. The State of Idaho denied this proposition and asserted that the challenge mounted by Mrs. Reed ought to be turned aside under the noninterventionist or "traditional" standard of equal protection analysis. In the state's view, the statutory preference for male executors could be tied to the legitimate governmental goal of simplifying the matters of probate procedure within the Idaho courts. This rationale was found persuasive by the Supreme Court of Idaho which dismissed Mrs. Reed's claim. On appeal, the United States Supreme Court, speaking through Mr. Chief Justice Burger, reversed. The Burger opinion found it unnecessary to decide the broad-ranging question of whether or not "sex" is an inherently "suspect" basis for classification. Surely, the Court must have been aware of the vast implication of such a holding. Rather, the form of the Court's opinion was to place the case under the traditional standard but then to grant relief. While the opinion is doubtless subject to conflicting scholarly analysis, I believe that the net result of the United States Supreme Court decision in *Reed* v. *Reed*, 404 U.S. 71, 75–76 (1971), is to create a third or "middle" standard of review.

While conceding that the Equal Protection Clause of the Fourteenth Amendment does not deny to states the power to treat different classes of persons in different ways, the Court was insistent that the operative impact of the Amendment was to deny states the power to "legislate that different treatment be accorded to persons placed by a statute into different classes on the basis of criteria wholly unrelated to the object of that statute. 'A classification must be reasonable, not arbitrary, and must rest upon some ground of

---

[10]"Legislatures are presumed to have acted constitutionally even if source materials normally resorted to for ascertaining their grounds for actions are otherwise silent, and their statutory classification will be set aside only if no grounds can be conceived to justify them." *McDonald* v. *Board of Election Comm'rs of Chicago*, 394 U.S. 802, 809 (1969). Accord, *Lindsley* v. *National Carbonic Gas Co.*, 220 U.S. 61, 78 (1911); and, *Morey* v. *Doud*, 354 U.S. 457, 467 (1957).

difference having a fair and substantial relation to the object of the legislation, so that all persons similarly circumstanced shall be treated alike.' " This "fair and substantial relation to the object of the legislation" criteria then permitted the Court to determine whether the difference in the sex of competing applicants for letters of testamentary administration bore the requisite relationship to the state objective sought to be advanced by the operation of the Idaho statute. Notwithstanding the further concession that the "objective of reducing the workload on probate courts by eliminating one class of contests is not without some legitimacy" the Court held that the fair and substantial relationship had not been established.

The test thus enunciated and applied in *Reed* v. *Reed* is free from the analytical strictures of either labeling the criteria or placing transcending reliance upon an evaluation of the plaintiff's adversely affected personal interest. Rather, the focus of the litigation is upon the more satisfactory issue of the relationship between the object sought by the government and the means selected to that end. If this test is placed in the context of a challenge to restrictive land use controls, it can be anticipated that the state will advance the enumerated goals or objectives of population stabilization, community identity, aesthetic and environmental determinations, and conservation of public money and services. Whether a two-acre zoning minimum would be held to bear a fair and substantial relation to the objects of this legislation remains to be tested.[11]

Federal Supremacy

In the arsenal of potentially available federal theories, one more remains: The Supremacy Clause. This rather interesting doctrine is peculiar to our federal system. It is a lesson of eighth-grade civics that the powers of the federal government must trace their origin to the Constitution, and in particular to Article I. All those powers which have not been conferred upon the legislative, the executive, or the judicial branches have, by the express provision of Article X, been "reserved to the states respectively, or to the people."

---

[11] This middle standard of Equal Protection analysis, whereby the classification of citizens for disparate governmental treatment is scrutinized to determine if it is "reasonable" and "rest[s] upon some ground of difference having a fair and substantial relation to the object of the legislation," has now been utilized for a second time by the Burger Court. In *Eisenstadt* v. *Baird*, 92 S.Ct. 1029, 1035–38 (1972), the majority used this analysis to strike down a Massachusetts law which forbade the distribution of contraceptive materials to the unmarried. In *Skinner* v. *Oklahoma*, 316 U.S. 535, 541 (1942), the Court had determined that the right to procreate constituted a fundamental personal interest. Use of the middle standard of judicial review enabled the Court to avoid testing *Skinner* to determine if the right to procreate a bastard achieved the same lofty constitutional plateau.

Within this context, the Congress of the United States is the supreme oracle of the general welfare only when it is able to trace its law-giving powers to the provisions of Article I or to the Amendments to the Constitution. When it is acting within that sphere, its pronouncements are supreme and must prevail when tested against inconsistent provisions of either state or local legislation.

A review of precedent law discloses that the United States Supreme Court has, on a number of occasions, utilized the Supremacy Clause as a vehicle for suppressing state and local ordinances that circumscribed the property acquisition policies enunciated by the Congress. Yet, in each instance to date, the operative effect of these decisions has been to provide an alternative to strict review Equal Protection for the vindication of claims of the black race. The authority of Congress to enact legislation aimed at ensuring to black citizens a parity of status with whites in an ability to purchase, lease, sell, or convey property is traced to the Thirteenth Amendment. That Amendment represents the first of the Reconstruction Era efforts to abolish slavery and the vestiges of slavery. By its specific terms, Congress is given power "to enforce this Article by appropriate legislation." The activities of the Congress in seeking this end, have been sanctioned by the Court under the "badge of slavery doctrine."

More than 100 years ago, the attention of the Congress to the plight of black persons seeking residential locations manifested itself in the passage of what is now Section 1982 of Title 42 of the U.S. Code. The terms of that legislative effort are simple and direct. "All citizens of the United States shall have the same right, in every state and territory, as is enjoyed by white citizens thereof to inherit, purchase, lease, sell, hold and convey real and personal property." The utility of this provision of the original Civil Rights Act of 1866 has been demonstrated in several contests with local ordinances as well as manifestations of private discrimination.

In *Harmon* v. *Tyler*, 273 U.S. 668 (1926), the United States Supreme Court invalidated a New Orleans ordinance that gave legal force to private discrimination by forbidding any Negro to establish a home in a white community, or any white person to establish a residence in a Negro community, "except on the written consent of a majority of the persons of the opposite race inhabiting such community or portion of the city to be affected." As a result of the decision in *Harmon* v. *Tyler*, as well as the most recent pronouncement of the Court in *Jones* v. *Mayer Company*, it seems clear that any zoning ordinance that operates to discriminate on the basis of racial classification is per se subject to being overriden on a Supremacy Clause theory.[12] In

---

[12]In *Jones* v. *Mayer*, 392 U.S. 409 (1967), the United States Supreme Court held to be actionable for both injunctive and other relief the decision by a private developer to

Harmon v. *Tyler*, the discriminatory nature of the restrictive land use ordinance was transparent. More recent federal court decisions have held the question of motive to be *irrelevant* in a case involving racial discrimination.[13]

In an extension of the *Harmon* rationale, it would seem that if an ordinance could be statistically shown to operate to the exclusion of nonresidents of a particular race it could be struck down under a Supremacy Clause notion as well as under the strict review standard of equal protection analysis. Yet if the Supremacy Clause doctrine is to be tied to demonstrable racial discrimination, it sweeps with no greater scope than that offered by the strict review standard of equal protection analysis. It has been implicit in all of my remarks that the universal quality of the discrimination produced by snob zoning ordinances rests upon a criterion of wealth. The substantial identity between the racial composition of ghetto residents and the low-income status that permits snob zoning ordinances to work their deterrent effect upon mobility suggests that Equal Protection and Supremacy Clause theories that would be broadly remedial in the area of racial discrimination may be of substantial utility in coping with the anti-social impact of restrictive land use controls.[14]

---

refuse to sell a home in a suburban St. Louis subdivision to the petitioner Jones solely, as was alleged, because Jones was black.

[13]The United States Court of Appeals for the Fifth Circuit has put the matter quite bluntly. In a civil rights suit alleging racial discrimination in contravention of the Fourteenth Amendment, "it is not necessary to go so far as to establish ill will, evil motive, or absence of good faith ... objective results are largely to be relied on in the application of the constitutional test" (*United States ex rel. Seals* v. *Wiman*, 304 F.2d 53, 65 [1962]). The immateriality of this factor stems from the positive, affirmative constitutional duty of governmental officials to pursue a course of conduct which would not result in racial discrimination (*Cassell* v. *Texas*, 339 U.S. 389 [1949]).

[14]A recent decision of the United States Court of Appeals for the Tenth Circuit in *Dailey* v. *City of Lawton, Oklahoma*, 425 F.2d 1037 (1970), reveals an interesting twist to this "substantial identity between low-income ghetto residents and minority racial status." In *Dailey*, petitioners represented a qualified sponsor of a low-income housing project which sought a zoning variance so as to locate in a predominantly white section of Lawton, Oklahoma. In addition to the sponsoring organization, which had been organized by the Roman Catholic Bishop, the petitioners included Mrs. Willy Mae Dailey suing for a class denominated as a low-income group of potential residents of the housing project consisting of "Negroes, Spanish Americans, and poor whites." The rationale of the United States District Court which ordered the City of Lawton to refrain from denying a building permit on the grounds of a zoning violation was that the evidence established the City's refusal to be primarily predicated upon a manifestation of racial discrimination condemned by the Equal Protection Clause of the Fourteenth Amendment.

This rationale of racial discrimination was adopted by the Court of Appeals which affirmed. The presence of poor whites among the petitioning group escapes any more than a passing mention in the opinion authored by Judge Breitenstein. This factor is most interesting, in light of the precedent law which would make the presence of whites a substantial impediment to the petitioner's ability to draw clear lines of racial classifica-

There is one very practical advantage offered by the utility of federal statutes made supreme under the terms of Article VI, Clause 2 of the Constitution, and that is the precision with which the statutes articulate a federal land use and housing policy. The presence of a clearly articulated federal policy to be accorded supremacy over any conflicting state or local land use legislation would relieve the Court of the vexing problem of formulating its own value judgments in response to a low-income petitioner's challenge. In

---

tion. In the absence of an ability to construct such proofs of racial identity, the "suspect" basis of the classification would not be made out, and review under the strict review standard of equal protection analysis could not be had. None of these problems troubled the United States Court of Appeals. What this portends for the future cannot be known. The defendant City seems to have raised issues of land use planning, among which were the alleged overcrowding of neighborhoods, local schools, and recreational facilities and the overburdening of local firefighting capacities were this medium- to high-density low-cost project located within the previously all white neighborhood. These defenses were rejected by the United States District Judge on the theory that they were nothing more than "conclusory assertions," and thus did not defeat the prima facie case of discriminatory intent which had been created by petitioners' evidence.

The opinion of the Court of Appeals leaves this conclusion and rationale undisturbed. The language of the opinion suggests that the result was reached under the "traditional standard," and yet the racial discrimination factor would surely entitle the petitioners to the interventionist strict review standard. The failure of either court to make the standard explicit is difficult to diagnose. Perhaps the presence of low-income whites among the class of citizens to benefit by the decree caused the court to downplay any discussion of standard selection, a discussion that would have occasioned the vexing issue of the impact of whites as included plaintiffs.

Further research reveals that *Dailey* is not the only recent decision to "piggy back" poor whites into the realm of the strict review standard. In *Kennedy Park Homes Association* v. *City of Lackawanna*, 318 F. Supp. 669, 671, 693–94, 697 (W.D. N.Y. 1970), the District Court engaged in a detailed exercise of the strict review standard. Under attack were spot zoning ordinances enacted by the defendant which operated to create parks out of land that the Roman Catholic Diocese of Buffalo was attempting to qualify as the site for a large federally assisted low-income housing project. The case is of interest, for the city attempted to justify its zoning change in terms of physical necessity (flood control), unreasonable strain upon the local sewerage system, need for open space and other recreational facilities, and the implementation of a comprehensive plan for urban renewal. None of these justifications were accorded the status of "compelling governmental interests" by a Court convinced that the underlying rationale of the City's denial was racial discrimination. Yet the case is remarkable in that the suit had been commenced by "low-income families," a group broken down to include the "elderly, Negroes, and Puerto Ricans." Assuming that whites were included within the class denominated as "elderly," the total silence of a Court which swept them within the purview of a decree founded upon a finding of racial discrimination is a remarkable omission in an otherwise exhaustive opinion.

On appeal, the United States Court of Appeals for the Second Circuit affirmed. 436 F.2d 108, 109 (1971). An opinion written by Associate Justice of the Supreme Court Tom Clark, Retired, emphasizes the racial basis of the discrimination. The Clark opinion acknowledges that the "complaint alleged that defendants . . . had declared a moratorium on new subdivisions, in order to deny decent housing to low-income and minority families, in violation of the Equal Protection and Due Process Clauses of the Fourteenth Amendment," but makes no mention of the "piggy back" phenomenon.

the absence of some clear direction from the Congress or the Executive Branch, a court will have difficulty in assessing the issue of whether low-income housing projects are most ideally situated within or outside of a ghetto area. If one pauses for a moment to contemplate the conflicting positions taken within the black community on the issue of integration versus the community control possible within racially segregated neighborhoods, the difficulties for a judge are made manifest. Fortunately for a court seeking direction, the Congress has spoken by way of supplementing the integration policies held by the Civil Rights Act of 1886. The diverse civil rights and housing acts of the mid and late 1960s reveal a strong bias in favor of both racial and economic mix within the diverse neighborhoods of a metropolitan area.[15] To the extent that these federal statutory provisions seek to promote and mandate racial integration, the cooperation of the federal judiciary in suppressing inconsistent value judgments contained in either state or local legislation is called for by the Supremacy Clause.[16]

[15] See for example: Title VI of the Civil Rights Act of 1964, 42 U.S.C. § 2000d; the Fair Housing Act of 1968, 42 U.S.C. § 3601 et seq. (July 1968 Supp.); Demonstration Cities and Metropolitan Development Act of 1966, 42 U.S.C. § 3301 et seq.; and regulations of the United States Department of Housing and Urban Development, particularly Title 24 C.F.R. § § 1.4(b), 2(2), and 205.1(g) of the Department's low-rent housing manual.

[16] Already, they have been utilized in such a manner on behalf of Negro and Mexican-American low-income residents of Lansing, Michigan. In *Ranjel* v. *City of Lansing*, 293 F. Supp. 301 (W.D. Mich. 1969), the Court enjoined a proposed referendum on a city council ordinance that achieved a spot zoning amendment to the comprehensive city zoning plan so as to authorize a federally approved low-cost housing project in a white neighborhood for Negroes and Mexican-Americans who lived in the ghetto. Petitioners contended, and the District Court agreed, that the proposed referendum, which sought to nullify the spot zoning ordinance, would amount to activity on the part of the City of Lansing inconsistent with the controlling expression of a federal low-income housing policy. Thus Judge Fox rested his opinion squarely on an application of the Supremacy Clause. As an alternative holding, Judge Fox enjoined the proposed referendum on the ground that the evidence revealed a motivation resting upon racial discrimination and thus offensive to the interventionist standard of Equal Protection review.

In articulating a vision of the proper socioeconomic policy for urban land use, the Court relied most heavily upon the contents of the Department of Housing and Urban Development's Low Rent Housing Manual. The provisions of that Manual instructed the local authority seeking to qualify for federal financial assistance and loan guarantees to seek a nonghetto location for any project. The spot zoning variance which had been approved by the Madison Planning Commission and city council would have permitted this federally financed "turn key" low-income housing project to be located in a previously all-white neighborhood. Judge Fox perceived in the proposed referendum a serious threat to this goal, a threat which would impede the federal policy embodied in the Low Rent Housing Manual.

On appeal to the United States Court of Appeals for the Sixth Circuit, the judgment of the District Court, insofar as it rested upon an application of the Supremacy Clause, was reversed (417 F.2d 321 [1970]). In the view of the Appellate Court, there was no question but that the express statutory provision of the diverse federal civil rights and

The most optimistic possibility to emanate from this study is the potential viability of the Supremacy Clause for successfully confronting the economic discrimination that inevitably results from all snob zoning schemes.

Proposal and passage of a federal "Low-Income Housing Location Act" would clearly set the stage for a broad assault upon the restrictive character of snob zoning ordinances predicated upon the Supremacy Clause.[17] Before substantial reforms could be achieved, a court, and ultimately the United States Supreme Court, would be called upon to determine whether such an act is within the legislative competence of the Congress. Clearly, the Thir-

---

low-income housing legislation should be afforded supremacy over the inconsistent value judgments embodied in state or local land use control legislation. Yet the Sixth Circuit emphasized a belief that Congress intended a healthy respect for federal-state-local comity, and to this end it was not to be presumed that the local zoning ordinances were to be set aside if, under any theory, they would be harmonized with the federal policy. The specific manifestation of this respect for "comity" was the conclusion on the part of the Court of Appeals that the Department of Housing and Urban Development's Low Rent Housing Manual did not "rise to the dignity of federal law" for Supremacy Clause purposes. The Court did not take the blanket position that no delegation of rule-making authority to an executive branch could result in regulations rising to the dignity of federal legislation; it seemed to draw a distinction between those rules promulgated after publication in the Code of Federal Regulations with an opportunity for the submission of written views which the Department is obliged to consider before promulgating a regulation in final form. The provisions of the Low Rent Housing Manual were not run through such a procedure, and as such were not "regulations or orders of general applicability" within the Court's understanding of that term of art. The defeat sustained on appeal by the petitioners in *Ranjel* is disappointing, but the counselling point is clear. Pressure should be exerted upon the Department of Housing and Urban Development to promulgate the contents of the Low Rent Housing Manual via the forms and procedures prescribed for the acquisition of federal regulation status. At that point, they would be the controlling source of value judgments and policy articulation capable of being asserted by the federal courts via the Supremacy Clause.

[17] The call for the enactment of a "national fair housing law" has already been sounded. In *Report of the National Advisory Commission on Civil Disorders* (1969), p. 263, the Kerner Commission noted:

"Enactment of a national fair housing law will eliminate the most obvious barrier limiting the areas in which nonwhites live, but it will not deal with an equally impenetrable barrier, the unavailability of low and moderate income housing in nonghetto areas.

"To date, housing programs serving low-income groups have been concentrated in the ghettos. Nonghetto areas, particularly suburbs, for the most part have steadfastly opposed low-income, rent supplement, or below-market interest rate housing, and have successfully restricted use of these programs outside the ghetto.

"We believe that federally aided low-and moderate-income housing programs must be reoriented so that the major thrust is in nonghetto areas. Public housing programs should emphasize scattered site construction, rent supplements should, whenever possible, be used in nonghetto areas, and an intensive effort should be made to recruit below-market interest rate sponsors willing to build outside the ghettos.

"The reorientation of these programs is particularly critical in light of our recommendation that six million low and middle-income housing units be made available over the next 5 years. If the effort is not be be counterproductive, its main thrust must be in nonghetto areas, particularly those outside the central city."

teenth Amendment sustains congressional activity seeking to "eliminate the badge of slavery." However, should the Congress simply declare that no state or local legislation could stand in the way of site selection for federally assisted low-income housing projects regardless of the racial composition of their tenants, a specific source of congressional authority comparable to Clause 2 of the Thirteenth Amendment cannot be readily identified. Clearly, the power of the Congress, legislating in pursuit of the general welfare, to ordain and establish federal low-income housing projects has not been seriously questioned. But the critical factor, which would be contained for the first time in the proposed act for the facilitation of low-income housing project locations, is the direct confrontation with state and local land use schemes.

If the United States Supreme Court were to uphold the power of the Congress to pass such legislation, the Court would not have to override its earlier decision that the shelter interest does not represent a "fundamental personal interest." True, the operative impact of sustaining the power of Congress to pass supreme legislation in the area would be the same as the declaration that a housing location interest was a fundamental personal interest. But the crucial governance distinction lies in the origin of that value judgment. The inclusion of a new addition within the ad hoc category of fundamental personal interest is attacked on every occasion as being the height of "judicial legislation." However, were the Congress to pass this proposed act, the responsibility for arriving at and articulating the underlying value judgments in such legislation would be where the framers envisioned it — with the Congress.

State Law Theories and Forums

In deciding upon the appropriate legal vehicle and in shopping for an appropriate forum, the advocate seeking to advance the interest of the economically disadvantaged is well advised to consider the more immediate machinery of the state courts.

From my brief review of federal constitutional theory and the activities of the federal judiciary it should be evident that two related problems invariably arise to prejudice the case for intervention.

The first is the question of "comity," which the United States Court of Appeals for the Sixth Circuit noted in *Ranjel.* Though vague in its dimension, the concept rests on the respect which the organs of the state and federal governments are to show one another. When the ordinances of local government are drawn into constitutional question before a federal tribunal, the doctrine of comity — with its attendant focus upon the dignity of the defendant as a branch of local government – militates against federal intervention. Judicial hesitance is especially pronounced when the ultimate relief sought requires the court to substitute its value judgments for those espoused by the legislative branch of state or local government. This is the "substance" versus "procedure" dichotomy.

The second problem that plagues a federal court is functionally related to the first. Where the low-income residents predicate their challenge upon either the Due Process or Equal Protection Clauses of the Fourteenth Amendment, a judge hesitating in the face of decision-making difficulties may be further influenced by the spectre of having to "freeze" his decision within the mold of a constitutional pronouncement. If an appeal must be made to one of the United States Circuit Courts of Appeal, or, ultimately, to the United States Supreme Court, this "constitutional freeze" problem is exacerbated. The higher one climbs within the stratosphere of appellate procedure the more irresistible is the conclusion that a judicial enunciation of minimum entitlement for a minority goes beyond resolving a local dispute and smacks of legislating for the nation.

To summarize, the difficulties encountered by a federal court begin with the issue of comity – whether or not to risk offense to a state government or one of its creatures. Having begun with this hesitancy, a United States district judge must assess the practical difficulties of *rendering* and *enforcing* a decision. Finally, there is the concern that there may be massive judicial over-reaction – that the experimental results propounded in the face of a constitutional claim may suddenly become the frozen pattern to which all levels of executive and legislative decision making must yield.

The difficulties that plague the federal judiciary are either totally absent or greatly reduced in their hindrance of the processes of a state court. Litigation initiated before a state judicial tribunal faces no comity problem. A contest between the federal judiciary and the executive or legislative branches of the state government is simply avoided.

The difficulties implicit in forming value judgments are likely to be less vexing for a state judge. Leaving aside for a moment his responsibility for the enforcement of the Due Process and Equal Protection Clauses of the Fourteenth Amendment – a judicial responsibility coextensive with that of the federal courts – a state judge may resort to the provisions of his state constitution or the enactments of his state legislature. Unlike the Republic, which has functioned since 1789 with the same written Constitution, most states have continually revised and updated their basic political charters. It is not unusual for such constitutions to have acquired specific provisions that either empower the legislature to develop land use policies or restrict the discretion of local government in the exercise of a zoning power. The types of specific state constitutional provisions that may be encountered include "open housing" declarations or a demand that regional need be taken into account in the course of framing local land use ordinances. If the constitutional provision is merely permissive, the "fair housing," "open housing," or "regional need" provision may be found within the enactments of the state legislature. At the present time Massachusetts, New Jersey, and New York have such statutory provision. In New Jersey, such a provision has been construed to be required by a clause within the revised state constitution. Such pronouncements – be they within the state constitution or a legislative enactment – represent a legislative determination of the basic value judgment, which permits the court to avoid an exercise of what amounts to a "legislative act." Once a court is convinced that the elected branches of state government have opted in favor of a "fair housing" policy, it is much easier for a judge to make such judicial decisions as will "most nearly effectuate and promote the intendment of the legislature."

Even if the text of a particular state constitution is devoid of specific reference to housing or land use policies, and the legislative enactments are equally silent on the topic, the burden of articulating federal constitutional theories of Due Process or Equal Protection weighs more lightly upon the officers of the state judiciary. The reason is simple. Under the doctrine of *stare decisis* their decisions do not sweep beyond the territorial limitations of the specific state in question. Thus, it is easier for a judge to assume an interventionist role when he recognizes that he is not making law "for the entire nation." I suggest nothing more than that the less awesome nature of the responsibility facilitates the conclusion that it might be experimentally exercised.

It is even possible to enter a state court with a challenge to a local land use ordinance on the theory that the Supremacy Clause requires the judges in every state to resolve discrepancies between federal policies and state or local ordinances in favor of the federal policy.

From the foregoing analysis, it is evident that no theory that could be asserted in a United States District Court is lost when the litigation is filed in a state trial court. Furthermore, the dynamics of the judicial decision making process militate in favor of a more activist response on the part of a more local judiciary. Yet the record of the past five years reveals that most "poverty law" advocates will crawl over broken glass to gain access to a federal forum. The time-consuming jurisdictional questions thus encountered are frequently counterproductive to the asserted reform goal. Admittedly, there are instances when the record of state tribunals reveals such a total antipathy toward reform that access to a federal forum becomes the only promising avenue for relief. However, recent activities of the Pennsylvania and New Jersey state judiciaries suggest that contests about the validity of local land use controls are not an area in which abstinence from state courts can be justified.

A landmark case — one that has gone further in providing an avenue of relief to the economically disadvantaged nonresident than any judicial development to date — was decided by a majority of the Supreme Court of Pennsylvania in 1965. In *National Land and Investment Co.* v. *Easton Township Board of Adjustment*, 419 Pa. 504, 532, that court declared: "The question posed is whether the Township can stand in the way of the natural forces which send our growing population into hitherto underdeveloped areas in search of a comfortable place to live. We have concluded not. A zoning ordinance whose primary purpose is to prevent the entrance of newcomers in order to avoid future burdens, economic and otherwise, upon the administration of public services and facilities cannot be held valid." It is interesting to note that the genesis of this doctrine, which is now proving of greatest advantage to the economically disadvantaged and the politically nonresident, is to be found in early cases wherein landowners who desired to utilize their land for an unpopular purpose (a trailer park, a billboard site, or funeral home) contested the validity of local zoning codes which effectively amounted to total exclusion of the asserted use. The position of the Supreme Court of Pennsylvania amounts to nothing less ambitious than the assertion of an affirmative duty resting upon those in possession of local political office to use the zoning power so as to facilitate absorption of "the increased responsibilities and economic burdens which time and natural growth invariably bring."

Recent decisions by New Jersey state courts reveal a slightly different rationale but a functionally identical result. In *Oakwood at Madison, Inc.* v. *Township of Madison*, 283 A.2d 353 (N.J. Super. Ct., 1971), the plaintiffs included two developers who owned vacant land and developable land in Madison Township, and six individuals, all with low income, representing as a class those who reside outside the Township and had sought housing there unsuccessfully because of the one- and two-acre lot minimum zoning requirements. Plaintiffs attacked the Madison Township snob zoning ordinance as being at variance with both the New Jersey state constitution and controlling provisions of state legislation that required the local entities of government to pursue the "general welfare" through the exercise of a zoning power. In the plaintiffs' view, the large-lot zoning requirement thwarted the general welfare because it failed to "encompass legitimate housing needs." The court agreed and noted earlier New Jersey decisions in which the "general welfare" had been broadened to include consideration for regional as well as local housing needs. By thus redefining the parameters of the "general welfare," the court had no difficulty in concluding that the low-income nonresident possessed standing to challenge the Madison Township zoning scheme. In summarizing its review standard, the court declared that such ordinances must be tested against the responsibility to reasonably promote a "balanced and well ordered plan for the entire municipality . . . in pursuing the valid zoning purpose of a valid community, a municipality must not ignore housing needs, that is, its fair proportion of the obligation to meet the housing needs of its own population and of the region. Housing needs are encompassed within the general welfare."

CONCLUSION

An asserted preference by the economically disadvantaged and politically inconsequential for litigation as opposed to legislative or executive lobbying is most understandable. Access to the courts provides a relatively direct and expedient means for resolving the specific grievances of a minority group, be that minority founded on economic or racial classification. Equally understandable is the hesitancy of a court to assume the role of a "super zoning board." This hesitancy is accentuated when low-income petitioners seek relief within a federal forum under a constitutional theory. In this instance, a federal court is asked to assume the role of a "zoning board of last resort" – an interventionist role that is criticized by some on grounds that it is undemocratic for judges enjoying lifetime tenure to substitute their value judgments for those expressed by the elected official of a far more immediate tier of government. In my opinion the greatest chance for success lies in using a theory that permits a court to conceive of itself as a partner providing support and enforcement for a fair housing campaign begun by the elected representatives of the people. Consistent with this proposition is the suggestion that, when recourse must be had to a federal constitutional theory, litigation should be based upon the Supremacy Clause. Whenever possible, serious consideration should be given to seeking relief in a state court where the quest is a direct appeal to the state courts to order their own house, and a national housing law is not at stake. Within these guidelines, there is reason for cautious optimism that the habitually disadvantaged, now for the first time possessed of a litigating capacity, may extricate themselves from the discriminatory impact of snob zoning schemes and at last attain "home."

ECOLOGY AND HOUSING:
Virtues in Conflict

RICHARD F. BABCOCK and DAVID L. CALLIES

Woe unto them that join house to house, that lay field to field,
till there be no place that they may be placed alone in the midst
of the earth! — Isaiah 5:8

We must put housing on the front burner. We must focus our housing
programs on housing for poor people. — Douglas Commission Report,
H.R. Doc. 34, 91 Cong. 1 sess. (1968), p. 30

It is probably unfair to suggest, as do these two texts, that the ecologists
have God on their side while the housing advocates, turning as they do to the
federal government, have gone to the Other Place, whence cometh *their* help.

The proposition might be put in more judicious if skeptical fashion: Any
beneficent public policy, if prosecuted vigorously, is bound to conflict with
an equally beneficent public policy. If Disraeli did not say that, he should
have.

RICHARD F. BABCOCK is a Chicago attorney specializing in
planning and housing law and author of *The Zoning Game*. He is immediate
past president of the American Society of Planning Officials, former Commissioner of the Northeastern Illinois Planning Commission, and Chairman of the
Advisory Committee, American Law Institute Model Land Development
Code project. Mr. Babcock has an A.B. from Dartmouth College and J.D. and
M.B.A. degrees from the University of Chicago.

DAVID L. CALLIES is a Chicago attorney specializing in planning
and municipal law. Mr. Callies has a Master of Laws degree (in English planning law) from the University of Nottingham. He is a former assistant state's
attorney for planning and zoning in McHenry County, Illinois, and author,
with Fred P. Bosselman, of *The Quiet Revolution in Land Use Control.*

The ecological crusade, if taken literally, will either stifle growth or will drive up housing costs; in either event the heaviest burden will fall on the poor. By the same token, the production of all the housing that is needed, at the right price and near job opportunities, may be expected to have adverse effects on the environment that has become so precious to the white middle class.

Given that each of these public policies should be pursued, compromise is a moral as well as a practical goal worth seeking.

Turning back to the text from Isaiah, we are not so sure it is wholly out of place. The environmentalists are, indeed, a pious clan, too righteous by half perhaps; but it is an understandable character trait considering the simple virtues they embrace. They are also in the mainstream of the American myth as Max Lerner has so pointedly observed:

> Americans have been of twofold mind on the question of their natural resources. They neglected and wasted them . . . ; and when they discovered the extent of their waste they grew panicky and gave themselves to an intense conservation movement.[1]

In contrast, the housing spokesmen, whether civil libertarians or home builders, do appear to be in a state of constant embarrassment, seemingly in perpetual league with the forces of darkness: Federal Housing Administration (FHA) policies that provided thousands of homes after World War II — and underwrote the lock-out effect in the suburbs — are now replaced by tax policies, federal and local, and corrupt or inefficient appraisal practices that present the federal government with thousands of foreclosures in the central cities.

Compromise is never easy and it is doubly hard when the one side appears to be riding a wave of national sentiment, particularly among the ascendant middle class, while the other side, the ill-housed, is largely inarticulate, under-represented and often dependent for satisfaction of its material needs not only upon distributive justice but also upon an increased productivity that too often makes headlines only in terms of oil spills or nuclear wastes.

Let us agree that if ecology must compromise with every group with which its goals conflict, it will cease to be a definitive public policy. It is equally certain that the same can be said of housing for the poor, be they white, black, or brown. And while "spaceship earth" may indeed erupt one day if we do not see to her proper maintenance, the eruption of those communities in which a large portion are damned to slum housing is no prediction; it is already a sordid part of our national history.

[1] *America as a Civilization* (Simon and Schuster, 1957), p. 112.

We are not setting up straw men. The conflict between goals is real; the solution is difficult. A few illustrations follow.

THE BATTLE JOINED: WAR OF THE ANGELS

Litigation Over Long Island: Don't Sue Us; We'll Sue You

Nowhere is the potential conflict more painfully obvious than in the litigation that has developed over the zoning laws of the local governments on Long Island, New York. On October 20, 1970, Suffolk County and 40 of its units of local government were served with a complaint filed by some of its citizens who were collectively, if somewhat cumbersomely, denominated the Suffolk County Defenders of the Environment.[2] In their complaint, the Defenders seek to have the United States District Court declare

> ... that the existing zoning laws [of the defendants] individually and collectively violate the rights of the plaintiffs . . . not only of this generation but of those generations yet unborn . . . in that each of such zoning laws permits the development of the natural resources of the County of Suffolk, in particular the land mass of Suffolk County, as merely a substrate for speculation, failing to determine the highest and best use of each area of real property in the County of Suffolk in accordance with modern principles of real property utilization, in particular in that such laws fail to establish objective criteria for real property development, based on the physiographic, hydrologic, geologic, meteorologic, and ecological characteristics of the Regional Ecological System of which such real property is an element.

(It is illuminating that while the complaint invokes most of the environmentalists' favorite suffixes such as "ographic," and "ologic," it is notably silent when it comes to those prefixes dealing with mankind such as "demo" and "socio.")

The complaint asks the court to restrain

> ... the defendants . . . from implementing or issuing construction permits under any existing law, ordinance or regulation, unless and until adequate provision is made to determine the ecological impact of such development on the Suffolk County Regional Ecological Systems has been fully determined in accordance with modern methods of environmental systems science.[3]

[2] Lance Phillips, "Suit Challenges Zone Laws, Complaint Served to 40 Bds." *The Long Island Advance*, Oct. 22, 1970, p. 1.

[3] Complaint, *Suffolk County Defenders of the Environment* v. *Suffolk County, et al.*, filed Oct. 8, 1970, U.S. District Court for Eastern District of New York, #70–C–1278.

Successful prosecution of this suit by the plaintiffs would halt substantially all development in Suffolk County, including housing for the rich and poor alike, until ecologically oriented ordinances were adopted. Such ordinances predictably would compel lower densities and therefore higher-cost housing. It is not surprising that according to newspaper accounts it was a proposed high-density development that had aroused the ecologists.[4] As a result of this suit, a team of "environmental specialists" has been retained in at least one of the defendant municipalities to formulate a zoning law "environmentally oriented, ecologically protected, sociologically responsible, economically feasible, administratively sound and politically practical."[5] (Note the order of priorities.) Pending such a challenging legislative exercise, the town will apparently withhold the issuance of any further building permits.[6]

But it is not the rich or even the moderately well-off for whom decent shelter near jobs is a desperate need. It is the low-income minorities. And that group does not intend to wait for a resolution of ecological or any other cosmic problems before pressing its demands for housing, especially on Long Island.

On March 24, 1971, the National Association for the Advancement of Colored People (NAACP) filed a suit in the U.S. District Court for the Eastern District of New York against the Town of Oyster Bay in Nassau County, which is cheek by jowl to Suffolk County on Long Island. The NAACP wants an end to exclusionary zoning and the implementation of a plan to provide housing for black persons and others economically deprived in and around Oyster Bay.[7] The type of housing sought is multi-family and federally subsidized, not likely to evoke hurrahs by the ecologists along the shore. In other words, the NAACP is suing to compel the dismantling of barriers to the construction of precisely the same sort of housing, in virtually the same area, as the Suffolk County Defenders of the Environment are suing to prevent.

Sierra Club, et al. v. *George Romney, et al.:*
Separate but Equal Access to Aquifers

In February of 1972, the Sierra Club, the Citizens for a Better Environment, and several other similar groups filed a lawsuit in the U.S. District

---

[4] Phillips, "Suit Challenges Zone Laws," p. 1.

[5] Carter B. Horsely, "Ecological Zoning Code Sought in Huntington Town Pilot Effort," *New York Times*, Jan. 25, 1971.

[6] See Fred P. Bosselman, "Ecology v. Equality: The Sierra Club Meets the NAACP," *Law and Social Problems*, vol. 2 (Fall 1971), p. 94.

[7] Ibid., pp. 93-94; Joseph M. Treen, "NAACP Sues to Annul Zoning, Integrate Oyster Bay," *Newsday*, Mar. 25, 1971, p. 5.

Court for the Western District of Texas against George Romney, as Secretary of the Department of Housing and Urban Development (HUD), and San Antonio Ranch, Inc. to halt the development of a new community outside San Antonio, Texas.[8] The proposed new community is planned to contain between 30 and 40 percent subsidized housing for low- and moderate-income families.[9]

According to the complaint filed by the Sierra Club the facts are these:[10] San Antonio Ranch, Inc. proposes to develop 9,318 acres of land approximately 20 miles from downtown San Antonio over a period of thirty years and at a cost of $50 million. Target population is approximately 88,000 persons in single-family and multi-family dwellings. HUD proposes to issue a project agreement to provide a loan guarantee for up to $18 million, under section 713 of the Housing and Urban Development Act of 1970, for financing "real property, acquisition and land development."

According to the complaint, 75 percent of the land area of the proposed new community sits on the recharge area of the Edwards Aquifer, a massive underground river that supplies all the water for San Antonio. The plaintiffs have taken issue with the environmental impact statement submitted by defendants — as required by the National Environmental Policy Act (NEPA) — alleging that the pollution potential for the aquifer has been inadequately studied, that alternatives to the particular location of the new community were not considered, and that what studies there were are incomplete and biased. And here is the plaintiffs' clincher: "The [environmental impact] Statement does not consider the alternative of attempting to keep this area in its natural condition through strict land use controls."

The plaintiffs are particularly concerned with the possibility of pollution from leaking sewer lines and contaminated storm-water runoff. They seek an injunction restraining HUD from issuing any loan guarantees until such time as the environmental impact statement is shown to be in compliance with NEPA.

Whatever the results for the environment, it is clearly going to be a while before this particular new community with its several thousand units of subsidized low- and moderate-income housing gets building.

While the contrast is often not clearly so stark, the conflict between housing and ecology is painfully apparent nonetheless in other localities as well.

---

[8] *Sierra Club, et al.* v. *George W. Romney, et al.* (U.S. D. Ct., W.D. Texas, Civ. No. SA 72 CA 77 (1972).

[9] Interview with Jack Underhill, Department of Housing and Urban Development, Washington, Mar. 9, 1972.

[10] All the following statements about this case are from paragraphs 12, 14, 15, 16, 18, 19, 25, 27, and 28 of the Club's complaint.

Boulder, Colorado: "Bosun! Pull The Ladder Up, I'm Aboard."

The City of Boulder is approximately forty miles from Denver in a valley in the foothills of the Rockies. It boasts a magnificent view of the mountains, I. M. Pei's pile for the Institute for Atmospheric Research, and the greatest percentage of Ph.D.'s per capita of any city in the country. For several years environmental groups have been urging various measures to preserve what they term the aesthetic and environmental qualities of Boulder. One of the most recent demands is a limitation on population growth. Boulder reportedly grew by approximately 6,000 persons during the last nine months of 1970, the highest proportionate area growth in the Denver Metropolitan Region.[11] The result has been an unrelenting attack by environmental groups against growth.

The controversy has pitted businessmen and a mixed bag of proponents of housing against the environmentalists such as People United to Reclaim the Environment (PURE). The Chamber of Commerce pointed out in a public statement issued October 16, 1970:

> 1. That the City is destined to grow. It is unrealistic to plan otherwise and counter to our historic precedents. The right to live in and engage in legitimate business enterprises in Boulder cannot morally or legally be denied anyone.
>
> 2. That there is a strong trend toward urban living. To meet this need construction of living units for all income groups should be encouraged.[12]

PURE, of course, tags the Chamber, and all like-minded groups, as greedy promoters. But the environmentalists do not know quite what to do about the housing limitations their policies would compel. While PURE responded to most of the Chamber's comments in great length and detail in a public statement issued November 8, 1970, it could manage only the following lame rebuttal to the call for more housing:

> 2. We agree that there should be construction of "living units for all income groups" but hope that the bulk of this effort can be done by replacement and renovation of existing dwellings rather than by extension of an already over-extended community.[13]

What did Boulder's environmentalists propose? Nothing short of limiting by an amendment to the City's charter the population of Boulder. Groups

[11]"Boulder Growth Tops Metro Area," *Boulder Daily Camera*, Jan. 31, 1971, p. 5–A.

[12]"Growth is Destined, Says Chamber Policy Statement," *Boulder Daily Camera*, Jan. 31, 1971, p. 14–A.

[13]"PURE Says Chamber View Against Environment, People," *Boulder Daily Camera*, Jan. 31, 1971, p. 15–A.

such as PURE proposed to make it illegal for outsiders to move into Boulder after an "optimum" population is reached. To that end, a question relating to population growth found its way onto the November 1971 referendum. The proposition read:

> Shall the Charter of the City of Boulder be amended by the enactment of a new provision thereto which shall read as follows:
>
>> The City Administration and Council shall adopt regulations and policies to stabilize the ultimate population of the City of Boulder near one hundred thousand.[14]

The proposition failed, but barely. (A sister proposition to limit the height of all buildings to 55 feet passed, pushed over the top by late returns from precincts near the University of Colorado, many of whose voting students live in high-rise dorms.)

It can be assumed that the proposition will come up again, and there is no reason to doubt that the environmentalists will be pushing to guarantee that Boulder will remain what it now is — a place for the rich and middle class, with little housing for the low- and moderate-income segments of the population.

Hawaii and Vermont: Ecology As a Congregationalist Imperative

New England exported evangelical fervor by the boatload to Hawaii in the early years of the nineteenth century. It now appears that Hawaii has returned the favor in the waning years of the twentieth century by shipping back to New England the passionate dogma of antigrowth.

Hawaii. Until recently the Hawaiian economy was based on agriculture, and the land area is totally overlaid with land use regulations controlled at the state level. A Land Use Commission decides which lands are to be used for agriculture, and which lands are to be preserved in a conservation zone.[15] The principal purpose for enacting this statewide zoning scheme was to protect agricultural lands from development and to contain urban expansion — especially Honolulu's spread into Oahu's central valley.[16]

There is evidence that the importance of agriculture is on the wane in Hawaii, leaving huge tracts of land in a "preservation" state — to the positive delight of conservationists who now have for all practical purposes *two*

---

[14]"Notice of and Call for General Municipal Election," *Boulder Daily Camera,* Oct. 17, 1971, p. 6.

[15]See Hawaii Rev. Stat. § 205–2; Eckbo, Dean, Austin & Williams, *State of Hawaii Land Use Districts and Regulations Review* (Report of Aug. 15, 1969).

[16]Fred Bosselman and David Callies, *The Quiet Revolution in Land Use Control* (Council on Environmental Quality, 1971).

preservation zones, which, when combined, cover an overwhelming majority of Hawaii's total land area. The result, according to developers, is a drastic shortage of land classified in the urban district, which is the only district in which large-scale residential development is permissible. Of the 100,000 acres for which reclassification to urban usage has been requested since 1964, only 30,000 acres have been so classified.[17] Today, developers estimate that the total remaining developable land zoned in the urban district is well under 10,000 acres for the entire state.

Moreover, county regulations, at least those of Honolulu on Oahu, generally require substantial and costly site improvements on developable land already made expensive by its scarcity. Developers estimate that a 6,000 square foot lot alone may cost around $6,000, and that required improvements, such as water, sewer, sidewalks, grading, and the like, will run at least another $10,000. For even the least expensive residence, land acquisition and improvements will run from 50 percent to 66 percent of the sales price of a home.[18]

These "preserve" and "improve" restrictions have contributed to one of the nation's most appalling shortages of housing and a substantial increase in the cost of what housing there is. In 1970, the median value of owner-occupied housing in Hawaii was $35,100 — more than twice the national figure of $17,000. Less than one-third of the state's housing is available even at the $25,000 mark! As for rental units, two-thirds exceed $100 per month.[19] Many developers assert that it is now impossible to construct *any* single-family housing in Hawaii for less than $30,000.[20]

Vermont. In 1970, the State of Vermont enacted an Environmental Control Law (Act 250) aimed at protecting Vermont from overdevelopment occasioned by a ski resort/second-home boom accelerated by the interstate highway system to Boston and New York City. The Act creates an Environmental Board and seven regional commissions whose function it is to review all proposals for major development in the state. Only the builder on a large lot (10 acres or more) escapes scrutiny, provided his project is sited below the 2,500-foot "fragile area" elevation.[21] In the board's two years of operation it has been principally concerned with assuring that appropriate "environmental conditions" are attached to the many permits for which affected developers must now apply.[22]

[17]Shelley M. Mark and Richard Poirier, *State and Local Land Use Planning: Some Lessons from Hawaii's Land Use Law* (Jan. 1971), p. 7.

[18]Bosselman and Callies, *The Quiet Revolution*, p. 26.

[19]U.S. Bureau of the Census, *General Housing Characteristics* (Feb. 1971).

[20]Bosselman and Callies, pp. 25–26.

[21]Act 250; 10 V.S.A. § 6001 et seq.

[22]Bosselman and Callies, pp. 59–71.

Whatever its eventual effect on the *environment* (and there are signs it may well be substantial), the Environmental Control Law is having considerable effect on housing — by raising its cost. Purportedly aimed at small-lot, high-density developments that characterize the second-home/ski condominium market, the Act and its regulations cannot help but affect the development of low- and medium-cost housing — also characterized by comparatively high densities. One corporate developer engaged in building a 400-unit second-home complex has estimated his permit preparation and review costs at between $20,000 and $30,000 *per year* over his period of construction.[23]

Nor is this the only potential conflict with housing goals. Vermont's Agency for Development and Community Affairs has long been concerned about both housing and development in the state's less-affluent areas. There is concern that the Environmental Control Law will not only impede construction of housing but also stifle economic development in the rural areas — with the result that the rural poor will pay for the environment proposed and sought by the relatively urban, relatively comfortable people living in Vermont's 30 towns containing over 2,500 people.[24]

San Francisco Bay: One Man's Pad is Another Man's Poison

In 1965, California created the San Francisco Bay Conservation and Development Commission (BCDC) for the purpose of regulating all development in and on San Francisco Bay.[25] The Commission was created subsequent to an environmentalist-conservationist coalition and crusade that probably rivals anything of its kind in recent history, spurred on largely by the vision of San Francisco Bay becoming the San Francisco River.[26] And in fact, development in the Bay Area has come to an abrupt halt due to the BCDC's efforts. But the blessing has been a decidedly mixed one for the area's poor. The low-lying areas near the waterfront on the Bay contain no less than seven of the eight Negro, and two of the three Latin communities, in the Bay Area.[27]

In the first place, some of the Bay Area to be filled was slated for housing — some of it specifically for the poor. In addition, the shift of construction pressure from the immediate Bay Area to the periphery of the area markedly affected the construction job market, which apparently provided many of the jobs for the residents of these communities. As one commenta-

[23]Interview with John Davidson of Quechee Lakes Corporation, Quechee, Vermont, July 1971.

[24]Bosselman and Callies, pp. 88–89.

[25]California Government Code, § 66600 et seq.

[26]"Saving San Francisco Bay: A Case Study on Environmental Legislation," *Stanford Law Review*, vol. 23 (January 1971), p. 349.

[27]Richard L. Meier, "Insights into Pollution," *Journal of the American Institute of Planners*, vol. 4 (July 1971), p. 216.

tor put it: "programs for saving the Bay, as conceived by the purists, will benefit those with 'view' lots, yachts, and interest in estuarine wildlife, at the expense of those least able to pay for and to defend their interests."[28]

POLEMICS AND ISSUES: I'D STOP SHOUTING
IF YOU'D ONLY LISTEN!

The conflict between ecology and most people would fill a book — indeed, several have been written on the subject. We don't propose to begin another here, yet a few points about this broader conflict may serve to put the ecology-housing conflict into perspective.

Generally, the "ecology first" enthusiast has a low opinion of his fellow man, which is why he may be willing to consign a goodly portion of mankind (usually that portion to which he does not belong) to perdition. An excellent example of such a protagonist is Ian McHarg, of *Design With Nature* fame, who has been quoted as follows: "Man is a blind, witless, low-brow anthropocentric clod who inflicts lesions on the earth."[29]

The ecological purist concludes that "man" must curb his excesses to "save the environment." This usually translates into saving the ecologist's environment at the expense of some *other* man's. It is the type of elitism that gives voice to the following from Robert and Leona Reinow's *Moment In The Sun*: "Over cries of outrage, the historic Morningside Park in Manhattan is giving way to a school."[30]

In Chicago's Garfield Park, the battle went the other way, and the attempt to put a school and housing for southside inner city residents therein failed. School for whom; park for whom? In the inner city, the school and housing is for the inner city resident, often black and poor. The urban park is often as not for the aesthetic titillation of the city's middle class, or even the suburban commuter, who can afford to concern himself about his aesthetic sensibilities although he wouldn't be caught using the park. In Chicago's Grant Park, the view is from the skyscrapers along Michigan Avenue, and the only residences in sight are the posh Outer Drive East and Lake Point Towers. Indeed, one of the heaviest users of Grant Park's athletic fields is a 20-team league made up of LaSalle Street lawyers, precious few of whom live in the city.

But there is a growing awareness, as the environmentalist movement becomes more strident, that ecology is indeed elitist. Jon Margolis recently wrote an article for *Esquire Magazine* dealing with the cry of the ecologists for an end to growth and its effect on housing. Margolis comes on strong:

[28] Ibid.
[29] Ruth Adams, *Say No!* (Emmaus, Pa.: Rodale Press, 1971), p. 143.
[30] Ballantine, 1969, p. 51.

Stop growing? But growing is the secret of our success. We have mass affluence, to the extent we have it, not because we took from the rich and gave to the poor but because we became — *we grew* — so much richer that even most of the poor live tolerably. They still get the short end of the stick, but the stick is so long now that one can get at least a fingerhold on that end.

. . . the conservationists are not on that end. They are not steelworkers or assembly-line workers or small farmers or hotel clerks. They are Wall Street lawyers and junior faculty and editors and writers and corporate vice-presidents. One does not become a conservationist until one has had the time and learning to care about whether there are eagles or Everglades. *Searching for their hundred-fifty-year-old Vermont farmhouses, conservationists wonder how people can actually want to live in a new $25,000 split-level in the suburbs, apparently never thinking that for most people the alternative is a three-room walk-up in the downtown smog.* The suburbs are open to them, as Vermont is to the more affluent, because of technology, because draining swamps and dirtying streams and damming rivers and polluting the air gave them high-paying jobs. Shouting about the environmental catastrophe, urging an end to growth, the conservationists are $20,000-a-year men telling all the $7,500-a-year men simply to stay where they are so we can all survive. Ethics aside, there is a serious tactical problem here; there are more $7,500-a-year men and they are likely to say no. True, money would go farther in a good environment. True, as Ian McHarg said, ecological planning can give any given area more high-paying jobs and more profits plus good environment. But for the nation as a whole, for the economy, the conservationist's dichotomy remains, and he has not faced up to it: if we do not stop expanding, we ruin the environment; if we do, we condemn the lower middle classes to their present fate. (Emphasis added.)[31]

As Richard Neuhaus has made clear in his *In Defense of People*, it is often a matter of the rich man's politics of choice versus the poor man's politics of necessity:

To whom, politically speaking, does the environmental issue belong? To the aristocrats, certainly. To the monied, misanthropic aristocrats who live in the city as much as need compels but find their 'real life' in getting away from it all. The presumably radical ecotacticians of the 1970's are in large part the heirs of a conservationist history that, in a thousand variations, has peddled the proposition that 'only man is vile.'[32]

The point is not that ecology as the middle class reads it is unimportant. And it is quite obvious that the social critics of the ecological renaissance find

---

[31] Jon Margolis, "Land of Ecology," *Esquire Magazine* (March 1970).
[32] Richard Neuhaus, *In Defense of People* (Macmillan, 1971), p. 30.

themselves being cozied up to by some suspect characters who, as in the cartoons, have dollar signs where their eyes ought to be. The point is that certain other goals of a *social* nature are *also* important — such as housing. Ecology insists upon not only center stage, but the *whole* stage, on the ground that *survival* is at stake. The ploy of raising ecology to the dignity of a moral principle and then declaring it to be a matter of *survival* is aptly put by Neuhaus: "Who has time for programs of social justice if indeed survival is at stake?"[33] The fairness of priorities, of balancing, goes out the window and "necessity" sets in. There is no time for anything else, including housing.

It is not that the poor don't care about environment; it is just that environment to them does not mean keeping the fishing holes free of beer cans or of saving Lake Michigan "for all of us," but of finding decent shelter reasonably accessible to a job. One angry black said it: "Ecology is a Racist Shuck." As black Professor Robert Chrisman sees it, having acknowledged its own ecological abuses, white America now refuses to grapple with solutions that are acceptable to the have-nots.

SOME PATHS TO A COMPROMISE: ONE HOUSE, ONE PARK

We have seven suggestions for modifications in our policies that would help balance the equities between housing and clean air and perhaps help persuade the poorly housed that the rest of us understand what *they* mean by the term "environment." These suggestions are:

1. Stealing a leaf from the National Environmental Policy Act, we propose that before an ecology-inspired regulation is given the force of law, or before a development with a residential component is modified or rejected for ecological reasons, or indeed, before any environmental regulation is applied to, say, an inner city rehabilitation project, a "housing impact statement" be required, setting forth: (a) the effect such a restraint would have on the supply, the cost, and the quality of housing in the community; (b) what attempt was made to find alternative methods of preserving the environment that would not so drastically affect the housing supply.

This "housing impact statement" would further indicate what sort of housing — what segment of the community — is bearing the biggest burden of an environmental protection measure: low income, moderate income, or upper income. The information for working out a compromise would be readily at hand.

2. Amend section 201 of NEPA to require a statement on the impact of the proposed project on low- and moderate-income housing and a statement

[33]Ibid., p. 114.

of whether the effort to preserve amenities such as open space, historical areas, and scenic values will have an adverse impact on the community's or region's need for low- and moderate-income housing. The United States Supreme Court correctly believes that Congress has given parkland a uniquely privileged position in the search for land for highways.[34] When the Bureau of Public Roads must choose between a park and ghetto housing for a right of way, presumably the housing is more vulnerable. We would repair that imbalance.

3. A few jurisdictions have given broad authority to state agencies to control growth by vetoing development that may cause environmental nuisances. Such is the case in Illinois where the Environmental Protection Board can and has clamped down on builders in the Chicago Metropolitan Area in sectors where sewer treatment plants were inadequate. Stop orders on sewer attachments have been ordered; controls imposed over hookups. In any case, where a program of restricted attachments is required we would amend the law to permit the agency, upon a finding of need, to give priority to builders of subsidized housing.

4. The so-called A-95 program offers a shopping basket of federal goodies to local governments. Federal money is available for open space, sewer and water systems, hospitals, mass transit, and a score of other capital improvements. Local applications are subject to review by a regional agency to determine the consistency of the request with regional plans. Clearly, it would be counterproductive to use this regional review leverage in all A-95 programs to compel communities to open up to low- and moderate-income housing, but at least in the case of requests for federal assistance in the acquisition of parks, and perhaps in some cases involving sewer improvements, the community should be required to submit evidence on the need (or lack of need) for low- and moderate-income housing and what it is doing about it. It seems quixotic that Uncle Sam should underwrite programs to provide greater amenities for suburbs that open their doors only to those who can afford a $35,000 house.

5. Our state laws, particularly our zoning and platting legislation, should be amended to require municipalities to designate those areas that are unsuitable for any housing because of topographic, locational, or other "environmental" reasons. This will help ensure that low-cost housing, when it is permitted, is not limited to the environs of the village dump.

[34]"But the very existence of the statutes indicates that protection of parkland was to be given paramount importance. ... If the statutes are to have any meaning the Secretary [of Transportation] cannot approve the destruction of parkland unless he finds that alternative routes present *unique* problems." (Emphasis added.) *Friends of Overton Park et al.* v. *Volpe*, 401 U.S. 402, 412–13 (1971).

This change in state law should go hand in hand with a change in the doctrine of presumption of validity of municipal regulations insofar as they affect housing. If a community has designated an area as suitable for housing, the burden should be on the municipality to demonstrate why only low-density (i.e., high-cost) housing is appropriate on the site. (Serrano and its brethren may remove one of the usual municipal arguments — namely, that low-income housing will impose an intolerable burden on the schools because of dependence on the real property tax.)

6. The state should take back from the municipalities some portion of the police power it delegated to them fifty years ago in the name of zoning. This state reassertion of power should include at least the authority to review and to overrule all municipal decisions concerning proposals for (1) subsidized housing, and (2) industrial development that will provide more than 100 jobs. The former scheme is essentially what the Massachusetts "anti-snob" law is all about; and it can be smoked out of the rhetoric of the Nixon Administration's National Land Use Policy bill now in Congress. These proposals for state intervention in housing and in major industrial development are both part of Article VII of Tentative Draft No. 3 of the American Law Institute's Model Land Development Code. In contrast with the glacial pace at which the states move into the housing field, they are falling all over themselves to respond to demands of the environmentalists that the salt marshes be saved. The states must only not act to preserve our *natural* resources from improper growth, they must also move to encourage growth when it is necessary to benefit our *human* resources and to put right long-standing abuses of municipal land use regulation.

7. Finally, we propose that the Sierra Club form a not-for-profit or limited-dividend subsidiary to construct 1,000 subsidized housing units a year. We have every confidence that the Club will see to it that this housing does not impair the environment. We have only two conditions: the housing must be reasonably accessible to jobs, and it must be in a temperate area where the housing will make demands on our sorely pressed energy supplies. In that way the Club, at least symbolically, will share the collective guilt of the rest of us over the risks of growth such as pointed up by those headline grabbers, the Alaskan oil pipeline, the next oil spill, and the overheating of the Great Lakes from all those nuclear plants.

These proposals don't strike us as Graustarkian. And, with the exception of our last suggestion, they do represent specific legislative changes as a useful substitute for yelling at each other. It is time to end the name-calling. We would do well to take heed from these three lines of Robert Frost:

> And so put off the weary day
> When we would have to put our mind
> On how to crowd and still be kind.

POSTSCRIPT

One month after the RFF forum, an event occurred that is the quintessence of all that we were seeking to illuminate in our paper. On May 12 in the United States District Court in Chicago, a group calling themselves Nucleus of Chicago Homeowners Association (NO-CHA), other property owner associations, and scores of individuals filed suit to enjoin Secretary of HUD George Romney, the Chicago Housing Authority, and other officials and agencies from proceeding with an announced plan to construct public housing on scattered sites in predominantly white middle-class areas in the southwestern areas of Chicago.[35] The scattered site housing program was being undertaken as a consequence of earlier orders of a federal judge in the same U.S. District Court in the well-known *Gautreaux* cases.[36]

The complaint in the NO-CHA case is nothing if not blunt; no euphemisms for them. It alleges:

11. As a statistical whole, low-income families of the kind that reside in housing provided by the CHICAGO HOUSING AUTHORITY possess certain social class characteristics which will be and have been inimical and harmful to the legitimate interests of the plaintiffs.

12. Regardless of the cause, be it family conditioning, genetics, or environmental conditions beyond their control, members of low-income families of the kind that reside in housing provided by the CHICAGO HOUSING AUTHORITY possess, as a statistical whole, the following characteristics:

(a) As compared to the social class characteristics of the plaintiffs, such low-income family members possess a higher propensity toward criminal behavior and acts of physical violence than do the social classes of the plaintiffs.

(b) As compared to the social class characteristics of the plaintiffs, such low-income family members possess a disregard for physical and aesthetic maintenance of real and personal property which is in direct

[35] *NO-CHA, et al.* v. *Romney, et al.*, U.S.D.C. N.D. Ill. Doc. 72C 1197.

[36] *Gautreaux, et al.* v. *Chicago Housing Authority*, 296 F.Supp. 907 (1969); *Gautreaux, et al.* v. *George W. Romney*, 448 F.2d 731 (1971).

contrast to the high level of care with which the plaintiffs social classes treat their property.

(c) As compared to the social class characteristics of the plaintiffs, such low-income family members possess a lower commitment to hard work for future-oriented goals with little or no immediate reward than do the social classes of the plaintiffs.

Social Class Characteristics of the Plaintiffs.

13. As a statistical whole, members of the plaintiffs' social classes, often described as middle class and/or working class, possess the following characteristics:

(a) As compared to the social class characteristics of low-income family members such as described above, members of plaintiffs' social classes emphasize obedience and respect for lawful authority and have a much lower propensity toward criminal behavior and acts of physical violence.

(b) As compared to the social class characteristics of low-income family members such as described above, members of plaintiffs' social classes possess a high regard for the physical and aesthetic improvement of real and personal property.

And what federal law do the plaintiffs say has been violated? None other than the National Environmental Protection Act. Specifically alleged to have been violated is section 102 of that Act, which requires the filing of an environmental impact statement before a federal agency undertakes "major Federal action significantly affecting the quality of the human environment."

Poor people will damage or destroy the quality of middle class environment.

ALTERNATIVES FOR FUTURE
URBAN LAND POLICY

MARION CLAWSON and HARVEY S. PERLOFF

Given the land use situation in the United States, what are the policy alternatives facing the nation? The preceding papers have made it clear that substantial parts of our total population are disadvantaged by the land use policy that has emerged over the past several decades, primarily from the independent action of hundreds of local planning and zoning bodies. The various minority groups that have been effectively excluded from living in new housing in suburbs are naturally unhappy over their situation and strive to do something about it. But other sectors of the total electorate are also unhappy about the situation, and they, too, seek to do something about it.

MARION CLAWSON is director of the land and water use and management program at Resources for the Future. He has written extensively on land use matters, and his books include *Policy Directions for U.S. Agriculture, Economics of Outdoor Recreation* (co-author), *Land for the Future*, and *Suburban Land Conversion in the United States*. He worked for twenty-four years with the Department of Agriculture and the Department of the Interior, the last five years of which he was director of the Bureau of Land Management. Since 1955 he has been with RFF. Born in 1905, he holds B.S. and M.S. degrees from the University of Nevada and a Ph.D. in economics from Harvard University.

HARVEY S. PERLOFF is dean of the School of Architecture and Urban Planning at the University of California, Los Angeles. An economist and planner, Mr. Perloff helped to develop the program of education and research in planning at the University of Chicago and served as its head from 1950 to 1955. From 1955 to 1968 he directed the regional and urban studies program at Resources for the Future. His books include: *Regions, Resources, and Economic Growth* (co-author); *Issues in Urban Economics* (co-editor); and *Alliance for Progress*. Mr. Perloff was born in 1915, and received his B.A. from the University of Pennsylvania and his Ph.D. in political economy from Harvard University.

The several papers recognize that land use measures are not solely responsible for the discrimination that exists or for the generally disadvantaged position of racial and ethnic minorities and the poor. Reform of land use planning and zoning alone will not cure the unsatisfactory conditions.

The earlier papers have also made it clear that various measures have been taken, or might be taken, that will lead to substantial modification in land use planning and zoning practices. The actual events are far more significant as indicators of change than they are for their accomplishment. Perhaps they presage a hurricane, perhaps they will subside. In this paper we explore some of the possibilities for change, make some tentative appraisals, and suggest some possible lines of desirable action. If change is coming, from what direction is it coming, at what speed, and at whose impetus?

Traditional land use controls have been under attack from several directions. Heyman, in his paper in this book, points out that municipal land use regulation is under attack by the environmentalists, the lawyers, market forces, the proponents of open housing, state governments, and the federal government. Fessler, in his essay, has traced the recent rise of legal services to the poor and shown how these services have enabled poor people to challenge governmental actions inimical to their interests. Dissatisfaction with the results of local land use controls has caused many states to adopt statewide or regional approaches. In Alaska, Colorado, Connecticut, Delaware, Georgia, Hawaii, Maine, Maryland, Massachusetts, North Carolina, Rhode Island, Vermont, and Wisconsin, either a new state organization or an existing agency is required to implement some degree of *statewide* land use planning or zoning, or both, or to carry out some sort of planning and land use regulation aimed at particular classes of land such as wetlands or tidal areas.[1] In addition, in some states, as in California with its San Francisco Bay Conservation and Development Commission, or California and Nevada with the Tahoe Regional Planning Agency, or New Jersey with the Hackensack Meadowlands Development Commission, or New York with the Adirondack Park Agency, a regional agency has been created to deal with some special problems of land use planning and control. These various measures are primarily directed at resource-use problems – the preservation of some unique resource or area. Their primary focus is ecological (or physical). This is not to imply that they are lacking in social consequences, but social objectives are not the primary aim. Their significance for our present purposes does not lie in their aims or in their mechanisms, or even in their results (which to date have been small), but rather in the fact that they do represent a distinct break with past sole

[1] Fred Bosselman and David Callies, *The Quiet Revolution in Land Use Control* (Council on Environmental Quality, 1971).

reliance on *local* land use planning. Some establish state controls that replace local controls; others provide a combination of state and local controls, with statewide concerns clearly dominant.

In a few instances state legislation has been directed primarily at the social issues of land use control — particularly, at the exclusionary aspects of local land use zoning. Massachusetts enacted a Zoning Appeals Law, which enables developers of low-income housing to apply to a local zoning appeals board for a comprehensive permit instead of applying to various agencies for the many permits required under local regulations. If the application is denied, the developer can appeal to a Housing Appeals Committee created at the state level, which has the power under the law to reverse the decision of the local zoning board. In New York, the Urban Development Corporation has the legal power to override local zoning ordinances and building codes that would otherwise prevent the Corporation from building housing for low-income groups.

The statewide and regional approaches to land use planning and control are, in general, too recent to have been fully tested for either their competence and efficacy or their legal powers. They are significant, however, as portents of a growing dissatisfaction with the operation of land use planning and zoning at the strictly local level.

Bills before the Congress in 1972 provide for a much larger federal role in land use planning. Senate bill 632, which passed the Senate in September 1972, included a statement of national policy, expressing a national interest in land use planning; provided a system of grants to states to enable them to conduct land use planning for certain critical environmental and development areas and to give some degree of supervision to units of local government in their land use planning; and provided for the establishment of a small new unit in the Department of the Interior to handle the federal grants. The bill as reported out of the Senate Committee had included severe penalties for states that did not carry on land use planning; by Senate action these were reduced to a simple withholding of the planning grants. This bill had been supported, with minor suggested changes, by the executive branch. A similar but different bill had been considered by the House Committee but was not acted upon by the House. Although many important differences remain to be ironed out, ultimate passage of national legislation on land use planning seems likely. Most of the discussion about national legislation has focused on environmental problems, but social problems can surely not be ignored if any machinery for land use planning is devised. Who is to benefit, who is to lose, who is to be excluded, and from where?

Every analyst who deals with the future faces several choices. Will he try to project or forecast the changes that he thinks are most probable, or paint a

picture of what he personally thinks is most desirable, or take some inter-
mediate and often poorly defined approach? We recognize the problem, and,
in what follows, we try to be explicit about our choices. We sometimes use
one approach, sometimes another. On the one hand, we do not accept trends
or forces as inevitable and unchangeable; one purpose of an analysis such as
this is to provide the basis for alternatives. On the other hand, we do not
believe that pure wishful thinking is likely to be productive; there must be
some consideration of reality.

As we contemplate the future of cities and of land use, we make one basic
assumption that underlies the rest of what we have to say here. In our
opinion, a nation that has undertaken changes in education, in voting, and in
civil rights such as have occurred in this country in the past twenty years or
so cannot long continue to turn its back upon discrimination in housing.
True, and to the surprise of those of us who lived through the New Deal, the
lead has been taken by the courts, and more particularly by the Supreme
Court. But it is a mistake to underestimate the degree of legislative, executive
branch, and general electorate support for the changes that the Court has
imposed. There have been grumbling and threats of revolt, and here and there
outright defiance of a court decision; but the dominant fact has been the
degree to which people generally have gone along with, if not positively
supported, the Court in its reforms. Despite some talk in recent months about
the new Supreme Court being likely to be a strict constructionist one, the
present Court has pushed educational desegregation further than its predeces-
sors did. The Court, like the public, will change its views over the next decade
or two; but there is perhaps as much reason to expect the Court to go
forward on the removal of racial and other barriers as to expect it to retreat.

In the remainder of this paper, we consider the possible directions of
change in land use controls, with only modest consideration either of how
such changes might come about or of the chances that they will. We are
convinced that some change is inevitable and that a reduction of discrimination in housing is highly probable, but we are not sure how these changes will
be realized or exactly when. The task of developmental statesmanship is to
explore and to invent alternative policies; choice is possible, and urban land
use can be what we collectively choose to make it.

PROCEDURAL REFORMS

One possible avenue for change in land use zoning and other land use
controls is procedural reform — procedures in planning, in zoning, in public

works, and in other measures that largely determine the public input into urban and suburban land use. Anyone even modestly familiar with these procedures knows how often they violate the accepted principles of good government and even legal requirements of due process. Babcock, in his book, *The Zoning Game – Municipal Practices and Policies,* has amply documented this for zoning.[2] Fessler, in his essay in this book, has also described some of the deficiencies of zoning. Planning and zoning actions are often taken in closed sessions, or without due notice to affected parties, or in contradiction to rules established by the organizations concerned; members of zoning commissions and other bodies act on cases in which they have an interest, direct or indirect, or enter into reciprocal trade with other members, each to advance the other's cases without direct action by the involved party; outright bribery is proven in some cases and suspected in many others. Zoning and other actions are taken without any standards, or are inconsistent with other actions by the same public bodies. All in all, there is scarcely a field of local government activity where procedural sloppiness and outright favoritism are more prevalent than in zoning and related actions. As Babcock has shown in his book, the local courts have been scarcely more consistent; many have shunned zoning cases and have let virtually anything slip by in order to avoid serious work and thought on zoning. Fessler, in his paper in this book, has described the reluctance of appeals courts to disturb administrative local zoning actions.

All this would seem to cry out for reform, and there may indeed be persons or groups who will work for reform on these grounds. Some political conservatives, for instance, may favor racially oriented local zoning but still be outraged at the slovenliness of local governmental processes. Legal attacks on land use zoning for its procedural inadequacies face great difficulties, as Fessler has shown. The basic problem is standing to sue; this is often denied to nonresidents of the county or other area concerned on the grounds that they lack the requisite personal interest or stake in the outcome. Yet the local gentry who do have standing to sue may have reached an informal agreement among themselves that no one will upset the cozy arrangements by which they benefit (or think they do). Outsiders from racial and income groups not represented in the county but de facto excluded by local zoning may find it extremely difficult to get their cases before the judicial machinery. Nevertheless, difficult as challenges to procedural deficiencies may be, one should not wholly foreclose them from judicially imposed reform, or judicial stimulus to legislative reform, or self-inspired legislative reform.

[2] Richard F. Babcock, *The Zoning Game – Municipal Practices and Policies* (University of Wisconsin Press, 1966).

Let us first explore some of the directions procedural reform might take, and then consider what, if anything, a new method might accomplish if adopted.

Since cities and counties exercise control over private land use by means of powers granted to them by the states, the states might arouse themselves to exercise some degree of control over the use of those delegated powers. One avenue would be to enact legislation that would spell out the legal and administrative procedures for planning, zoning, and other controls over private land use. One element here might be a statement in the law of the kinds of considerations that should be faced, and discussed, in development plans for an area. For instance, the law might require that the plan state its goals, that it explore and present evidence on its benefits and costs to affected groups, and that it include some governmental procedure adequate to implement its objectives. One might here draw an analogy with the environmental impact statements required under the National Environmental Policy Act of 1969 and subsequent amendatory measures. The local government to which legal power to control private land use had been delegated might be required to analyze the economic and social impact of its regulations. State legislation might also spell out such procedures as due notice of action, public hearing requirements, provisions for appeal, and others. While these might not alter current practice in some of the better-managed local zoning and planning bodies, they might raise the standard of practice in many others. If any such legislation were adopted by any state, the grounds for appeal from planning, zoning, and related actions would be laid.

This type of state action would be vastly more effective if interest groups of various kinds, whether resident within the local area or not, had clearly established standing to sue. This might be specified in the same or in other legislation. However, the effectiveness of the concerned citizen organization should not be exaggerated; few organizations are equipped to fight all the battles for racial minorities, and still fewer are equipped or willing to fight battles for economically depressed groups. Nevertheless, states could go a long way in bringing a procedural orderliness to local government actions in the zoning and related fields.

A state law governing local zoning might include a special measure requiring that specific zoning actions conform to, or at least not violate, an area's general plans and policy "frameworks," and that these, in turn, be established only by proper procedures of hearing and appeals. This would provide some guide for specific zoning actions. Zoning board members could no longer state that cases were heard "on their merits" without defining a "merit" and subjecting their definition to citizen review in open hearing.

Conformity to general plans and policy frameworks would help to reduce the arbitrariness and favoritism of local zoning actions. This would be particularly effective if local plans and policy frameworks set out local plan objectives and principles of developmental action in specific terms and if the local plans showed the relationship of the local unit to the metropolis in economic, social, and political terms as well as in physical and service terms. Tying zoning to general plans would not guarantee wisdom or fairness. General plans are also subject to prejudiced and parochial thinking. But at least the zoning rationale and purposes would have to be formed in the open.

State legislation might go further and provide that appeals from local governmental planning and zoning action be heard by a body outside the area concerned. This might be a state body like the Massachusetts Housing Appeals Committee or a metropolitan-wide body such as a subsidiary of a metropolitan Council of Government. Or it might be a special court — after all, special courts have been established to decide other special types of problems. If an appeals system of this kind is to be effective, it should be open not only to the parties directly involved, and perhaps the professional staffs of the planning and zoning organizations, but to any interested citizen group as well. Here, the right of citizen groups to bring class action suits would be extremely important if not critical. A principle might easily be established that any citizen within the larger area served by the appeals board could have the right to appeal.

A system of appeals from local planning and zoning actions to an agency of a higher unit of government that serves a larger area would have some similarities to the procedures under the British Town and Country Planning Act of 1947 as amended (including the amendments still pending, but likely to be adopted).[3] In Great Britain, under this act, local units of government prepare land use plans for their area of jurisdiction. If a tract of land is designated on the map for residential or other development, this in itself is "planning permission," and its owner is thereby granted the legal freedom to develop it in accordance with the plan. If the map shows that a tract is to remain in some undeveloped use, then "planning permission" has been refused. There is no separate step of land use zoning such as we have in the United States. The plans have to be approved by the appropriate Minister in London (originally, the Minister of Town and Country Planning, later the Minister of Housing and Local Government, and now the Minister of the

<hr />

[3]This and other references to the British experience come from Marion Clawson and Peter Hall, *Planning and Urban Growth: An Anglo-American Comparison* (Johns Hopkins University Press for Resources for the Future, forthcoming).

Department of the Environment). Refusal of planning permission has almost
always meant a substantial loss in land value compared with the value of the
same land with planning permission; any citizen feeling aggrieved by such loss
of value could appeal to the Minister who could, if he chose, hold a public
inquiry into the matter. If the local government sought loans or grants for
public housing — and about half of all housing since World War II in Britain
has been publicly built — the approval of the Ministry for the loan or grant
was required. Thus, in effect, the Ministry had three opportunities to review
the local plans. The Ministry could, and in fact almost always did, modify the
plans before granting approval. This process was very time-consuming; the
delays in planning review were very great. In 1968 an act provided that
thereafter local authorities would prepare "structure" plans, or statements of
general policy, showing trends and broad patterns of future development;
these are approved by the Ministry, as before. The detailed proposals to
implement the structure plans come in local plans, which are not normally
approved by the Minister, although he has the legal right to intervene. This
process in Great Britain has reduced the arbitrariness and parochialism of
local planning, and — though such conclusions must be largely subjective — it
seems greatly to have reduced fraud, bribery, and personal profiteering from
the individual's actions as a public official. The *overall* social consequences
may not be much better than the results in the United States, but for different reasons.

If appeals from local planning and zoning action could be taken to a body
with jurisdiction over a wider area — at least a metropolitan area — the metropolitan-wide effect of local actions might receive consideration. Thus, the
type of large-lot zoning that may seem defensible when practiced on a small
scale by one suburban municipality would be seen to produce significant and
undesired effects when practiced by all suburbs in the metropolis. The appeals process *might* be able to force consideration of regional interests and
results in this way.

When one begins to contemplate the possibility of appeals from zoning
and other land use controls being made to regional or statewide bodies, the
recent California and Richmond, Virginia, school cases assume paramount
importance. These decisions may or may not be upheld on appeal to higher
courts and, even if upheld, must be fleshed out with additional decisions. In
the Richmond case, the court rejected the defense of school integration
within counties when this led to segregation between counties. In effect, the
court was sweeping county boundary lines, at least for some purposes. Many
boundaries of local government arose from historical accident. If carried to its
logical end, the court's attitude would reject the defense of suburban cities or
counties that they were not responsible for a segregated housing situation in

the larger metropolitan community. Again, one should not assume that the potentials of these school cases will be realized — whether one regards this as good or as bad. The decisions to date are significant as straws in the wind rather than as actual firm results. But it surely is not inconceivable that the highly localized land use zoning we have known for about half a century might be changed materially in the future.

There are those who take a dim view of the efficacy of procedural reform. In their view, legislation prescribing proper procedures may force local governments to do properly and neatly what they had previously done sloppily and with frequent favoritism, but the end results will be the same as far as the poor and the racial minorities are concerned. This view assumes that procedure can be made subservient to ends and that, given the ends, legally defensible procedure can be found that will attain the ends. Some might go further, and argue that there would be insufficient interest and power to require local governments to live up to the improved procedures established by law. One can surely sympathize with the "procedural pessimists," for good procedure alone does not guarantee wisdom, fairness, or positive results.

We take a rather different view of the advantages of procedural reform while admitting the arguments of the pessimists. We think that procedures do matter, that the end product of governmental action is directly affected if not governed by the processes of government, and that the reform of procedures will affect the outcomes of the processes concerned. If some or all of the foregoing procedural reforms for zoning and other land use controls were adopted, a different pattern of land uses would result. One key feature of a reformed procedure would be the use of public hearings or other open review of actions by local governmental bodies; anyone familiar with public hearings knows that they are no panacea — often attended only by the directly interested and by the crackpots, often eliciting nothing but junk testimony, often ignored when the decisions are made. But the mere possibility that a public hearing will be held, or can be insisted upon by opponents, surely acts as a strong restraint against favoritism and illegality.

If zoning had to be based upon general plans and policy frameworks, and if both had to conform to certain legal standards and be arrived at by a governmental process subject to citizen scrutiny, then at least one could say that the results represented the considered decision of the people of the area or of the unit of government making the decision. This would reduce the ill-considered actions and those in the personal interest of one of the actors; it would by no means guarantee a socially enlightened action. But, when combined with review at a higher and geographically wider level, it would be less locally oriented and more considerate of the metropolitan or regional interest. We think these differences would be real gains.

SUBSTANTIVE REFORM

The dividing line between procedural and substantive reform is obviously not a clear and sharp one, yet there is some difference between efforts to make old established approaches work better and efforts to institute new and different approaches. The preceding section was concerned, in the main, with measures to improve the working of the zoning and other land use controls that have existed for the past half century or so – to make these controls work more effectively, more democratically, less parochially. Now we consider some new measures to replace or supplement the old ones.

First, we must consider and dismiss as unworkable any suggestion to abolish land use zoning. The experience of Houston, Texas, where private covenants have largely governed land use, is sometimes cited as evidence that public zoning is unnecessary and costly. Comparatively few persons, we judge, would accept this view. We do not. Private covenants may raise more problems than they answer; in particular, their social accountability is weak. On a more practical level, private covenants do not exist on hundreds of square miles of residential areas in the United States, and the negotiation of such covenants among the many landowners in such residential areas would be impossibly difficult. Were zoning to be abolished for these areas, their residents would feel that they were not adequately protected from intrusion by nonconforming and discordant uses. Thus, should land use zoning be totally overthrown by some court decision, we think that legislatures would immediately act to restore it in some legally acceptable form at least for the areas where zoning has existed for many years. We think that a total rejection of land use zoning is both undesirable and politically unacceptable. Reform, not abolition, seems called for.

Proposals for drastic reform of land use zoning fall in a very different category than proposals for its abolition. In "Requiem for Zoning" and "The Future of American Planning" John Reps sharply criticized land use zoning as it has worked in practice, but he proposed major changes to cure or reduce its demonstrated deficiencies.[4] Our own proposals, in the paragraphs that follow, bear considerable resemblance to his. Without attempting to review or appraise his proposals, we proceed to develop ours, merely warning the reader that ours are not wholly new.

One major substantive change would be the provision that every land use plan or land use zoning ordinance require every residential development to

---

[4]John W. Reps, "Requiem for Zoning," *Planning 1964: Selected Papers from the 1964 ASPO Planning Conference*; and "The Future of American Planning: Requiem or Renascence?," *Planning 1967: Selected Papers from the ASPO National Planning Conference* (American Society of Planning Officials, Chicago, 1964 and 1967).

include some provision for low-income and/or racial minority populations. This requirement upon land use planning and zoning might conceivably be imposed by a court decision or by legislative action arising either spontaneously or in response to court pressure. In fact, an ordinance requiring residential builders to include housing for low-income families was adopted by the county government of Fairfax County, Virginia, in 1970, but was not upheld in a court test. If mandatory mixing of a majority and minority groups were proposed, two major questions would immediately arise. Should it apply to economic classes as well as to races? For what unit of area should it be applicable? These questions merit consideration at this point.

Racial discrimination in housing surely still exists, and is likely to be struck down whenever it is too overt or whenever it can be proven — not an easy task. But dealing with income discrimination is vastly more difficult. How much good would it do poor people of any race or ethnic group to have discriminatory land use controls abolished if they cannot afford to buy or rent housing of standard or better quality? Elimination of bias in zoning would remove one obstacle to their ownership or occupancy of better housing, but their limited ability to afford something better would remain a barrier, unless removed by other measures. Thus, requirements in land use plans and in zoning ordinances that provision be made for racial minorities and for the poor would not, in itself, produce much housing for these groups. Other measures would be needed, as Weaver has pointed out in his paper in this book.

Perhaps more important is the question: At what geographic scale should a mixing of income classes and/or races be required in land use plans and zoning ordinances? Should it be required at the subdivision, suburban satellite town, or metropolitan scale? If the requirement is imposed at the subdivision scale, the developer would have to provide some housing at specified price levels for poor and/or racial groups, with no discrimination in sales to the latter. The required amount would probably not exceed a relatively small percentage of his total housing construction. Presumably, the developer's profit prospects are such that he would not provide this housing unless he had to — if he would, there would obviously be no problem. If the developer must suffer some reduced income by providing housing for low-income and/or racial occupants, then he must make up this loss by higher prices or larger profits from the other houses he builds; their purchasers are, in effect, bearing the social cost of providing housing for the low-income and racial groups involved. Is this the proper incidence of such costs? Is this the proper scale of mixing? Will small numbers of persons from low-income and racial groups find their best social opportunities in otherwise high-income subdivisions? Such questions clearly challenge the idea of mixing at the subdivision level.

Mixing at the suburban-city or suburban-county level would avoid some, but not all, of these difficulties. If a unit of suburban government were forced to make provision for both low-income and racial groups in its land use plans, it would have somewhat more flexibility than a single subdivision developer. Since the low-income workers would often be the service employees for the higher-income residents, provision of land on which housing could be erected for them could be justified on grounds of simple equity and of the efficiency of people living reasonably near their jobs. It has been stated that less than 10 percent of the garbage collection staff of Montgomery County, Maryland, actually live within the county. Here are regularly employed public employees receiving low but not substandard wages, who are forced to commute long distances because there are no practical housing opportunities nearby. Such extreme separation of home and work place may be attacked on both efficiency and equity grounds. In the case of suburban counties, a strong case could be made that their land use plans and zoning should provide land for housing for all major groups of workers in the county. Provision of housing within their means would involve its own problems; appropriately zoned land is essential but may not be sufficient. At the level of the suburban city, especially the small one, a requirement to provide land for low-income housing might be more difficult to meet and perhaps less defensible. In each case, an attempt to provide for all would raise the question of whether there is any place in the future for the exclusive high-income residential area. If there is, how large can it be without creating social consequences unacceptable to a large proportion of the electorate?

The case for requiring land use planning and zoning to take account of the needs of racial minorities and low-income groups is strongest at the metropolitan level. If genuine planning exists or can be created at the metropolitan scale and if land use zoning is either formulated or subject to review at the metropolitan scale, provision could be made for housing all income classes within reach of job opportunities, public services, and recreational and cultural facilities. This would undoubtedly produce some separation of housing by income levels, and probably by race also — in each case, perhaps more de facto than proclaimed. But such metropolitan planning and zoning does not exist today; possibly a series of court decisions would provide the impetus to legislation which would provide for it.

There are various ways in which lower-income and minority groups can be helped to achieve better living and working conditions. One is for large-scale public purchase of undeveloped suburban land to be made available for subdivision, sale, or lease to private developers. The idea would be for some public body to purchase undeveloped suburban land or land for the construction of balanced satellite communities, well in advance of the need to develop it, and to attain a desired pattern of suburban or new town growth by making this land available for private development.[5] As Reps has pointed out in his paper, a number of specific proposals to this end have been made in recent years. Public ownership of land for urban development is an old and well-established American practice that has fallen into some disuse in recent decades but which might well be revived.

One issue in implementing such a proposal is: What proportion of the potential development land should the public agency buy — all of it, most of it, or just some? The argument can be advanced that sound suburban development requires control over land use on all land, hence the public agency should buy all the developable land. Certainly it can be argued that a few intermingled tracts of private land might go a long way to thwart the general plans for an area. On the other hand, purchase of *all* development land would surely raise many difficult political as well as economic problems. The negotiations and problems involved in buying land from every holdout might become intolerably complex and time-consuming; public agencies as monopolies may become as barnacle-encrusted as private monopolies; and a public agency that was forced to meet all demands and requirements for buildable land might face unnecessary problems in dealing with developers. Considerations of this kind have led to the suggestion that the public body avoid a monopoly position but buy enough land to be the major factor in the suburban land market — something on the order of 60 percent of development land, for instance.[6] In the case of land purchase for the development of satellite communities or new towns, a stronger case can be made for 100 percent public ownership.[7]

Closely related to the question of how much land to buy is the question of how far in advance of the time of expected development to buy. Land likely to be developed soon is also likely to be the object of some developer's plans and not easily acquired. Its price is likely to be high. Land not likely to be developed for some years can be bought more readily. Owners may even welcome a good buyer. For this type of land, the price is likely to include some allowance for risk or uncertainty as to timing and ultimate form of development. Since a public body might be in a position to make its own forecasts come true, a price that is attractive to a seller might also be a good

---

[5] Bernard Weissbourd, "Satellite Communities: Proposal for a New Housing Program," *The Center Magazine* (Center for the Study of Democratic Institutions, Santa Barbara, California), January and March 1972.

[6] Marion Clawson, *Suburban Land Conversion in the United States: An Economic and Governmental Process* (Johns Hopkins University Press for Resources for the Future, 1971), pp. 358-59.

[7] Weissbourd, "Satellite Communities," pp. 11-13.

bargain for the purchaser. But purchase far in advance of development calls for a relatively large capital investment and postpones the political or social payoff of the program for several years.

Public purchase of development land for later resale or lease to private developers implies substantial fiscal problems for the unit of government buying the land. A public agency cannot expect to buy much land at the market price that prevailed before it began its purchases; its act of land purchase pushes up the land price. Calculations based upon desired acreage of land and upon appraised land prices prevailing before the land purchase program starts will prove far too low. The public agency cannot operate as if the market were determined by others and that it only accepted the market prices, when in fact the scale of its operations would largely determine that market. If any public agency seeks to buy a substantial acreage of land on the assumption that the pre-program going prices will continue throughout the program, it is in for serious disillusionment — as federal, state, and local park executives learned long ago.

When the public agency that has bought land for development purposes begins to sell that land, or lease it on long-term leases, its disposal actions then push the market price for land downward. In the long run, a program of public land purchase and disposal may lower land prices on a net basis; that is, prices may average less for the long run than they would have if there had not been a public land purchase program. But the effect in the short run may be different.

One argument that has been used against public land purchase for development purposes is that public purchase takes land off the tax rolls, hence imposes a financial burden upon the local unit of government that loses the real estate tax that the private landowner would pay. But this argument ignores the fact that the public land purchase pushes up the price of the land not bought, as well as of that actually purchased. If the tax assessment procedures are efficient and alert, land will be reassessed promptly as land values rise; and tax revenues from the remaining private land will rise also. A fairly extensive program of public purchase of land need not lower tax receipts from private land at all. In many instances, the unit of government that buys the land will be able to obtain some receipts from various forms of temporary land use, pending permanent development for some purpose.

In any discussion of public agency purchase of land for development, one immediate question is the power of eminent domain. Must the agency have the legal power to take land from its owners by payment of a fair compensation but without the owner's consent? Political obstacles often preclude the large-scale use of this legal power even when it is available to an agency. But it can be argued that a public agency that is to acquire land for suburban development must have the power of eminent domain, both to acquire critical tracts and to permit serious bargaining with private landowners. To some extent, real estate tax programs and extending (or withholding) public facilities can be made to substitute for eminent domain as a means of bringing private landowners to the bargaining table.

Another major question is: What public agency should buy the land, make plans for its development, dispose of it by lease or sale to private developers, and generally use the land program as the mechanism for the realization of plans for the development of the area? A suburban satellite city or a suburban county, unless relatively large in area and population, is likely to lack the governmental revenues or credit, the administrative expertise, and the political stability to undertake a program of large-scale acquisition of lands. In general, regular governmental agencies, at any governmental level, are likely to be poorly organized to carry out such programs. Special land agencies or development authorities may be more appropriate. Mixed public and private corporations may have many advantages, including the possibility that present landowners may wish to acquire an equity participation in the corporation in return for their land, because this land venture may improve their tax position. Such corporations might operate with fewer bureaucratic hindrances also. State and national corporations, as well as regional units, have been variously proposed as best able to carry out a land development program. For each of these proposals there are pros and cons that should be thoroughly analyzed.

If a major program of suburban land acquisition were undertaken by an established unit of local, regional, or state government or by a newly created instrument politically responsible to one of these levels of government, what are the prospects that the acquisition and disposal of lands would be managed with more skill and higher standards of performance than they are now? Are not the same individuals and groups likely to run the new agency and to continue to serve their personal interests? Obviously, neither a new program nor a new agency will serve as a magic wand, but they have something to offer. A program of land acquisition, planning, and disposal would provide new tools for suburban development — positive tools that would supplant the negative tools of zoning and enable dedicated and able people to do a vastly better job than has been done in the past. With a new agency and a new program that could, and probably would be forced to, operate in the public limelight, the kind of preferential treatment that often destroys the effectiveness of land use zoning would be immensely more difficult.

As one contemplates the history of urban land use change and urban growth over the past quarter century or so and the kinds of suburbs that have resulted from the processes involved, one is forced to conclude that nothing less than major public involvement in the suburban land market will make any real difference in the kinds of urban growth that will take place. Better planning, more carefully operated land use controls, reorganization of local government, and many other proposed reforms are helpful but not sufficient, and must be supplemented by a program of public land purchase to achieve a real change in urban growth and land use.[8] If we are dissatisfied with the kinds of suburbs that have been produced in these years and want to change them, we must be prepared to adopt adequate measures.

Another major substantive change in urban land use policy would be the restructuring of private speculation in suburban land. The sprawling nature of suburban growth is a direct outgrowth of private speculation in land, and the exclusionary character is an indirect result of the same speculation. The speculation, itself, grows directly out of three kinds of programs that reward and encourage speculation in land: (1) zoning, which restricts the supply of land to a greater or lesser degree; (2) a system of charges for public services that penalizes neither withholding land from development nor jumping to distant tracts for development; and (3) various forms of preferential tax treatment for land speculation. These three programs deserve more detailed treatment.

Zoning and other land use controls, when effective, are a restriction upon the supply of buildable land; one is tempted to say "an artificial restriction," in the sense that they are manmade, not inherent in the physical land availability. But, it is also well to note that all markets for all commodities are artificial to a degree; they operate within a framework of laws and institutions made or governed by public action. Even where zoning is so weak that it can usually be overthrown by a determined assault it exerts a substantial effect upon land prices. It takes both money and time to appeal a zoning decision. If the demand for buildable suburban land is modestly inelastic (as we judge it is, in the absence of any rigorous analysis of the question), the price of suburban land moves upward more than proportionately to the decrease in supply resulting from zoning. A 10 percent reduction in the effective supply of land would push land prices per acre up more than 10 percent – perhaps a great deal more. If one intervenes to affect the supply of buildable land, he must either accept the price consequences or intervene adequately to offset or prevent them.

Two characteristics of the typical system of local government charges for public services also favor speculation in suburban land. First, usually no charge is made for availability of services not yet taken advantage of; and, second, charges do not reflect differences in location and the costs arising from them. When a sewer line is extended beyond a piece of idle suburban

8 Clawson, *Suburban Land Conversion*, pp. 355–63.

land, usually no charge is made for the availability of such service, until a new house on the lot is connected to the sewer. The owner of this land has all the advantages of sewer availability, with no costs on his part, until he chooses to use the service. The same relationship is true for roads, schools, water supply, and other services typically provided by the local government. When building does occur and such services are utilized, the charges do not reflect location and the costs associated therewith. That is, the sewer charges for houses in a subdivision a mile beyond the nearest housing are not likely to be any higher than they would be in the lots adjacent to the presently developed area. These two aspects of charges for local governmental services serve to encourage the discontiguous subdivision type of sprawl. Under a different system of charges, sprawl could be discouraged.

Favorable tax treatment for suburban land speculation arises in several ways. Numerous studies have shown that unimproved suburban land is typically treated with great tenderness by the assessors, even though most states have laws requiring that the idle land, like other real property, pay local real estate taxes based upon the full market value of the land. In cases where it is hard to distinguish the real market price from inflated claims, the assessor's caution may be defended, at least in part. Frequently, however, there is a lag in reassessments, and land with a rapidly rising price pays taxes based upon values of some years earlier. In many cases, outright favoritism is suspected but cannot well be proven. Often the landowners and the assessors have mutual interests. In some states favorable tax treatment has recently been extended to "farmland" in suburban areas, and tax farming has become profitable.

Land speculation gets favorable treatment in federal taxes also. Real estate taxes are deductible from income in calculation of federal income tax; so is interest paid on money borrowed to finance land speculating. Also, with some exceptions, gains from land sales may qualify for treatment as capital gains and be taxed at a distinctly lower rate than ordinary income.

Each of these preferential tax treatments for suburban land speculation could be removed by government action. Local real estate taxes could in fact as in theory be based upon the full market value of land; federal income tax laws could be changed so that real estate taxes and interest could not be claimed as a deduction if the land were relatively unimproved; and capital gains on unimproved land could be treated as ordinary income.

Adapting measures that make private speculation in suburban land a less profitable practice would result in much lower prices for building lots, as well as in much more closely settled suburban areas, which would make for certain economies in provision of public services. Under these conditions the building of lower-priced houses becomes possible. When building lots are expensive, a developer tends to build more expensive houses so that the land price is not an unreasonably high proportion of the total price of house and lot. The provision of lower-priced new suburban houses would open the suburbs to people of somewhat lower incomes. It would not solve the problems of the poorest people, but it might ease them somewhat, as the housing vacated by the near-poor would become available to a lower-priced group. The filter-down process might thus be made to work faster and more to the advantage of the lowest-income persons.

A discussion of possible substantive changes in urban and suburban land use planning and control would not be complete without a brief reference to the situation in the older sections of inner cities and the possibilities for facilitating private action in urban renewal. Public urban renewal programs have not been as effective in supplying housing to those who need it as it was hoped they would be. The time between the purchase and clearing of a site and its rebuilding for any purpose has too often been unduly long — land has sometimes lain idle for years. In a large proportion of the cases, the price at which the public agency could sell the land was substantially less than what it had paid for the land and for site clearance; large public subsidies have been necessary, and these have gone to the owners of the decadent properties — hardly a group in financial need of public subsidy. When cleared sites were redeveloped, the resulting residences were usually far too costly for occupancy by the former residents of the area, and these people were pushed into other decaying residential areas. The whole process has been clouded by racial overtones; in many instances the displaced population was black, while the new residents were white. "Urban renewal has been black removal." And, finally, the scale of public urban renewal has been too small to cope with the large backlog of decayed urban centers and with the constant accumulation of slum areas as old housing becomes virtually uninhabitable. For all these reasons, some new approaches that would enlist private business as well as public efforts in urban renewal seem called for.

Various devices might be adopted to make private urban renewal more feasible economically.[9] The developer might be given the power of eminent domain, under carefully prescribed conditions so that land assembly would not continue to be as difficult and as time consuming as it is now. Taxation of real estate might be shifted more toward the land and less toward the improvements, thus removing one major obstacle to rebuilding. Provision might be made for accumulating a demolition fund for each building by an override on the mortgage payment or by special taxes; this would be effective

[9]Marion Clawson, "Urban Renewal in 2000," *Journal of American Institute of Planners*, May 1968.

for buildings that still have a fairly long life ahead of them. Owners of seriously deteriorated housing might be given subsidies for demolition purposes as a means of speeding up rebuilding. While these and other measures might facilitate rebuilding of slum residential areas, they would have to be supplemented by other public programs such as rent subsidies or income maintenance if they are to help produce new housing for low-income people.

IN CONCLUSION

The essays in this book have shown that land use controls, particularly zoning, have operated — and are still operating — to exclude low-income and racial minorities from many urban areas, particularly from many suburbs. Current land use controls are under heavy new attack from several quarters: from the environmentalists, from professional associations of lawyers, from large business firms that operate in the residential-building business, from various proponents of open housing, from state governments, and from the federal government. The motives and the objectives of these groups differ somewhat, but they are united in their opposition to existing land use controls. The road to substantial revision of the land use planning, zoning, and control process is a rocky one; assaults on existing practice may be made on various grounds, yet may not be uniformly successful. Powerful economic and political groups have much to gain from present arrangements and will resist change. The several challenges to existing practice made thus far are more significant as straws in the wind that suggest how social attitudes are changing and may be effective than they are in actual results. The conclusion of several of the authors, and one with which we agree, is that change is coming, but its timing, its exact form, its origins, and its final results are unclear at this time.

We believe that social change is within the control of our whole society, that choices are possible, and that the course of events is not immutable. In this essay, we have outlined some of the possibilities for modifying land use controls for the next generation. Our analysis is neither all-inclusive nor greatly detailed. Others can doubtless think of different approaches or restructure our ideas in major ways. In any case, new approaches would have to be spelled out in detail before they could be applied, and experience in their use would almost surely reveal the need for refinement.

For urban and suburban land use, as for so many other facets of modern life, the future promises to be interesting, even exciting. It may not always be simple or easy, but surely ways can be found to modify urban land policy so that it will better meet future needs.

INDEX

241